EDUCATING YOUNG CHILDREN IN A DIVERSE SOCIETY

Edith W. King
University of Denver

Marilyn Chipman
Metropolitan State College of Denver

Marta Cruz-Janzen
Denver Public Schools

Allyn and Bacon
Boston • London • Toronto • Sydney • Tokyo • Singapore

Editor in Chief, Education: Nancy Forsyth
Editorial Assistant: Christine Nelson
Production Administrator: Susan McIntyre
Editorial-Production Service: Ruttle, Shaw & Wetherill, Inc.
Cover Administrator: Suzanne Harbison
Composition Buyer: Linda Cox
Manufacturing Buyer: Megan Cochran

Library of Congress Cataloging-in-Publication Data

King, Edith W.
  Educating young children in a diverse society / Edith W. King,
Marilyn Chipman, Marta Cruz-Janzen.
      p.   cm.
  Includes bibliographical references and index.
  ISBN 0-205-14789-5
  1. Multicultural education—United States. 2. Early childhood
education—Social aspects—United States. 3. Educational
anthropology—United States. 4. Curriculum planning—United States.
I. Chipman, Marilyn. II. Cruz-Janzen, Marta. III. Title.
LC1099.K49   1994
370.19′6′0973—dc20   93-5189
                                                             CIP

Printed in the United States of America

10 9 8 7 6 5 4 3 2 1   98 97 96 95 94 93

To the memory of Dorothy Berke
Edith King

To my children, David, Michael, and Sarena;
my husband, Aaron; and my mother, Lois.
Thank you for your love throughout the years.
Marilyn Chipman

To all my elementary school teachers in Puerto Rico
who taught me to believe in myself.
To my husband, John, and daughter, Eva,
whose love, faith, and encouragement keep me going.
¡Gracias!
Marta Cruz-Janzen

Contents

Foreword

Nothing inherent in culture itself, or in other forms of human diversity, creates pedagogical problems. Diversity is the norm in human society, even where homogeneity appears on the surface. It is *that attitude of the educator* toward diversity that creates problems in the education setting. When educators do not notice diversity, when they give negative notice, or when they lose the opportunity to give positive notice of the natural diversity that is always there, they create a bogus reality for teaching and learning.

Politicizing diversity contributes to practices of inequity in education. The two primary areas of inequity are in the *process* and in the *content* of education. The content problem in education is primarily a validity problem. Will the curriculum faithfully reflect the truth of the human experience—the *whole* truth? Will the experience of any segment of the society be ignored, falsified, or defamed? Neither chauvinism nor shame is a natural outcome of a truthful rendition of the human experience. Pluralism is the norm and will be unavoidable if the truth is to be told. Critical thinking about the content of education is dependent on the accuracy and completeness of the content.

The primary process issue is that of equal access to school services, and this begins in the first years of schooling. The distribution of high-quality teaching and support services should be equitable for all groups beginning with these first years of schooling. Exemplary programs should not be a refuge for the wealthy or an exclusive preserve for any one racial, ethnic, or gender group. Conscious and sophisticated monitoring of education services to locate and eliminate inequities is the responsibility of every educator from the preschool on.

Awareness of diversity within human society is a necessity for anyone interested in the knowledge base of early childhood education. The strength of this book lies in the presentation of diverse cultural experiences as a natural source of ideas and stimulating creativity and, for many, a natural source of the variety that enhances the environment. The world is now and always has been an environment of physical and social diversity. A respect for that and an appropriate response to it can enhance education for all. King, Chipman, and Cruz-Janzen raise many issues for early childhood educators and propose plausible practices to respond to the reality of diversity.

Asa G. Hilliard, III, Ed.D.
Georgia State University

Preface

Living in our contemporary world grows vastly more complex with each day, with each new event, with each change in technology. As in every aspect of society, early childhood education experiences these impacts. For more than two decades, the authors of this volume have been deeply involved in and committed to the education of young children, their parents, their teachers, and their care givers. Moreover, all three authors were drawn into education that centered on young children and on multicultural issues because, as mothers and educators, their offspring had been affected profoundly by the early childhood education process. Just as early childhood education has experienced dramatic changes in recent years, the field of multicultural education has been redefined and reorganized continually in the light of societal upheavals. As educators, we recognized an urgent need to provide a text that would infuse "the diversity perspective," into the teaching of all young children.

CHILDREN'S SELF-PORTRAITS: A MULTICULTURAL PROJECT FOR THE CLASSROOM

Many positive comments have been received regarding the children's self-portraits included in this text. We thought the reader might want to know how they were created. Nancy Gallavan, whose students produced the self-portraits, gives the following account:

The changing enrollment has transformed our school over the last five years from a predominantly middle class, white suburban neighborhood school to one that reflects wide diversity. The students now come from all social classes and many ethnic groups. The spirit of friendship and harmony is a result of concerted efforts by the administration, staff, students, parents, and community to join together in the pursuit of education of the highest quality.

Much thought has been given to educating this diverse student body so that multicultural education has been integrated into all areas of the curriculum. It is not presented as a separate subject area, but as an extension of activities and discussions vital to every aspect of learning. Staff members have discovered a wealth of resources and information through the incorporation of materials on diversity and the help of committed adults from the community.

The children's self-portrait project arose in my class from interest in human diversity and the danger of stereotyping individuals and groups of people. The project was first explained to the children and a letter was sent home describing the educational purposes and outcomes of such a project. While creating their self-portraits the children spent considerable time studying their own features in front of a large mirror I had placed in the room. They spent much time viewing their eyes, noses, and mouths from several angles.

I encouraged all the students to use differing colors as they cut out and attached their features with paste to the large paper which formed the base for their self-portraits. These activities presented opportunities to discuss the physical attributes associated with different ethnic groups and the need to avoid stereotyping individuals. They finished the creation of the self-portraits by adding a simple piece of clothing, choosing their own favorite colors. Some students then attached jewelry such as earrings or necklaces to their portraits. A few others constructed eyeglasses if they wore them regularly. Other children who needed to wear eyeglasses would not include them in their self-portraits because they felt they were not as attractive when wearing glasses. This reminded me that these children, as most people, need constant reassurance of the acceptability of their personal appearance.

This self-portrait adventure was integrated into a combined reading, writing, and social studies unit presented during the month of December. This was a particularly fruitful time since so many celebrations emphasizing multicultural and global customs, traditions, and holidays occur in this month. Every December I have opportunities to visit the children's homes and meet with their families. A home visit with a family of a student I had taught in the previous year empha-

sized the value of the self-portrait project. My former student, now quite a young lady, eagerly took me to see her room and her study area. There, placed on the wall above her desk in an elegant frame hung her self-portrait. I knew then that I should repeat the self-portrait project in my classroom every year so the children could learn from the efforts of this type of self-expression.

Acknowledgments

In writing this book, the authors were continually inspired and encouraged by the students enrolled in their education courses, seminars, and programs over the past years. Some were in preservice education, while others included experienced early childhood teachers, administrators, consultants, school psychologists, parents, and undergraduates and graduates with majors other than education.

We wish to specifically cite by name some of these students, colleagues, and associates whose contributions to this volume were invaluable. We want to thank Margaret Huxley of Manchester, England, for the models and insights into the importance of gender socialization in early childhood; Janice Luellen for her outstanding research on young Native-American children; and Robin Glaser, officer of the U.S. Air Force Academy, for his insights as a father in a culturally-different setting. Others whose input provided unique aspects of early childhood education and research were Seng Seok Hoon of Singapore, Nasma Hussein of Kuwait, and Peter Woods of the Open University, England. Our thanks also go to Nancy P. Gallavan of the Cherry Creek, Colorado, public schools and her students, whose lively and unique self-portraits illustrate the book, and to Marjorie Milan and Janette Astacio and their staff and students in the Denver public schools.

We want to thank our editors at Allyn and Bacon, Nancy Forsyth and Christine Nelson, as well as Jim Ruppel, who continually provided us with encouragement and counsel. We thank the educators who reviewed the manuscript: Gail Bollin, Westchester University and Linda Medearis, East Central University. Finally, much of the inspiration and commitment to bring this project to fulfillment came from our own children.

About the Authors

The senior author of this text, Edith W. King, is Professor in the School of Education, University of Denver, where she specializes in sociological, multicultural, and comparative education. Her teaching includes courses on the child in society; on ethnicity, social class, and gender in education; and on qualitative research methods. For the past fifteen years, King has organized travel seminars for educators to study early childhood and elementary education in international settings. Additionally, she has investigated the effects of ethnicity, gender, and social class on education in nations around the globe, including doing field work in schools and universities in Singapore, Kuwait, Hong Kong, Britain, and Canada. As a senior faculty member at the University of Denver, King has been the major adviser for a growing number of dissertation research studies of young children that combine aspects of ethnicity, gender, and social class. Throughout her professional career she has authored numerous articles, as well as developed monographs, pamphlets, and media materials on child socialization, multicultural education, sociological theory, and cross-cultural perspectives in education. Among the books she has authored are *Teaching Ethnic and Gender Awareness: Methods and Materials for the Elementary School; Administering Early Childhood Education* (with Joseph Stevens, Jr.); *Twentieth Century Social Thought* (with R. P. Cuzzort); *Educating Young Children . . . Sociological Interpretations; The World: Context for Teaching in the Elementary School;* and *The Sociology of Early Childhood Education.*

Marilyn Chipman is a professor in the Department of Early Childhood and Elementary Education, and the past Area Coordinator of the

Early Childhood Teacher Certification Program at Metropolitan State College of Denver, Colorado. She has been appointed as the Race Coordinator for the federally-funded Rocky Mountain and Northern Plains States Desegregation Assistance Center, an outreach of the college. In this capacity, she provides assistance and training for K-12 school districts in a six-state region. Dr. Chipman's background includes teaching young children in public schools in California and in Colorado, where she was nominated for the Teacher of the Year Award. In addition to her commitment to early childhood education, Dr. Chipman develops curriculum, teaches courses, and conducts seminars in the area of cultural diversity for both preservice and experienced teachers, administrators, support staff, and for parents and community leaders. A recognized consultant in multicultural education, she speaks on the local, state, and national levels to audiences from both inner-city and rural areas. Her research and prior publications have addressed the impact of the educational experience on students of color from pre-school through the graduate level in academe. She has received numerous awards. Dr. Chipman holds a B.A. degree in Sociology and Psychology from the University of Denver; a M.A. degree in Early Childhood Education from California State University, and a Ph.D. in Education Curriculum and Instruction from the University of Denver.

Marta Cruz-Janzen is the principal of Remington Elementary School, Denver Public Schools. She is a doctoral candidate in the College of Education, University of Denver, specializing in curriculum leadership and multicultural education. Cruz-Janzen was the Gender and Race Equity Consultant at the Colorado Department of Education, where she provided technical assistance to K-12 education districts in the state of Colorado. Her career with the Denver Public Schools has also included teaching, advising, and providing technical assistance in bilingual/English as a second oral language (ESOL) education. Before coming to Colorado, Cruz-Janzen taught bilingual education in the New York City schools. She received her B.S. from Cornell University and her M.A. and M.Ed. from the Columbia University Teachers College. She has been selected Vice-Chair of the National Coalition for Sex/Race Equity in Education (NCSEE). Marta is also a member of the National Association for Bilingual Education (NABE) and a member of the Board of Directors for the Colorado Association for Bilingual/Bicultural Education (CABE). She has conducted presentations on gender and race equity, and the interface of gender and race issues, at conferences across the country. Cruz-Janzen's research and field work have focused on young children and gender/race issues in bilingual/bicultural settings.

1

RECOGNIZING DIVERSITY IN EARLY CHILDHOOD EDUCATION

As we approach the twenty-first century, voices are proclaiming, "What we need now for educating all children, especially our very youngest, is a *diversity perspective!*" Is this emphasis on diversity just another label for cultural pluralism, multiculturalism, and multicultural education, or is this a new and more propitious stage in the evolving dynamics of educating our society's children? In the past three decades much has changed in teaching about ethnic diversity, cultural pluralism, and multiculturalism. First known as ethnic heritage studies or bilingual/bicultural education during the 1960s and 1970s, the focus was on language and cultural differences. Children who came to the school not speaking or understanding the English language were considered deficient, culturally disadvantaged, and in need of remediation. This concept of cultural disadvantagement was redefined in the 1980s to promote a valuing of cultural difference, encompassing not only race and ethnic diversity, but also gender and social class affiliation. Multicultural education, as attested to by the titles of a proliferation of textbooks, has become the umbrella term for dealing with many types of differences in our society and in a global context, as well. These attributes include differences based on ethnicity or race, social class, religion, gender, age, disabling conditions, and intellectual abilities. The definition of *multicultural education* has been broadened to include teaching "special" children—the physically disabled, the mentally retarded, the emotionally disturbed, and the gifted and talented.

In this book we have chosen to use the term *diversity perspective*. We define the *diversity perspective* as the concept that, in early childhood education, we must infuse a positive awareness and inclusion of differences in the education of all young children. A diversity perspective calls for the application of knowledge about ethnicity, social class, and gender to issues, problems, viewpoints, theories, and programs surrounding young children.

In 1987, in an important and forward-looking book, *Teaching and Learning in a Diverse World: Multicultural Education for Young Children*, Patricia Ramsey wrote that the majority of early childhood programs in the United States were racially, culturally, and socioeconomically homogeneous. As a result of these conditions teachers often questioned the appropriateness of multicultural education in these types of settings. Ramsey went on to assert that the goals of multicultural education are most relevant to children who are growing up without the opportunity to have contact with people different from themselves. "In a sense, their classroom experiences have to compensate for their social isolation. Teachers in these settings frequently are perplexed about how to make the diversity of our society and the world seem real to their children" (p. 3).

THE AUTHORS' PURPOSE
IN WRITING THIS TEXT

This text is primarily for aspiring and current teachers of young children. In this book it is our intention to provide information, strategies, techniques, innovative ideas, and most importantly, encouragement for teachers, administrators, educators, and parents in implementing this fresh and essential *diversity perspective* into programs for young children. In America at the close of the twentieth century we now know that multicultural education is deeply entwined with the recognition of the importance of ethnic identity, social class affiliation, and society's new awareness of gender issues. Further, we cannot eschew the impact that Americans with disabilities have made on society, resulting in the Americans with Disabilities Act (1991). Therefore, we must also focus on the children who start life with disabling conditions that affect their lives.

We are mainly concerned in this book about informing and developing awareness and sensitivity to ethnicity, gender, and social class as these forces affect young children. Early childhood education begins with birth. Our text, however, encompasses the ages of three to eight years, those years when children attend nursery schools, preschools, kindergartens, and the primary grades of the elementary school. Although our major attention is given to examining ethnic, gender, and social class differences, attention is devoted to discussing "special" children and their needs. Authors of recent texts on multicultural education that mainly focus on teaching older students at intermediate, middle, and high school levels stress that the past conceptions of diversity are expanding to include differences based on more than ethnicity, class, and gender. Yet, our knowledge of how these differences affect children in school or impact teacher education have not been well articulated or insightfully researched (Baruth and Manning, 1992; Cushner, McClelland, and Safford, 1992; Nieto, 1992). Extensive data provide us with the picture of our school populations growing more and more ethnically diverse and being from lower socioeconomic levels. On the other hand, those who go into teaching, and especially into early childhood education, are predominantly middle class, white, and female. We need to encourage members from different and diverse groups—people of color, especially men, and people of less advantaged economic circumstances—to aspire to careers in early childhood education.

Our initial purpose in writing this text for pre-service and in-service teachers of young children, administrators, parents, and others interested in early childhood education was to fill a distinct void in the literature of multicultural education and teacher education. In searching the available resources for our college-level courses, we became acutely aware of the pressing need for a textbook—that would address questions and concerns regarding teaching very young children about the wide diversity that now characterizes American society. Not only do young children perceive and react to physical, cultural, and ethnic difference, they also are keenly aware of gender and social class differences. These considerations are part of daily life, beamed to children in their homes through the media and embedded in their socialization in the family.

In our search for resources for novice and experienced teachers on teaching about diversity, multicultural education, and pluralism in early childhood education, we found many articles but only a few books. These included Patricia Ramsey's (1987) innovative book highlighted above; Louise Derman-Sparks and the Anti Bias Curriculum Task Force's (1989) practical handbook on the anti-bias curriculum, subtitled "Tools for Empowering Young Children"; and King's *Teaching Ethnic and Gender Awareness: Methods and Materials for the Elementary School* (1990). Especially in the *Anti-Bias Curriculum,* the point is made that it is not enough for the teachers and parents of young children to merely teach tolerance. In this important handbook for early childhood educators, examples and anecdotes are recounted quoting the hurtful remarks, ethnic and gender slights, and biases and prejudices that even three- and four-year-olds display. This gives us ample evidence that a proactive, anti-bias curriculum is imperative in the earliest years of schooling. This book affirms throughout its pages that adults must make it clear that it is not acceptable for even the very youngest children to exhibit discriminatory behavior. Adults must examine their own prejudices, stereotypes, and biases and model appropriate behaviors and attitudes for the children they rear and teach.

The Use of Accounts and Anecdotes of Childhood Experiences

To bring to our readers the nature and depth of early childhood encounters with ethnicity, social class, and gender identification, we have drawn on our own and other adults' firsthand accounts, anecdotes, experiences, and remembrances. The chapters of this book are filled with "stories" to illustrate and exemplify the concepts, ideas, strategies, and theories in early childhood presented on the pages that follow. These remembrances of childhood experiences—some extensive, others more brief—are all poignant, pivotal, and unforgettable in shaping the lives and careers of those who experienced them. These accounts serve to instruct us in the same way that stories and storytelling are used and even featured in early childhood education to provide yet another way to learn and remember important lessons.

ORGANIZATION OF THE CHAPTERS

Educating Young Children in a Diverse Society begins with this introductory chapter and is followed by nine more. Chapter 2 focuses on the importance of viewing multiculturalism and multicultural education from the new perspective of diversity. Awareness of diversity is inherent in early childhood socialization, a socialization in modern society that now embraces ethnic and racial differences, gender identification, and social class affiliation.

Chapter 2 also includes an extensive investigation detailing observations over a period of time in a bilingual early childhood classroom. This encourages a thoughtful examination of how powerful and how early in children's lives comes the recognition of ethnic, linguistic, gender, and social class differences.

In chapter 3, the necessity for developmentally appropriate practice is spotlighted. The theoretical and historical basis for developmentally appropriate practice is discussed and analyzed from a diversity perspective. The incorporation of diversity through developmentally appropriate activities for early childhood education is presented.

Chapter 4 extends the discussion of historical and theoretical views including the impact of emergent literacy on customary methods for teaching language development. We highlight what experts have traditionally considered to be the three major approaches to curriculum for children three to eight years of age and the concomitant supportive curriculum materials for these programs. We present a critique of these three major views of curriculum for young children from a diversity perspective, examining the implications of each type of curricular framework for the ethnic, gender, and social class biases inherent in the early childhood education philosophies that undergird these three major approaches.

The crucial nature of ethnic, social class, and gender identity is highlighted in chapter 5 through accounts, anecdotes, childhood remembrances, and stories. Two pieces in this chapter are in-depth and detailed; others are briefer statements of how individuals experienced firsthand the impact of ethnic and racial affiliations, gender identification, and the subtler effects of social class biases and prejudices.

This leads the reader to examine the concept of culture and its importance for early childhood education in chapter 6. This chapter also contains an extensive examination of a unique and exciting exemplary early childhood program for Native American preschoolers, "The Circle Never Ends" curriculum of the Denver, Colorado, Indian Center.

Chapter 7 concentrates on the critical nature of gender awareness in early childhood education, including the subtle nature of gender stereotyping that starts early in the socialization of our children. We discuss how gender biases are perpetuated in our culture and arise daily in our preschools, kindergartens, and early elementary grade classrooms. This chapter ends with a true, poignant, and telling story of two Spanish-speaking six-year-old girls and their unforgettably cruel experience on the playground of an American elementary school, totally within the view of the teachers who were responsible for their learning and social development.

In chapter 8 we present the significant but seldom discussed sociological view of the young child. Applying the theories of sociology and the writings of the famous sociologist Erving Goffman to early childhood education brings forth conceptions of prejudice and the discrimination experienced by children as young as four, five, and six years of age. Again, anecdotes and accounts illuminate the impact of this discrimination so early in life, which can stem from racial, ethnic, gender, or disabling conditions.

Our text would not be complete if we overlooked the importance of research and evaluation as this relates to the teaching of young children. This topic is the major intent of chapter 9, where studies of teacher as researcher in early childhood settings are presented and discussed. Additionally, the import of naturalistic, qualitative research for illuminating promising practice in teaching ethnically diverse children in early childhood programs becomes apparent in the discussion of exemplary research projects involving children under eight years of age, their teachers, and parents.

This text ends with chapter 10, devoted to examining where the education of young children must take us in an interdependent world.

FEATURES OF THE TEXT TO PROMOTE TEACHER DEVELOPMENT

We wish to point out to our readers some special features contained in each chapter of the book that are designed to promote educational awareness and professional development. At the conclusion of each chapter the reader will find a summary of the major points in the chapter. This is followed by a section labeled "Key Concepts" where the important terms, concepts, and themes brought out in the chapter are listed and defined. These key concepts, ideas, and themes stressed in the chapter are actualized in the activities section of each chapter beginning with chapter 2. This section is appropriately labeled "Issues and Actions." It is our hope that the users of this text will take up the issues, questions, projects, and assignments listed at the close of each chapter and carry them out in their own classrooms, school settings, homes, and neighborhoods. Finally, each chapter ends with a list of suggested readings for teachers, parents, educators, and administrators as resources and background for the material developed through the book.

SUMMARY AND OVERVIEW

Ethnicity, social class affiliation, and gender identity affect everyone. These dynamic forces affect our behavior in the social spheres of our lives. They affect how we spend our money, how we vote, even where we live or where we go out to dine. Implicitly we use ethnicity, gender, and social class as a filter for forming our identities, opinions, and attitudes toward others.

Individuals function on a continuum of ethnic affiliation, ranging from no recognition of one's ethnicity in daily life to an almost complete identification with an ethnic, religious, or nation-state group in all activities, choices, and designations of self-identification. Because ethnicity and gender are so central to people's images and concepts of self-identity, those working with young children need to be aware of the importance of multiculturalism, gender equality, and wide diversity in expanding the young child's opportunities to learn. That is, requirements or cultural conditioning inherent in the family and in the religious, linguistic, or ethnic group a person identifies with may influence his or her learning options.

James Banks states this with acumen when he writes:

> *Each of us becomes culturally encapsulated during our socialization in childhood. We accept the assumptions of our own community culture, internalize its values, views of the universe, misconceptions, and stereotypes. Although this is as true for the child socialized within a mainstream culture as it is for the minority child, minority children are usually forced to examine, confront, and question their cultural assumptions when they enter school.*
>
> *Students who are born and socialized within the mainstream culture of a society rarely have an opportunity to identify, question and challenge their cultural assumptions, beliefs, values, and perspec-*

*tives because the school culture usually reinforces those that they learn
at home and in their communities.*

*Consequently, mainstream Americans have few opportunities to
become free of cultural assumptions and perspectives that are
monocultural, that devalue African and Asian cultures, and that
stereotype people of color and people who are poor, or who are victim-
ized in other ways. These mainstream Americans often have an
inability to function effectively within other American cultures, and
lack the ability and motivation to experience and benefit from cross-
cultural participation and relationships. To fully participate in our
democratic society these students and all students need the skills a
multicultural education can give them to understand others and to
thrive in a rapidly changing, diverse world (Banks, 1992, p. 35).*

It is the goal of this book to bring together understanding, knowledge, and appropriate educational instruction on multiculturalism and
gender and social class awareness with that diversity perspective. It is the
goal of the authors to provide the means for the teachers, educators,
parents, and all those who work with, nurture, and care for young
children to develop appreciation for diversity. Educating for diversity is
essential. Human nature cries out for personal dignity and recognition.
This is vital for learning. Teaching that incorporates a knowledge of
cultural, gender, and social class awareness contributes to preparing the
future citizens of the nation and the world.

REFERENCES AND SUGGESTED READINGS

Banks, James. *Multiethnic Education: Theory and Practice* (second edition). New-
ton, MA: Allyn and Bacon, 1988.
Banks, James and Banks, Cherry (eds). *Multicultural Education: Issues and Perspec-
tives*. Newton, MA: Allyn and Bacon, 1989.
Banks, James. "Multicultural Education: For Freedom's Sake" *Educational Leader-
ship*. Jan. 1992, pp. 32–35.
Baruth, L. G. and Manning, M. L. *Multicultural Education of Children and Adoles-
cents*. Newton, MA: Allyn and Bacon, 1992.
Chipman, Marilyn. "Curriculum Decisions in the '90s: The Impact upon the
African American Child" Paper presented to the National Black Child De-
velopment Institute, 1990, Washington, DC.
Chipman, Marilyn. "African American History Month: A Time for Discovery"
Today's Catholic Teacher, February, 1991. pp. 24–27.
Cushner, K., McClelland, A., and Safford, P. *Human Diversity in Education*. New
York: McGraw Hill, 1992.

Derman-Sparks, L. and the A. B. C. Task Force. *Anti-Bias Curriculum: Tools for Empowering Young Children.* Washington, DC: National Association for the Education of Young Children, 1989.

Hilliard, Asa. (editor) *Testing African American Students.* Morristown: Aaron Press, 1991.

Hilliard, Asa. "Teaching and Cultural Styles in a Pluralistic Society." *National Education Association.* Vol. 7, No. 6, 1989. pp. 65–69.

Hilliard, Asa. "Why We Must Pluralize the Curriculum" *Educational Leadership.* Vol. 49, No. 4, 1992, pp. 12–16.

King, Edith. *Teaching Ethnic and Gender Awareness: Methods and Materials for the Elementary School.* Dubuque, IA: Kendall/Hunt, 1990.

Nieto, Sonia. *Affirming Diversity: Sociopolitical Context of Multicultural Education.* New York: Longman. 1992.

Ramsey, Patricia. *Teaching and Learning in a Diverse World.* New York: Teachers College Press, 1987.

Weis, L.; Altbach, P. H.; Gail Kelly and Hugh G. Petrie. *Critical Perspectives on Early Childhood Education.* Albany: State University of New York Press, 1991.

2

THE IMPACT OF ETHNICITY, GENDER, AND SOCIAL CLASS ON YOUNG CHILDREN

This chapter considers in detail the impact of ethnicity, gender, and social class, the central elements of the diversity perspective discussed in chapter 1, in the lives of young children as they enter the school setting. Most adults in our society have highly selective recollections of experiences during their early childhood years. When asked to recall memorable events they may focus on occasions with a grandparent, a nursery school teacher, or a specific aunt or uncle. Adults tend to idealize these recollected situations and the characters involved. This selective memory of adults weakens and limits their recognition of the importance of their socialization process in the early childhood years. Adults have limited empathy and appreciation for the extent of very young children's perceptions about social situations, interpersonal relations, and the turmoil, tensions, and troubles that surround human beings from time to time. Since young children have less ability to communicate their feelings and impressions verbally, adults do not realize the extent of their understandings of the social scenarios unfolding around them. Maryellen Goodman detailed this in her imaginative volume, *The Culture of Childhood: Child's-Eye Views of Society and Culture,* published over twenty years ago,[1] as did King in a previous work (King, 1973).[2]

Young children are socialized at very early ages into the "ways of their society," the values, attitudes, roles, and statuses of the adults that surround them. Take, for example, the following insightful and amusing remarks of a five-year-old when asked to describe his family:

> *My father teaches education, which is a service. My father works at University Hall. My mother is just a housewife, so she produces services. She tries to help with school work. My mother is very nice. My sister doesn't produce ANYTHING—BUT TROUBLE!*

Other five-year-old children, whose parents were in higher education, responded as follows when asked about their fathers' employment: "My dad is a teacher that teaches teachers to be teachers," and "My dad is Dean of Arts and Science. He came up the hard way. First we came to this campus and he was just a teacher, then he did another job. Then he became dean!"

These children, who attended a laboratory school on a college campus, show keen perceptions about the social, economic, and political life of the adult world that surrounds them. They were certainly aware of the roles and statuses of the society and campus community in which their families were immersed. These anecdotes provide an introduction to this chapter that focus on the crucial nature of socialization in early childhood, not just in the home with family members and friends, but during the child's first schooling experiences, as well.

SOCIALIZATION IN EARLY CHILDHOOD

What is socialization? Socialization is the dynamic process that brings a human being into the human group. It occurs throughout an individual's life. Socialization causes a person to internalize the ways of the culture, to accept and affirm the values, traditions, folkways, mores, and attitudes of the broader society. We learn to eat certain foods, wear specific types of clothing, and speak the language that we do as a result of socialization. Elkin and Handel (1989) define socialization as the process by which we learn the ways of a given society or social group so that we can function within it. Sociologists and psychologists assert that every person is born into a human group that shapes or socializes him or her during childhood and on into adulthood. Through socialization, social reality is internalized by the individual. Hence, the individual's self-perceptions and identity are being formed through these encounters with everyday experiences. Social scientists point out that significant others (usually parents and teachers) interpret the meaning of experience in the social world for the child and influence the socialization process in important ways.

Sociologists, anthropologists, and social psychologists list the sources or agencies of socialization as the family, the school, the peer group, and, of course, the contemporary network of the mass media. In their text on socialization, *The Child and Society: The Process of Socialization* (1989), Elkin and Handel write that socialization occurs in many settings and in interactions with many people organized into groupings of various kinds. They note that these groups—the family, the school, peers, and the mass media—exert pressures on children and thereby impact on their preparation for life in the society.

Social scientists have filled many erudite volumes with research and writings about the family, the peer group, and the mass media as agents of socialization. Somewhat less attention has been devoted to the importance of the school and its personnel on socialization, particularly in early childhood. In this chapter we examine socialization in early childhood by looking at factors that affect children early in their lives. These aspects of socialization can be defined in the following categories: *gender, ethnicity,* and *social class.*

Gender Stereotypes Start Early

If young children are highly aware of the social life that goes on in their midst, then they are certainly cognizant of the sex role behavior that is appropriate in the culture. Parents and teachers play a central role in this process because they continually provide children with models of behavior, reinforcing gender-appropriate behavior and suppressing behavior that may appear inappropriate (Maccoby and Jacklin, 1974).

Sociologists are aware that children learn about sex role behavior very early during the first year of their lives, certainly long before they have entered school. They learn gender-appropriate behavior through the patterns that we take for granted, such as the rougher physical play that male babies are subjected to versus the delicate handling and coddling that female babies experience. Early on boys are dressed in different colors from girls, and their toys are chosen based on gender from birth. We generally expect female babies to be quieter and more docile, while encouraging male babies to be assertive, noisy, and boisterous.

Consider this anecdote: The nursery school teacher asked Rosemary, "What will you be when you grow up?" She replied: "I can be a mother. I can be a nurse. I can be an actress. I can be a wife and my name will change to Rosemary 'Something-or-Other'." This four-year-old female child in American culture already is aware that she gives up her surname for the name of the man she will marry.

When examining how gender stereotypes start early, how often, in the early childhood classroom, do the girls sit to the side while the boys move chairs and blocks or the housekeeping corner's furniture? How frequently do teachers of young children plan rhythmic activities with the galloping for boys only and the tiptoeing for girls only? Those who work with young children recognize that by the age of four or five, preschoolers embrace the traditional gender stereotypes so that even before kindergarten and first grade girls have been socialized to expect their future roles will be only as wives and mothers, while boys have a wide range of options that do not necessarily emphasize being a husband and a father (Best, 1983).

Race and Ethnic Awareness

Every person is born into a human group that shapes or socializes her or him during childhood. As noted, through socialization the individual internalizes the values, attitudes, meanings, and social constructions of the family, the locality, and the wider culture. Thus, an individual's self-perceptions and identity are being formed through his or her encounters with everyday life (Berger and Luckmann, 1966; G. H. Mead, 1934). Each day, young children leave their homes, where they are immersed in the specific ethnic enclave of their family, to go to school. These first school experiences are most often patterned after the majority society. Young children are expected, even in the very first days of attendance at these schools, to perform their roles as pupils adhering to the shared meanings of the broader American society. Furthermore, some young children have the additional burden of interacting with adults who speak only in the English language.

Many of these young children return home, sometimes to "their section of town," to resume family life in the ethnic group with its own cultural patterns and traditions, and perhaps even to a different language or dialect for the rest of the day and night. This scenario describes the young child's initiation into our widely diverse, multicultural American society. Early in life many youngsters learn that reality is being a marginal person living with two everyday realities, one at school and one at home. Teachers of young children have only recently begun to recognize that people frequently occupy several provinces of cultural meaning, and this is not necessarily deleterious. Yet, some still declare that if a child's ethnic affiliations are not those of the majority society, there are bound to be cultural differences. To educators of the majority society, these differences mean cultural *disadvantages*.

Studies continue to demonstrate that young children, as early as three years of age, are aware of ethnic differences. They are aware of skin color; hair texture; shape of eyes, noses, and mouths; and general physical differences. One may ask young children of majority group affiliations or predominantly white backgrounds, "Who are you?" and the child might reply, "I am Mary Smith," or "I am Johnnie Johnson." If one asked the same question of a preschooler in New York City or Trenton, New Jersey, you might receive the reply, "I am *black* and *beautiful!*"; while in Los Angeles or San Diego, a five-year-old girl might say, "I am a Chicana." Contemporary American society is becoming more culturally aware, and young children recognize and discuss ethnic and racial differences. It is all around them—on the television, in their schools, on the buses, often in their family and neighborhood settings. *Ethnicity* is defined as a sense of peoplehood and commonality derived from kinship patterns, a shared historical past, common experiences, religious affiliations, language or linguistic commonalities, shared values attitudes, perceptions, modes of expression, and identity (King, 1990). Young children are already forming their ethnic affiliations and ethnic identities as they are being socialized in the home, in the neighborhood, and in those first weeks at school.

Awareness of Social Class

What do we mean when we speak of *social class* or socioeconomic status? One cannot examine the lives of people without touching on the social class structure of the group or subgroup in a society. Economic wherewithal is tied to accumulation of material goods and the amassing of treasured art as wealth. What is treasured and valued comes from the worth imbued to the material good, such as cash, precious metals and jewels, stocks, bonds, and properties (real estate), through a cultural definition of what is valuable. Further, accumulation of wealth and status means power and superiority over other groups. Social and economic status tends to give one group power over another and leads to attitudes that one ethnic or racial group is inherently better than another because it is richer and holds a higher social status. Material wealth not only endows an individual or a group with greater social status, but often it is also accompanied by wider political power. Socioeconomic status (SES) is defined as a measure that combines a person's education, occupation, and income to derive that person's ranking in the social structure (Cuzzort and King, 1989).

When considering abstract theoretical postulates such as socioeconomic class it is helpful to present concrete examples. The following account of a fifteen-minute observation in a classroom of young children, with interpretive notes, provides an illustration of the "hidden agenda" of the impact of social class status on both children and adults.

The Classroom Setting

It is early in the school year, a crisp, sunny autumn morning. The new second graders (seven-year-olds) file into the highly organized classroom, filling their assigned seats in the neat rows very quietly. Each child is expected to fold hands together, keep lips still, and face forward with an eager look, awaiting the teacher's signal that the attendance count is about to begin. The teacher makes it clear she will wait until every child is "ready"—hands folded, not talking, eyes front. The children obey, although there is some rustling of coins and a few whispers as a loose nickel is retrieved. Attendance is taken. The lunch count is made.

The Classroom Drama

The teacher then brings out a small box from her desk. It has a colorful emblem on it. She asks the children if they remember what the box is for. One girl raises her hand and is called on by the teacher. The child responds that this the UNICEF box to collect contributions for children "all over the world who are not as fortunate as we are." Now the teacher asks, "And who has brought a contribution for our UNICEF box this morning?"

The same girl jumps up quickly and rushes up to the teacher waving a dollar bill. "I have a dollar!" she declares proudly. The teacher then asks the child to write on the chalkboard the amount of her contribution: $1.00. The child does so, and the teacher turns back to the class, saying, "Very fine, Gail. You brought a whole dollar contribution to our box and you wrote the amount correctly on the board. Now who else has a contribution today?"

Some shuffling and a little hurried whispering takes place. Then a boy at the rear of the room raises his hand and is recognized by the teacher. "I have a nickel," he says rather wistfully, as though he expected the teacher to reject his contribution after the magnificent one before. "Very good, Alphonso. Come up to the front of the room and drop your *nickel* [emphasized] in our UNICEF box and write down on the board your contribution under Gail's. The teacher continued: "Boys and girls, we will see if Alphonso can add the amount correctly and you do it with him at your seats."

Rather slowly Alphonso approaches the front of the room and places his contribution in the box, then attempts to do the addition. The teacher continues to solicit the children for money to put in the UNICEF box, but no other volunteers seem evident.

Where Does Social Class Come into the Scene?

In analyzing the implications and ramifications of this brief classroom drama, several aspects of social class awareness and socioeconomic status are revealed. The children in this classroom setting should be further described. These second graders come from a range of ethnic affiliations and socioeconomic levels. Of the twenty-nine children in the class, six are African-American bused in from one section of the city, and seven others are of Hispanic heritage bused from another area where Southeast Asian immigrants have come to reside as well in the high-rise public housing facilities both ethnic groups share. Six more children of Vietnamese and Laotian families from these housing projects arrive on the same buses. Crosstown bussing has been employed to achieve integration in this neighborhood school. The school is located in a mainly white upper middle-class subdivision of single homes in a large Southwestern city. Children from the school's immediate neighborhood come from families whose parents are professionally employed or owners of businesses. The affluence in the homes of these white children is reflected in the objects and games they bring for the "show and tell" time that followed the "charity" episode describe above. One has to ask to what degree a climate of materialism is being developed in this group of seven-year-olds by a seemingly well-intentioned teacher?

This teacher appeared most intent on creatively developing an *arithmetic lesson* out of a mundane activity like contributing to a charity. One wonders how she would have reacted if her school principal asked her to contribute to the United Fund or some other such charitable function publicly in front of the school staff. It can almost be assumed that she would call this an invasion of her personal privacy to be as charitable as she chooses. Yet, did this teacher realize that she was placing the seven-year-olds in her classroom in an embarrassing and socially difficult situation? As is frequently the case, many adults do not stop to consider that young children, too, are socially sensitive to exploitive situations that involve monetary or material bases.

This is an example of how money in the form of power and status relations is subtly introduced into a classroom of young children. The unexamined social forces of the broader society sometimes function to create malicious results unleashed by a well-intentioned, middle-class teacher attempting to inculcate in her pupils the majority society's definition of charitable actions—together with the learning of addition in mathematics.

In the initial pages of this chapter we have presented an introduction and background for the examination and discussion of young children's socialization through their gender, ethnicity, and social class affiliations. Now follows a detailed account of observations over a period of time in an early childhood classroom. This effort by a sensitive early childhood educator and researcher enables the reader vicariously to experience what life is like in an early childhood setting. This account examines the dynamic interactions and the impact of the *diversity perspective* (discussed in chapter 1) on gender awareness, ethnicity, and social class membership of both the young pupils and the adults who teach and care for them.

A STUDY OF INTERACTIONS IN A BILINGUAL EARLY CHILDHOOD CLASSROOM

A series of visits over a period of several months were made to a bilingual early childhood education class for the source of the information reported in this study. This class was housed in an public elementary school that enrolled approximately 400 children in kindergarten through third grade. This school was located in a largely Hispanic community of a major city in the American Southwest. The visits were made during the afternoon class with an enrollment of seven boys and eight girls, in the age range of four to five years. All the children were of Hispanic background. Twelve children were Spanish monolingual speakers; one was Limited English Proficient (LEP), and two were dominant English speakers. All the parents spoke Spanish at home and at school, so the children experienced the influence of a second language in their daily lives.

The Classroom Setting

The classroom appeared very inviting and exciting to those who entered the room (see Figure 2-1). It was colorful and attractive, filled with ethnic folk art from the traditions of those who used it. The teacher had hung four big "piñatas" (three stars and a witch) from two room-length, diagonally crossed wires immediately overhead. The children had made colorful hats from crepe paper that also hung across these wires, alongside exquisite embroidery artwork from South America. Pictures of the children adorned some of the bulletin boards as did the attendance record cards. A goldfish swam in a small illuminated tank by the sink. A variety of manipulatives allowed for improvement of eye-hand motor coordination and new concept development. The room was full of places for inquisitive minds and exploring eyes. It was a room that validated children and their experiences. The early childhood curriculum of this school district was considered exploratory and developmental and designed to provide pre-kindergarten, lower socioeconomic children with enriching experiences to support and enhance their later formal education in the public schools.

The teacher and her aides were warm and nurturing, making the children feel loved, valued, and appreciated. The teacher was firm in her expectations, yet gentle. She used a variety of materials and strategies to capture the children's interest. In this classroom parents and visitors always seemed welcome. There were no obvious signs of a "hidden curriculum" except for the playhouse or housekeeping corner. In recent years this cornerstone of the early childhood program has become the center of controversy. Some primary teachers consider the playhouse a segregating and gender-biased area that should not be part of any primary education program.

General observations indicate that boys and girls in early childhood classrooms need more exposure to new behaviors and attitudes about the playhouse. The children's play in that area is conditioned by the general role expectations already internalized. Unless we show them otherwise, stereotypic behaviors become increasingly supported and ingrained through their play. A classroom playhouse is not in itself a problem but that without careful monitoring it *could* become a powerful force for the promotion and perpetuation of socially acquired biases and stereotypes. It appears that early childhood education teachers need increased awareness and knowledge about the socialization of young children and skills in the creation of fostering environments that pro-

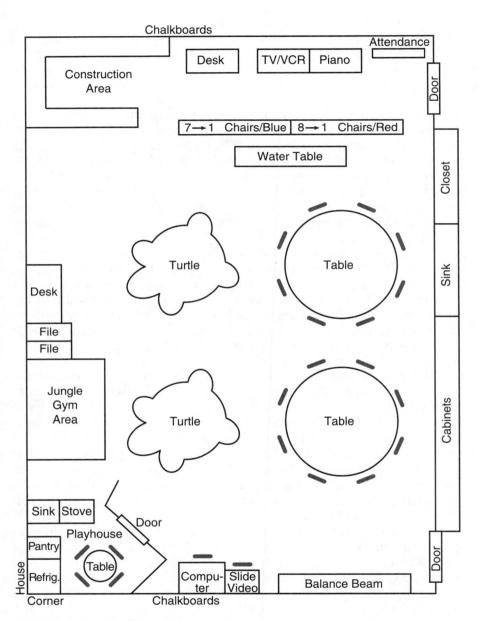

FIGURE 2-1 Classroom Arrangement

vide opportunities for growth and the acquisition of bias-free behaviors. A classroom playhouse could provide a fine resource for ending biases and reinforcing the acquisition of new values because children liken it to their home environments where they feel safe. It is not the playhouse itself that presents these stereotypical images but the socializing behaviors that children bring from outside and display in the classroom, often unnoticed and without adult direction.

Some Comments on the Observer's Role

As difficult as it was, the researcher decided to remain an objective observer during the visits and not become involved with the children. She tried to have the children feel at ease with her while not being too obvious or disrupting the flow of their activities. The children knew that she was there observing them, but they generally paid little attention to her. It was recognized that by mere presence one was an influential factor in the classroom. Children occasionally came to the researcher for support or acknowledgment.

To help the reader interpret the material more clearly the descriptions of the classroom setting, the ongoing activities, and the interactions of adults and children appear in italics, while the observer's commentary, remarks, and impressions appear in normal script. It is important to note that the children and their teacher, the paraprofessionals and parent-aides carried on verbal conversations mainly in Spanish. The observer/researcher is fluent in Spanish and also is especially aware of and sensitized to the colloquialisms, speech and gestures, and their nuances and cultural meanings. These cultural meanings are highlighted for the reader, as well, throughout the account that follows.[3] Here begins the narrative account of the researcher covering her series of visits over several months in the bilingual early childhood classroom.

Initial Visits to the ECE Classroom

On the first day the researcher visited with the teacher for about half an hour before students began arriving to review background information and establish a vision of the students—both as individuals and as a group.

Soon, students started arriving with their parents. The parents usually came in the room to greet the teachers and bid their children farewell. Most parents brought their own children and said hello to the teacher and other adults in the room. They were visibly comfortable within this classroom environment. They were very interested in meeting me and learning of my purpose(s) in the room.

I was able to communicate with them in Spanish and meet a crucial twofold need: (1) to create affective and effective communication with the parents, and thereby (2) to dissipate any discomfort or apprehension. Although many did not appear to understand my objectives clearly, they nonetheless showed interest and enthusiasm. They welcomed me into their classroom and school community. After this, parents often came to greet me and ask about my progress. I enjoyed sharing some of my observations and getting their impressions. Most expressed their belief in educational equality. Although they often agreed that boys and girls were very different behaviorally, they did not indicate awareness of the socialization forces deeply ingrained within their societal and school cultures.

There were many hugs and kisses between parents and children, reminiscent of a first day of school. The children all seemed happy and excited about being in school and did not protest when the parents left. They would also hug the teacher and aides. Many could hardly wait for the parting protocol to be over in order to begin exploring the classroom. They would look anxiously about the room at all the activities taking place while their parent(s) continued to bid them farewell. Some simply broke loose from their parent's grip and said their farewells as they rushed to their selected area.

Two boys immediately went to the wooden jungle gym and began dangling upside down from their feet or climbing to the top. Lucy and Gloria went directly to the "playhouse" and began setting up. They started moving furniture and hanging pictures. Lucy came in with her "baby doll" and placed the doll on her seat before going to the playhouse. Later, two girls showed me that this doll was a boy and had genitalia to prove it. I smiled as I remembered the dolls I had as a child. When dolls came out with a semblance of breasts, the public went into an uproar.

Soon some boys joined the girls at the playhouse. The girls then began to tidy up while the boys did most of the moving and hanging of pictures. As more students arrived, another boy and girl joined the two girls at the house. Joe came in and sat at a round work table where wooden puzzles had been laid out, while a new boy, Oscar, arrived and wandered around the room appearing indecisive about an activity. He went to one of the round work tables but did not seem to find anything satisfactory there and finally joined the boys' group in their activities moving furniture at the playhouse.

Five boys moved to the "water table." This table contained spray bottles, suction toys, containers, and other "water toys." Two girls then moved to one of the round work tables to work on puzzles already laid out, while two other girls moved over to the computer with the male parent volunteer. Bob played on the floor with large, carton building blocks. Mary joined the boys at the water table. The boys were messy and squirted water on each other. Yet, they did not squirt Mary, who was neat but quiet. While the boys laughed and interacted with each other, they avoided interacting with her, nor did she speak to them. A conflict developed between two girls in the playhouse. Soon, Gloria and her friends left the house to create their own house at the opposite side of the room in the building area. They brought baskets of play food and fruits. They hung a few pictures and even hung a telephone receiver from an empty cookie jar to resemble a wall phone. It was interesting to watch each "play-house team" recruit boys and girls to their side against the other. After a while, the girls were still in their opposing teams while the boys joined forces to take goods from both houses and "tease" the girls. The boys appeared to enjoy this game against the girls. The girls were concerned with allegiances and the rules they created while the boys quickly forfeited the rules and decided to have fun together. Whereas the girls queried each other verbally for loyalty ("Don't play with her. She is not in our group."), the boys almost had an unspoken bond and soon organized themselves into the same team.

By 1:00 p.m., when all the students had finally arrived and the afternoon session was officially in session, one girl was sitting at one of the round work tables working on a puzzle with the female teacher aide. Five boys and one girl (Mary) remained at the water table, two groups of two girls played at two separate houses, one boy and girl played at the jungle gym, and a boy continued to play with the large building blocks on the floor. The teacher joined the students at the water table. Immediately Mary complained to the teacher that one of the boys had taken her water spout forcibly. I thought it interesting that she had not voiced any complaints before. The teacher asked the boy whether he had done that. He acknowledged that he had. The teacher asked him to return the spout, which he did, and the playing continued as before, with the boys playing together and the girl playing on a corner of the water table alone.

I found Mary's action strategic and almost predictable as she probably suddenly believed herself in a position of power over the boys with the teacher present to protect her. Although boys also vie for adult attention, the girls appeared to seek adult protection more than the boys. I wondered what her behavior would have been had the teacher not joined the group and given her a sense of empowerment. I thought of "Cinderella" waiting for "Prince Charming" to rescue her and deliver her to safety and how we socialize girls into believing the myth that *nice girls* get rescued to live happily ever after.

Bob asked to watch the video *Peter Pan*. The teacher had told me earlier that this boy was a true "father's son" and demanding to view the movie each day was his way of asserting his rights and power over the other students and even the adults in the room. I was told that he often demanded things. *The boy insisted on loading the video himself. The teacher and the male parent volunteer guided the boy through verbal instructions and cues. The adults pointed to things but never did anything to load the video themselves or show him how to do it. Lucy stayed at the playhouse the entire afternoon. She wore a dress and played with a doll. She often held the doll as she briefly ventured outside the house. Gloria, who had obviously claimed the second house, also ventured in and out of it but did not stay all the time. It appeared that rather than play together in the same house, these two girls preferred to establish separate jurisdiction at separate houses. They also "battled" for playmates or other girls who would join their individual cause against the other girls' group.*

When the female aide finished "helping" one girl with the puzzle, she moved next to another girl to help her, even though the girl appeared to be doing well alone and did not request the assistance. She never offered assistance to a boy who was also sitting at the table. The teacher sat at a round table to show a girl how to tie yarn and create patterns. Soon other girls came to that table.

It appeared that teachers and other adults do things for girls while allowing boys to do things for themselves. They also instructed boys verbally on how to do things but physically showed girls.

While the two girls remained at their respective playhouses, the boys created a game of taking fruits from one house to another. Sometimes the girls would instruct them on which items to take from the opposing house. The boys worked together and enjoyed this game of breaking the rules, being secretive, and disrupting the girls. They also climbed up on the jungle gym to spy on the girls playing inside the playhouse. The girls knew that the boys were indeed breaking the rules and taking their fruits but seemed to motivate and encourage their activities. The girls giggled, while appearing to conceal their laughter, as the boys sneaked to take their fruits. Yet, the girls often signaled each other and watched the boys from the corner of their eyes as they approached, took the fruit, and left with their loot. Three boys got very large rubber balls and played with them. The video continued to play while it appeared that the students were not really watching it. The female aide told me that she felt that they needed the sounds, and that just like the playhouse, background sounds and activity probably made them feel safe and at home.

The teacher opened the "sand turtles" and soon two girls were playing there. It appeared that the teacher was the key initiator of activities for the girls. The boys pretty much got the toys they wanted, when they wanted, or created their own activities. They decided what they wanted to do. Boys begin to distance themselves from teachers and caretakers, especially female ones, around this age. They also begin to distance themselves from girls. Later, in the first and second grades, boys distance themselves more and eventually detach themselves emotionally. They begin to rely more on other boys for guidance, leadership, and emotional support, whereas girls continue to be dependent on the teacher until later years (Best, 1983). The girls appeared to wait for the teacher's initiative and leadership, except in the playhouse, while the boys enjoyed playing games and breaking rules. Educators need to create activities that encourage girls to take more initiative and make their own decisions.

The areas of activities preferred by the girls appeared to be the playhouses and the round work tables for puzzles, cutting, and coloring. With the exception of the playhouse, girls selected adult-dominated areas. The areas of activities for the boys appeared to be the water table, the jungle gym, the construction area, and the front open space of the room (in front of the television) where they could throw or roll their balls, build with LEGOS, or roll around on the floor with each other. It was interesting that the boys commanded the most, the largest, and, seemingly, the most strategic parts of the room. These were areas where they could create their own rules or break old ones. Areas preferred by boys were not specified for them by adults.

The boys tended to move about and change activities faster than the girls. They also appeared to organize their games more cooperatively and decided on their activities independently of the adults. They appeared to organize their activities naturally and without much struggle, whereas the girls showed difficulty deciding what they were going to do and who they were going to do it with. The boys moved in and out of boys' groups without hesitation, whereas girls negotiated and pledged allegiances to one particular girl or girls against others. There was also no set pattern to these allegiances and girls moved from one play partner to another without apparent motives or predictability. Even though boys also quarrelled, they resolved their disputes quicker, even with fists, and continued playing, whereas girls ended the game when a dispute arose, sought the teacher's help, or recruited new girls into their personal circle against other girls' groups. When the boys "fought" physically, it was usually the girls calling the fight to the teacher's attention. After a boys' fight was over, it was not uncommon for them to resume playing together. The girls did not "fight" physically as much as the boys, but constantly searched for the teacher's intervention in their quarrels. Once a girls' quarrel was over, they avoided each other and proceeded to recruit supporters to their cause.

Bob got a book and asked the teacher to read it for him. The boys, more than the girls, went to the teacher to ask or demand things, whereas the girls appeared to wait for the teacher to initiate an activity or relied on the teacher for praise or protection. The boys' language appeared very clear, decisive, and commanding: "Read this for me," "I want (this or that)," "I want you to do (this or that)." When asking for things, many of the girls used language that was more imploring and whining. Many of the girls also tended to create a distinctive facial and body expression when asking for very special things they wanted.

Lucy came to show the teacher a pendant she was wearing. The teacher praised the pendant and told the girl that she looked pretty. After the teacher praised it, she appeared satisfied and left to play back in the house.

I thought about that for a while, wondering about other ways to praise female students for attractive items of clothing without attaching the physical object(s) to the personal value of the student. How can we praise the physical appearance of students, particularly females, while helping them realize that (1) they possess personal individual characteristics that are equally or even more valuable than their physical attributes, and (2) their individual personal attributes are not dependent on their physical appearance?

Mary finally left the water table and went over to the house but didn't talk to anybody there. After observing the activities briefly, she then walked over to a seat and sat alone. After a very brief moment, she walked over to the playhouse again, watched the girls playing there for a short while, then walked away once more. When the teacher took out the LEGO boxes, the boys immediately grabbed them and started building. Mary joined them. Again, the boys interacted as they played, but did not speak to this girl. She played with the LEGOS alone. When the teacher joined the group, this girl again complained to the teacher that her box didn't have as many LEGOS as the boys' box. The teacher looked into her box and the other boxes and immediately emptied some LEGOS from them into hers.

I found it interesting that this girl was always well-behaved and quiet, was obedient to adults, and never argued with the other boys or girls in the classroom. She walked away from troublesome situations. At first, I thought that she was just more mature than the other children. The teachers described her as a very good and bright student. Further, I remembered that this girl was often asked to accompany other girls to the lavatory. She appeared not to partake in the girls' games of allegiance and exclusion. She sometimes appeared to simply go about her business almost unnoticed by anyone, adults included. I, personally, did not notice her much at first either, until I witnessed the incident at the water table. Then her behaviors became very intriguing as I tried to understand the ingrained stereotypes that molded them. She spent a lot of time around the boys' circles even though they did not interact or pay much attention to her. I surmised that she was more attracted to the boys' activities than the girls.' The boys disturbed, even fought, with some of the other girls, but not with this girl. They did not chase her away from their circle but ignored her. When she played with the girls, she appeared to lose interest quickly. The girls did not often solicit her participation in their games. The teacher and the other adults in the classroom did not interact much with this girl either, except to ask her to assist someone or escort another girl to the lavatory.

Research shows that acquiescent female students receive less attention than boys and that the most intelligent female students receive the least attention from teachers (Grayson and Miller, 1990). This is related to their apparently untroublesome behavior and conformity to our accepted female stereotypes and expectations. This girl has obviously learned that adults around her will protect her and provide for her wants and needs. Being a *nice girl* means being quiet, passive, and submissive. Being a *nice girl* also means that others will protect you and provide for you.

I was at a loss trying to explain the children's attitudes and behaviors towards her. Were the children mirroring adults' perceptions, attitudes, and behaviors toward this girl?

Later two other girls joined the teacher in this group. They interacted only with the teacher. I asked the boys playing with LEGOS what they were doing and they were quick to respond that they were building houses, firehouses, stores, or cars. One boy built a truck and began to roll it on the floor to show me how it worked. The boys played with the toys they built. Further, I noticed that sometimes boys put toys together without really knowing what they were, then tried them out to see what they could do with them. The boys used their imagination to add utility and versatility to their toys. Girls were more conventional.

I asked one girl to tell me what she was doing and she responded that she did not know. She was, with the teacher, placing animals on a LEGOS platform, but could not tell me what they were doing or why. I tried to establish a pattern to the activity, but after observing for a while, I could not do so. The animals were of all kinds and were being placed without an apparent pattern. Later, I asked a second girl in that group, but she too responded that she did not know what she was doing. The teacher asked them as well, but the girls in this group were not able to respond.

I began to look for patterns to explain some of the behaviors I was observing. All the girls had long hair. Two wore braids, five wore pony tails. Only one girl wore sneakers and was casually dressed for play. I noticed that this girl was the only one who earlier had joined the boys at the jungle gym. The rest of the girls wore dress shoes, which were slippery and difficult to run and play in. They wore more formal clothing, which they obviously could not soil or tear, even their pants suits. Only three girls wore pants while the rest wore dresses with many ribbons, bows, and lace. All the boys wore comfortable, everyday playwear such as jeans and sneakers.

A girl asked to go to the bathroom and the teacher asked Mary to go with her. Later, a boy wanted to go to the bathroom. The teacher escorted him to the door, opened it, but let him go alone. The aide explained that usually girls go to the lavatory in pairs, whereas the boys are sometimes permitted to go by themselves. The two girls held hands as they left the room.

Day Two of the Initial Visits

Later in the week I returned to the classroom. On this day Lucy came in wearing a dress again and immediately went to the playhouse. She wore a very elaborate white, red, and blue dress with a blue apron, red dress shoes, and strands of silver stars on her hair. She even wore blush and some lipstick. Only two girls wore dresses or skirts. The rest wore dressy pants still unsuitable for play. All wore dress shoes. The boys again were dressed comfortably and appropriately for rough floor play.

Mary joined two other girls on the floor to work with wooden puzzles. The male parent volunteer drew pictures of cars with three boys on the back chalkboard. Males (parents and volunteers) present an invaluable asset in the classroom. They can serve as effective role models for both male and female students. This male parent volunteer usually helped the teacher by doing work alone (cutting, coloring, or preparing things to decorate the classroom with) or helped the girls with technological equipment, such as the VCR and the computer, by actually turning them on. Yet he *explained* the process and encouraged the boys to use these things on their own.

Unintentionally, this male was reinforcing biases and stereotypic behaviors. What would happen if this male role model received awareness and skills development training that would enable him to work with the girls designing and building cars or other mechanical toys? What would happen if this male held a lesson on cooking or participated in other stereotypical female activities? I spoke with him on numerous occasions about the need for equity awareness and training in the early childhood classroom. He agreed but didn't know how to go about initiating change. As a male parent volunteering to spend time in his daughter's classroom every day, he represented a powerful role model. He seemed to already hold a foundation for more extensive equity training.

The aide began to build a LEGOS house with a boy and two girls. This time when I asked one of the girls what they were doing, she responded quickly and accurately—they were building a house. Perhaps, building a house is a much more concrete idea for the girls because of their socialization than placing animals on a surface. Girls can be encouraged to build and create mechanical objects that have practical applications as boys do.

I did not observe girls initiating activities with LEGOS or other building materials like the boys did. Their building activities tended to be initiated by adults. Often the teacher or aides put out large wooden puzzles in the construction area. This attracted both boys and girls, but again it was an adult-initiated activity that attracted the girls to boy-controlled areas. This was also true for the water table.

Boys acquire mechanical abilities from male role models and through manipulating toys that require and develop mechanical skills. Girls could also learn how to put things together and take them apart and understand how they work. These experiences and knowledge set the foundation for mathematical and science concepts, as well as higher-order thinking processes. Math and science readiness is linked to pre-school games and toys (blocks, construction sets, cars, trains, model kits, tools) that lead to understanding and familiarity with apparatus and interest in how things work. Males tend to have more experience with such toys than females (Schubert, 1983).

After a while, the girls gravitated to the playhouse, with Lucy at the lead. They played with the dolls and Lucy carried a purse around the room with her imitating an adult. Lucy came to show me the stars on her hair. I remembered that she was the same girl who during my first visit had shown the teacher the pendant she was wearing. It appears that this girl seeks attention in the form of praise for her appearance. Whereas Lucy never approached me on the first day, perhaps she felt more at ease with me today and wanted to secure my praise as well. I rarely observed boys seeking teacher or adult praise for their clothing or physical appearance. Once one boy flaunted a buckled cowboy belt he was wearing. The aide simply responded that it was very nice, but never told him that *he* looked good with it or that it made him more handsome. I thought of not praising Lucy but quickly realized that such action would have upset the established pattern in her life and classroom. I decided to praise her clothing but added that I like *her* better because I believed that she was very intelligent. Then I asked her if she considered herself smart. She smiled, agreed, and walked away satisfied.

Again, Lucy brought a stuffed bear. It appeared that the girls, more often than the boys, brought stuffed dolls or animal toys to school. I did not see any of the boys bring toys from home, except for miniature cars and *"Transformers"* (robot-shaped toys whose form can be changed). We condition boys to be "men" the minute they enter school, yet promote girls to remain "cute little girls" even after they enter school.

Boys, beginning in first grade, are pressured into increasing distancing from girls and anything labeled "feminine." Girls come to school "already primed for the archetypical feminine role" (Best, 1989). Girls are ready and waiting for the opportunity to help others, whereas boys are socialized to be taken care of. Girls complain about their weaknesses (when a boy is too aggressive or they don't have as much as the boys), whereas boys are socialized to either take or demand more regardless of what anybody else gets. Girls and boys also learn to make career and life choices deemed appropriate for their sex (Best, 1989).

On this second day, three boys became very interested in cutting magazine pictures. This was probably influenced by the fact that this was a teacher-initiated activity and she again specifically asked them to join her. One boy stayed constantly at the water table. Two girls (Mary included) joined him, but again the girls interacted with each other but not with the boy. The boy pretty much played without paying much attention to them.

I wondered if perhaps some adult-directed activities would encourage the boys and girls to interact more with each other in self-selected activities. Leaving the children to self-select activities and groupings is a valuable self-development process, but in a gender-biased society, I thought, perhaps continuous self-selection is not developmental but detrimental to the establishment of a wholesome individual. I realize that assigning tasks and groupings can also be harmful, but perhaps a balance could be reached to support individual growth through decision making and the self-establishment of priorities and support the acquisition of new values and behaviors that will enhance a more pluralistic self-concept.

The girls staged a bridal parade. Lucy dressed as a bride with an improvised white veil and bouquet. As she marched from the playhouse around the classroom some of the other girls marched behind her holding her veil and dress. They sang, hummed, and marched to the rhythm of a Spanish song. They didn't know all the words but I later identified it as a Spanish wedding march ("Valsoviana") originated in Seville and very traditional of the Southwest. There was much joy and laughter in this activity. The boys watched amusedly but none joined the girls. The bridal group marched back into the playhouse and the girls finally left the house to watch the video Corduroy, *which is about a little girl who befriends a cuddly teddy bear.*

I found it interesting that the boys showed more interest in the video *Peter Pan* (adventure and danger) whereas the girls were more interested in *Corduroy* (love and nurturance). *Corduroy* was also the book of the month. Lucy told me that her teddy bear was also named Corduroy. *About one hour into the session, the female aide was still building LEGOS houses with a boy and a girl. The teacher joined four girls at the water table. The teacher asked the girls what would happen if she added soap to the water. The girls quickly added that they could wash the "trastes" or dishes. Again, this would have presented an excellent opportunity to dissipate some gender biases and introduce some new behaviors: What else could we do instead of washing dishes? The teacher added soap and the girls pretended to be washing the dishes or clothes. She showed them how to wash their hands and emphasized the need to do so before eating and after going to the bathroom. She modeled the hand movements (rub hands around and around). She later explained that personal hygiene and disease prevention was part of the curriculum.* I enjoyed the way she introduced and integrated the curriculum as part of the children's play. Gender equity can also be an integral and natural part of every curriculum and activity.

Later Visits to the ECE Classroom

Later in the spring, I visited the class again. After reviewing my earlier observations with the early childhood bilingual teacher and her aides, we decided to intervene and implement measures to change the students' attitudes and behaviors toward the playhouse, the construction area, the jungle gym, and each other as boys and girls (see Figure 2-2). The teacher, paraprofessional, aide, and even the male parent volunteer appeared excited about this new awareness. They explained that even though they were cognizant of gender disparities within their classroom, school, and society at large, they initially hadn't realized that they contributed to them or that they could change them favorably. They were eager to acquire new knowledge and skills that would enable them to provide equity and excellence in education for *all* students.

Because the playhouse had essentially become segregated by gender, with mostly girls playing inside while boys attempted to sabotage their activities from the outside, a way was needed to open up the area for all students. To stop the girls' secretive behavior in the playhouse, the walls of the play house were opened and pushed out so all activities taking place there could be seen by everyone in the room. This also enabled all the adults to enter it. The jungle gym had been preferred by the boys, but because it was right next to the playhouse, it was especially utilized by the boys to spy on and disrupt the girls' secretive activities in the playhouse; therefore, it was decided to move it to another part of the room away from the playhouse. The jungle gym was placed in an open, central area of the classroom where it could be more accessible to both boys and girls. It was acknowledged that the girls' secretive activities triggered the boys' disruptive behaviors, which further encouraged more secrets from the girls.

To encourage initial involvement in the playhouse by all students, one of the large round work tables was placed right in front of the entryway. Everyone sitting at this table could see the playhouse and all the activities taking place there. The teacher and other adults in the room often initiated activities with the students at this round table. Children sat at the round tables regardless of gender, especially when called by an adult to engage in activities together. Children expected to find teacher- or adult-initiated, teacher-directed activities there. Whenever children were lost for something to do, they went to one of the large work tables and sat. Even when nothing was specifically set out for them, they waited for an adult to come and provide or suggest an activity. This was also where parents sat and worked or observed when they visited the classroom. Other areas of the room were "owned" by the users.

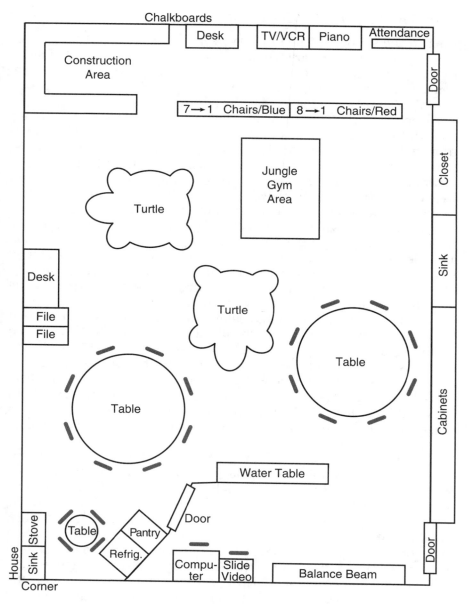

FIGURE 2-2   Classroom Arrangements

By both boys and girls engaging in adult-initiated activities at this table, it was hoped that the students would feel more positive about continuing their activities *together* in the playhouse. The presence of adults attracted students to different play areas regardless of the students' perceived ownership of it. The girls worked in the construction area whenever an adult also worked there or initiated an activity. Adults, restricted by their size, seldom entered the playhouse.

The boys had always preferred the water table as a play area. The teacher wanted to include something that was preferred by the boys in the playhouse as a way of interesting them in it while removing the behavior that had been established on the jungle gym. Therefore, we moved the water table right next to the playhouse, inside the area between the house and the round work table. To our dismay, the girls immediately tried to claim it as a sink to wash the dishes. Realizing that this was counterproductive, the teacher and the aide quickly moved the water table to the other side of the playhouse. The adults definitely did not want the boys to feel like "their" work area had been usurped. It was clear that the popularity of some areas or equipment was directly related to their location and the students' perceived ownership. Resources are usually owned by the primary users (Huxley, 1990). Although the adults ultimately wanted to end the "cycle of ownership" and exclusions, it was realized that changes had to be gradual. The teacher and her aides decided to give this new classroom arrangement some time and then review whether and how it had affected students' activities.

Returning Several Weeks Later

After a few weeks, I went to observe the class again. The new classroom arrangement had been maintained. I found more boys and girls playing together in the playhouse, the jungle gym, and the construction area. The teacher and the other adults in the room agreed that more boys were indeed going into the playhouse than before. The girls' secretive activities appeared to have been reduced and the boys were no longer interested in stealing the girls' play food or disrupting the girls' activities in the playhouse.

I was still very concerned about the girls' inappropriate clothing and shoes. Even though warmer weather was prevalent, most girls still wore dresses and dress shoes rather than the comfortable play clothes the boys wore. The new central location of the jungle gym appeared to have had an impact. It was interesting to observe more girls playing in the jungle gym even if they were not appropriately dressed for it.

I did not observe more boys and girls playing together in the construction area, and activity at the water table appeared to have been eliminated altogether. The teacher indicated that as the year progressed and warm weather approached, the children were merely shifting their interests. The children were learning songs and rehearsing for their year-end program.

Yet, when boys and girls played together in the playhouse, they still engaged in stereotypical behaviors. They played "mom and dad." *Three boys and one girl (Mary) sat at the round table drawing and coloring. The girl suggested to a boy, "Let's go to the playhouse and play 'mama y papa'/'mom and dad.'"* To my surprise, the boy actually went with Mary to the playhouse. This is the same girl who always joined boys' activities but who, previously, received little acknowledgment from them. *Soon they were joined by other boys and girls. The girls cleaned, cared for the baby dolls, and constantly fussed at the boys for their behavior, which was very typically male. The boys sat around while the girls cared for them and served them food or scolded them. The girls engaged in play gossip about fictitious neighbors "Esa mujer de al lado . . ./That woman next door . . ."). The boys scolded the "mom" and the children, moved furniture and hung pictures or misbehaved. The girls threatened to spank the children who were misbehaving and to "tell Dad when he comes home." Sometimes the boys played house pets such as cats and dogs while the girls still played "moms." The girls or "moms" yelled at the children or the "dad" to take the animals out of the house because the animals were "messing things up." The girls pretended to push/drag the offending pet ("Largate, perro sucio"/"Out, dirty dog") out of the house but always waited for the "dad" to accomplish the task most effectively. It was interesting to observe the "pet" resist the females' push and tug, yet follow the boys' lead out of the house. Often the boys playing house pets slept on the play bed, under the kitchen play table or "hung around" being taken care of by the "mom" or just plain misbehaved. Part of the game was clearly the girls' expectation that the "dad," pets, or children would misbehave, giving them something to fuss or complain about.*

Again, the girls were the helpers and caretakers while the boys were expected to be cared for or break the rules and misbehave. Often the girls chased each other out of the house ("This is my house!"/"This is my baby!"/"This is my husband!") and fought each other. If one girl was the "mom" and a boy the "dad" the other boys and girls were either the children or pets. When a girl refused to be a part of this scheme, she became the neighbor who came to visit and was either welcomed or often rejected by the "woman of the house" when she knocked on the door. If she came in the house without first knocking, she was quickly reminded by the other girls in the house that this was not her house and that she needed to knock and wait to be invited before coming in.

The boys showed little concern about who or which girls came in or went out of the playhouse. They came and went as they pleased and did not remember or were reminded by any boy or girl that they needed to knock on the door before being admitted. The girls established unspoken rules about who was admitted to the game, whereas the boys just stepped into or out of the game if and when they felt like it. They appeared to be unrestricted by any rules and almost seemed to fall into the situation, casually enjoying it while redefining or changing the rules regardless of the girls. On the other hand, the girls appeared overwhelmingly concerned about who was playing and with whom (loyalty). When the boys got tired of the game, they just walked away and did something else, whereas the girls fussed with each other and complained to the teacher that so and so "doesn't want to play with me anymore. She doesn't want to be my friend."

Even though the boys appeared to break the rules more often when playing with girls, they seemed to be better able to play together and organize their games with other boys than the girls with other girls. The girls argued and disagreed with each other more often. They quarreled over playmates and friends and playthings, such as the play food and the baby dolls.

This in-depth account of a series of observations in a bilingual early childhood program over a period of several months is presented to give readers the unique opportunity to intimately view the social interactions that occur in such classrooms. The observer described and discussed how gender impacted young children and the responsible adults in this early childhood school setting. This detailed study lends support to a recognition of the complexity of socialization in the early childhood years. This micro-ethnography discloses the myriad pressures and conflicting messages given to children about the social world they live in and the expectations the adults that surround them hold for their behavior in the home and in the school.

SUMMARY

The chapter began with a caveat for adults concerning the perceptiveness of young children to the social, economic, and political life of the adults that surround them. Anecdotes and examples attested to the process of socialization of children early in life to these conditions. Gender, ethnic, and social class awareness of young children was discussed and documented. This presentation of the major aspects of the diversity perspective was followed by an in-depth study or micro-ethnography of a bilingual early childhood classroom. This chapter highlighted the educational philosophy and the intentions, actions, and interactions of responsible adults in the early childhood classroom and their impact on young children in educational settings.

KEY CONCEPTS

Early Childhood Education   According to guidelines established by the National Association for the Education of Young Children (NAEYC), this term encompasses the experiences of children from birth through age eight. As used in *this* textbook, the term applies to youngsters between three and eight years old. It includes both formal, structured experiences within a school setting, as well as the informal learning that takes place everywhere within a child's social and physical environment.

Early Childhood Education Programs   The five recognized educational units in early childhood include: *Preschool:* Usually a setting for half-day, two or three days per week; considered to be "enrichment;" serving youngsters as young as 2 1/2 years. *Kindergarten:* The highest, culminating level in preschool, or the beginning level of a regular public or private elementary school. *Primary Grades:* First and second grade. Some schools include third grade to be certain to include youngsters up to eight years of age. *Child Care:* The setting serving children with the widest age range (infants and toddlers through age twelve as in after-school programs). It also has the longest schedules (often 6:00 a.m. through 6:00 p.m., with the children remaining more hours than the teachers). *Head Start:* This early childhood program is federally-mandated. It attempts to address the educational, physical, and social needs of preschool children who are economically underprivileged.

Socialization   The dynamic process that brings human beings into the human group, causing an individual to internalize the ways of the culture and to accept and affirm the values, traditions, folkways, mores, and attitudes of the broader society.

Ethnicity   A sense of peoplehood and commonality derived from kinship patterns, a shared historical past, common experiences, religious affiliations, language or linguistic commonalities, shared values, attitudes, perceptions, modes of expression, or identity.

Gender-/Sex-Appropriate Behavior   Initially based on biological distinctions between males and females, those processes that structure the statuses, roles, and activities in a society and then become further developed and interpreted through culturally defined norms, attitudes, and values.

Socioeconomic Class   A measure that combines a person's education, occupation, and income to derive that person's ranking in the social structure.

Interaction of the Forces of Socialization   The consequences of the interaction of an individual's gender, ethnic, and social class affiliations on life chances, educational opportunities, general growth, and development.

Bilingualism in Early Childhood The conditions under which young children are exposed to speakers of differing languages or dialects, so that their early speech patterns are shaped by speakers of two or more languages.

ISSUES AND ACTIONS

On various occasions we are asked to recall significant remembrances or incidents from our childhood that have influenced us in adulthood. Presented in this chapter were some anecdotes that contained young children's remarks about the economic and social class status of their parents or families. To get a sense of what this means from your personal perspective spend a short time with the following activity:

1. Write down one or two anecdotes from your childhood memories of an incident where your parents' or family's economic or social class status was revealed. Try to think about how the incident came about. Who were the individuals involved? Is this a positive memory or an embarrassing one for you? How did the others involved in the occurrence react? Has the incident had a long-lasting impact on you, shaping your attitudes and values, or has it become insignificant to you? Discuss your anecdotes with others and see what reactions it draws from them.

2. If you do not wish to delve into your own childhood, write down one or two anecdotes that you recall or have heard others detail about young children's awareness of the social, political, and economic scene that is occurring around them (for example, during a presidential election or during a news media blitz). Share these anecdotes with fellow students or the teacher. Discuss the implications for child socialization that these stories raise.

3. Possibly the incidents or anecdotes that you recall also bring forth significant memories related to gender awareness or ethnic affiliation awareness in your childhood. Write down or recount these memories and discuss them with a friend or colleague. Are these accounts similar to the ones presented in chapter 1, or are the topics quite different? What conclusions can you come to about the nature of child socialization based on your own remembrances?

4. We hope that after reading the in-depth case study of the early childhood classroom you are stimulated to observe young children, either in the school setting or at informal play, with an emphasis on their expressions of gender stereotyping. Plan such a project with options for diverse ethnic group involvement if possible. Write down in detail your observations,

impressions, and comments. Share your project with others. If you have access to an early childhood classroom consider intervention strategies as described in this chapter. Plan such strategies and record the results of your efforts. Discuss the effects and results with other teachers or parents.

ENDNOTES

1. Goodman, Mary Ellen. *The Culture of Childhood: Child's-Eye Views of Society and Culture.* New York: Teachers College Press, Columbia University, 1970.

Goodman was a gifted and learned anthropologist who wrote with an extensive knowledge of the anthropological literature on childhood socialization in cultures and societies around the globe. Her most well-known and precedent-setting book was *Race Awareness in Young Children,* a cultural anthropologist's study of how racial attitudes begin among four-year-olds, first published in 1952 by the Anti-Defamation League of B'nai Brith. Early childhood educators owe a great debt to this perceptive social scientist for her pioneering work in race relations in the earliest years.

2. King, Edith W. *Educating Young Children . . . Sociological Interpretations.* Dubuque, IA: William C. Brown, 1973.

In this volume the author provides many examples and classroom accounts of young children's experiences from a *sociological viewpoint,* during a time in the education literature and lore when cognitive development and educational psychology held sway.

3. The authors are indebted to the teacher and her staff and the children of the early childhood education program described here. Their patience, cooperation, and enthusiasm are greatly appreciated for the study included in this text.

REFERENCES AND SUGGESTED READINGS

Banks, James. *Multiethnic Education: Theory and Practice* (second edition). Newton, MA: Allyn and Bacon, 1988.
Banks, James, and Banks, Cherry (Eds.). *Multicultural Education: Issues and Perspectives.* Newton, MA: Allyn and Bacon, 1989.
Baruth, L. G., and Manning, M. L. *Multicultural Education of Children and Adolescents.* Newton, MA: Allyn and Bacon, 1992.
Berger, P., and Luckmann, T. *The Social Construction of Reality.* New York, Anchor Books, 1966.
Best, Raphaela. *We've All Got Scars: What Boys and Girls Learn in Elementary School.* Bloomington, IN: Indiana University Press, 1983.
Cuzzort, R. P., and King, E. W. *20th Century Social Thought* (4th edition). New York: Holt, Rinehart and Winston, 1989.

Derman-Sparks, L., and the A.B.C. Task Force. *Anti-Bias Curriculum: Tools for Empowering Young Children.* Washington, DC: National Association for the Education of Young Children, 1989.

Elkin, F., and Handel, G. *The Child and Society: The Process of Socialization* (fifth edition). New York: Random House, 1989.

Garcia, Ricardo. *Teaching in a Pluralistic Society: Concepts, Models and Strategies* (second edition). New York: HarperCollins, 1990.

Grayson, Dolores, and Miller, Pamela. *Gender Ethnic/Expectations and Student Achievement.* 1990.

Huxley, Margaret. Practical Steps towards Gender Equality with the Under-Fives. England: *Early Years;* Fall, 1990.

King, Edith. *The World: Context for Teaching in the Elementary School.* Dubuque, IA: William C. Brown, 1971.

King, Edith. *Educating Young Children . . . Sociological Interpretations.* Dubuque, IA: William C. Brown, 1973.

King, Edith. *Teaching Ethnic and Gender Awareness.* Dubuque, IA: Kendall/Hunt, 1990.

King, Edith. *Teaching Ethnic and Gender Awareness: Methods and Materials for the Elementary School* (second edition). Dubuque, IA: Kendall/Hunt, 1990.

Lubeck, Sally. *Sandbox Society.* Philadelphia: Falmer Press, 1983.

Maccoby, Eleanore, and Jacklin, Carol. *The Psychology of Sex Differences.* Stanford, CA: Stanford University Press, 1974: 277–302.

Mead, George Herbert. *Mind, Self and Society.* Chicago: University of Chicago Press, 1934.

Milner, David. *Children and Race Ten Years On.* London: Ward Lock, 1983.

Ramsey, Patricia. *Teaching and Learning in a Diverse Society.* New York: Teachers College Press, 1987.

Schubert, J. B. "An Interactive Approach to Infusing Equity: A Teacher Model." Unpublished paper presented at the American Educational Research Association Meetings, April, 1983.

3

DEVELOPMENTALLY APPROPRIATE PRACTICE AND MULTICULTURAL INSTRUCTION

In chapter 1 we defined the diversity perspective in early childhood education as the infusion of ethnicity, social class, and gender aspects in our teaching. In this chapter we examine the importance of developmentally appropriate practice and its relation to this diversity approach. The following anecdote illustrates the topic.

> *Seated at the breakfast table, Janine, a young mother, showed her husband a cartoon appearing in the morning paper. It depicted a half dozen or so three- and four-year-olds in line waiting for the teacher to open the door of their preschool. All the boys and girls were dressed in business suits and carried identical small briefcases. Both parents laughed at what they perceived to be a humorous scenario.*
>
> *An hour later this same young mother dropped their toddler off at the day-care center. She intentionally had arrived a few minutes early because she wanted to talk to the director. Janine had heard something about an early childhood learning program that purported to teach infants to read sight words. Janine wanted to volunteer to organize a fund-raising event among the parents so that the director could purchase this teach-your-infant-to-read program for use at their day-care center. She mentioned to the director that some of the parents had been voicing concerns that "all the children do is play" and this might be a way to respond to some of these types of complaints.*

This anecdote provides an example of how Janine and so many other parents are not aware of what is termed "developmentally appropriate practice" in early childhood education. What is this all about and why is it so vital to the design of the early childhood education curriculum? This chapter focuses on the crucial nature of developmentally appropriate practice for young children and the recent perspective of emerging literacy. A number of parents, like Janine in the account above, are quick to judge preschool and kindergarten teachers on how successful they are in getting their students to excel. While she felt that the cartoon was preposterous, she unwittingly was trying to make the pre-school director move the youngsters along at a faster pace.

THEORETICAL BASES FOR DEVELOPMENTALLY APPROPRIATE PRACTICE

The Ascendancy of Emergent Literacy

Over the past several years there has been growing criticism by experts and researchers specializing in early childhood education of the emphasis on reading readiness. This emphasis on readiness, especially for language development and early reading, has led to a massive use of reading readiness testing and early labeling of children. The dangers of these insistent pressures to assess very young children are clear. Many kindergarteners experience daily routines that are dominated by phonic workbook activities that trace the letters of the alphabet as well as coloring in little pictures on "ditto" sheets. Some preschoolers must sit through tedious drills that teach auditory and visual discrimination skills in a manner that is isolated from all they are familiar with in their daily life.

Early childhood experts assert that young children need to be involved in meaningful acts of learning to communicate, which includes comprehending the spoken work, speaking, then reading and writing. The emergent literacy perspective has recently begun to challenge the concept of reading readiness:

> *This [emergent literacy] perspective, based on current research in the areas of reading, writing, listening, and speaking, casts serious doubts on the underlying assumptions of reading readiness. On the basis of school and home ethnographic studies, case studies, and structured interviews of children from a variety of ethnic and social backgrounds, educational theorists and researchers, as well as scholars from the fields of linguistics and psychology, have begun to think about literacy in a new way. (Hodges, 1991, p. 155)*

This new way of thinking about literacy recognizes that very young children, even two-and-half and three-year-olds, come into early childhood education with a background of language experiences, including recognizing written symbols and prewriting efforts, from their home and neighborhood environments. Ollila and Mayfield (1992) stress that emergent literacy includes an awareness of print and writing and other uses of language. It is a multidimensional and complex process that stems from the children's active participation in efforts to communicate with those around them. This new concept of literacy in the early years varies from child to child and includes speaking, listening, reading, and writing as parts of a language process that is emerging from the child as a result of environmental stimulation.

To provide an example of emergent literacy we can cite the proud grandmother who is adamant that her 2 1/2 year-old grandson can read because he tells her, as they are driving around the neighborhood to shop, she has just gone past K Mart and will reach McDonald's at the next turn and he wants to *eat*!

The Importance of Play in Early Childhood Education

The intimate relationship between what is "serious" language learning and just what is learned by very young children through daily experiences brings us to the importance of play. Is play just frivolous childish activity? "Play is the child's work" is a familiar saying among early childhood educators. Modern educational methods have recognized the importance of play in the growth and development of children. Philippe Aries (1962) points out in his book, *Centuries of Childhood,* that historically the child was considered "frivolous" for the need to play, and through the centuries children were allowed this stage of play and frivolity only until about seven years of age. Today we realize that play is a natural and necessary medium for the internalization of values and for the construction of concepts and relationships. The child's social development is encouraged through play. Play is a means of discovering one's own identity, relating to others, understanding other viewpoints, learning to use symbols in thinking, and internalizing the ways of the society through imitating adult roles and situations.

The importance of play, particularly for socioemotional and cognitive development, has figured prominently in early childhood theories and methods. Rousseau, the French philosopher, wrote continuously of the need to allow children the freedom to explore, to discover nature, and to roam openly in their environment—in other words, *play!* Additionally, games, toys, finger plays, and manipulative materials have been mentioned as innovations in the writings about young children's learning by those famous founders of early childhood education—Pestalozzi, Froebel, and Montessori.

Early writings of Jean Piaget, the famous Swiss psychologist, focused strongly on the importance of play. The toddler of two or three years of age emerges from solitary and parallel play patterns into the stage of more cooperative and collective play at about four years of age. Piaget theorized that from about four years to about seven years of age children engage in forms of play characterized by imitation of adult occupations and pastimes.[1] These activities of young children were described in chapter 2 of this volume by our observer of the bilingual early childhood program and its engaging housekeeping corner experiences.

The behavior of children at play is highly consistent with Piaget's theory on the development of moral values and ethics. Early childhood games also pave the way for children to develop reversibility in their mental operations, in Piaget's terms, particularly in games and singing games where the roles of various characters or the leader and the chorus are interchanged. This so often occurs in favorite nursery and kindergarten songs and rhymes.

Piagetian Theory of Cognitive Development

In the previous discussion about the importance of play in early childhood education programs we have referred to Piaget and his theories. Let us now describe the theory of Jean Piaget as it relates to young children and underscore the insights and understandings that these concepts of young children's learning give adults. Piaget sees the individual as an action-oriented, searching, seeking, continually adapting organism. Children learn through the interactions of spontaneous, active play with the environment and the people around them. The emphasis is placed on the individual as an active rather than a passive learner.

Piaget identified three distinct stages of cognitive growth that follow infancy. He labels infancy as the *sensorimotor* stage. The next three stages he calls the *preoperational,* the *concrete-operations,* and finally, the *formal operational* stage. In the preoperational stage, ages two and a half to seven years, the child is still exploring the environment and sees the world in egocentric terms. At this stage children's perceptions lead to the greater acquisition of language and concepts of space, time, classification, seriation, and enumeration. Children have not developed an understanding of the conservation of matter and of reversibility. The child continues to assimilate information and accommodate the new knowledge to that which has been acquired. The young child still relies on intuitive thinking for many explanations of natural phenomena. The world children perceive seems to be a constant, unchanging environment.

Piaget's next stages involve children as they reach the ages of eight years and beyond—the stages of concrete operations and then formal thinking. We will not detail and discuss these stages and the implications they hold for cognitive-perceptual aspects of learning here, but it is important to realize that Piagetian theory covers the intellectual development of the individual from infancy to adulthood. Piaget's influence on educational thought, first as a biologist and later as a psychologist and moral philosopher, was grounded in the evolutionary conception of stages in human development. His theory of intellectual and moral development in human beings has become, in recent years, one of the most important foundations in early childhood education.

The British Primary School Approach

Early childhood education also has been deeply influenced by the British Primary School method, which has alternately been called "open education" and the "integrated day."[2] The British Primary School approach also is based in the Piagetian theory of cognitive development and the central role that "child's play" holds in the cognitive and social development of young children. No discussion of early childhood education would be complete without reference to this highly praised and emulated approach to working with young children. As a handy working description, let us characterize the British Primary School approach in early education as a philosophy that regards all children as active learners, individuals who can demonstrate to their teachers their learning needs and wants. The daily program is planned in large blocks of time to allow the children to explore and investigate topics in which each one is interested. The classroom is arranged in "interest" centers, not with fixed desks and a teacher front and center. The rooms of the school are open to the outside so that there is an indoors-outdoors feeling in the classroom. Much of the children's work and topics come from the community and the local environment that surrounds them. Field trips are frequent, and the children go out into the community to learn from their parents and local citizens as well as their teachers. Older children work with younger ones in multi-age level classes. Physical activities and movement education are integral parts of the curriculum. There is a focus on play and games in learning, both physically and mentally. It is not difficult to detect the influences of Rousseau's naturalism, John Dewey's progressive education, Maria Montessori's didactic materials, and Piaget's learning theory in the methods of the British Primary Schools.

DEVELOPMENTALLY APPROPRIATE PRACTICE IN THE CURRICULUM

Now let us examine the implications of the British Primary School approach and the importance of play for developmentally appropriate practice in early childhood education. Often curriculum reform is impacted by myriad factors outside education itself. The perceptions (often misconceived) of legislators and lobbyists carry strong influences on decisions made for the schools. Unfortunately in recent years there has been a trend away from "open education" and recognition of the importance of "play" for young children; rather, we have seen an increased emphasis on the acquisition of "academic learning" in early childhood programs. However, there does not appear to be an accompanying body of research to indicate a change in the ways that young children learn. On the contrary, professionals in the field continue to affirm that young children need concrete, play-oriented experiences to ensure that optimal learning takes place in the first years of life. Curricula that impose an academic regimen coupled with intensive testing and evaluation of young children have been the center of protest recently. Early childhood educators have championed the cause of open education, play, and investigative learning for young children.

Professor Philip Gammage of the University of Nottingham declares in his article titled "Children Don't Get Taller By Being Measured" (1991) that the *child* lies at the heart of learning:

> *I believe in what [David] Elkind has called "developmentally based practice." This phrase of Elkind's can be summed up very simply as meaning that, above all, the curriculum cannot be imposed from outside but must take into account the entering characteristics of the learners. This latter is not just a nod in the direction of children's passing interest; it is fundamental to the sensitive match and to real ownership of the learning experiences by the child. (Gammage, 1991, p. 22)*

Leading American child psychologists such as David Elkind, David Weikart, and Benjamin Bloom have emphasized that curricula for young children are best designed from a clearly developmental perspective. They have pointed out what experienced teachers of young children know: that growth and development involve a mix of the cognitive, social, physical, and emotional aspects in early childhood programs. Therefore, in planning the early childhood curriculum, the basic developmental needs of youngsters must be kept well in focus. The recent "Position Statement" of the National Association for the Education of Young Children indicates that, while many factors determine the quality of an early childhood program, a major determinant is "the extent to which knowledge of child development is applied." (Bredenkamp, 1987)

There are two levels of developmental appropriateness for us to keep in mind. The first is based on *age*. As a child grows, specific physical, linguistic, emotional, social, and cognitive changes take place. Research in child growth and development over decades has documented these assertions. Within the range of normal development, these age-related changes are predictable. Therefore, activities and lessons can be planned based on verifiable knowledge of age-related occurrences.

The second level is based on individual differences. Within the predictable normal range of development based on age, individual differences occur among human beings. These are due both to "nature," or inherited characteristics, and to "nurture," the environmental influences that impinge on the individual. The child's social background influences the prior knowledge brought to the classroom setting. A child's reactions to past experiences as well as to new ones are reflective of differences in personality. The *rate* at which a child develops physically, linguistically, cognitively, socially, and emotionally may vary. Activities for classrooms of young children should be planned with individual variations in mind.

AREAS OF THE EARLY CHILDHOOD CURRICULUM AND DEVELOPMENTALLY APPROPRIATE PRACTICE

The physical, linguistic, cognitive, emotional, and social growth of the child should be addressed through careful planning. Four major aspects of the young child's curriculum to be considered are the following:

- emergent literacy and the language arts;
- motor skills;
- socialization among peers and with adults;
- the broadening of cognitive and perceptual knowledge

It is also important to note that the integration of content areas is imperative and in the best interests of the young learners. Science, mathematics, and social studies are interwoven with music, art, and oral language. Counting and sorting occur as naturally outside on the playground as they do in the classroom. What are the contrasts between those programs that reflect developmental appropriateness and those that do not? Let us examine some specific areas and some pertinent examples in each of the aspects listed above: language arts and emergent literacy; social/emotional aspects; and cognitive/perceptual aspects.

Emergent Literacy and Language Arts

In language and literacy development, developmentally appropriate practice dictates that the children are given myriad opportunities to listen to stories and poems, as well as to dictate their own; to role-play life's situations; to share experiences freely; to produce original drawings and paintings and then discuss them extensively; and to take field trips or merely walking excursions and then communicate their observations verbally. These language activities lead the youngsters in a natural sequence to literacy. As they become emergent readers and writers, they will value the connection between their spoken words and the symbols they can put on paper to be read by themselves and others (Morrow, 1993).

As we have noted before, inappropriate practice is observable in early childhood classroom activities that emphasize such things as rote singing of the letters of the alphabet and the days of the week; the excessive use of "ditto" worksheets for the children to practice "coloring within the lines;" or the exact copying of words from a chart onto penmanship paper.

Motor Skills

Gross motor skills are enhanced in the developmentally appropriate setting by activities planned to provide exercise for the larger muscles of young children. The children spend ample time outside in open space for running or in using the apparatus designed especially for their needs. Fine motor control is gained by cutting, lacing, tying, stringing, and producing "masterpieces" from their own creativity with the use of fat pencils or felt-tip markers. In the setting characterized by inappropriate practice, children's outside play is withheld as punishment for some classroom offense or may be limited to a small adjacent play area with insufficient space for the entire class to participate during the short time allotted for flexing larger muscles and more robust exercise. Fine motor activities are limited to tracing the dash marks on penmanship ditto sheets, or the like.

Social/Emotional Aspects

In this area, developmentally appropriate practice dictates the use of positive rather than negative reinforcement strategies. Children are given alternatives to enable them to internalize acceptable behavior. The providing of choices and the modeling of a better way to act leads children to develop skills for resolving problems on their own. Positive social interactions with classmates are encouraged, while hurtful or taunting behaviors are clearly discouraged. It is in the area of social/emotional aspects that understanding the perspective of others and of the social world that surrounds the child begins to take place within the young child. Through imaginative play, storytelling, and creative dramatics young children begin to take the role of the other. They learn the importance of understanding themselves in relation to their families and their peers. The development of an awareness and understanding of others' perspectives is important if children are to operate effectively in their social environment. Children try out and feel what it is like to function in differing statuses or situations. These activities help to prepare young children to enter into the complexities of contemporary life.

On the other hand, inappropriate practice is observable when the teacher intervenes as the instant problem solver or when children in conflict are separated physically from their peers as punishment. Social interactions are kept to a minimum by classroom rules such as "no talking in class" and "do your *own* work by *yourself*."

Cognitive/Perceptual Aspects

In the developmentally appropriate classroom, this area is enhanced by the presence of "discovery learning." Here, the teacher serves as an "enabler" or "facilitator" by providing the environment and the experiences that lead to learning. The children experiment with concrete materials, observe the life cycles of plants and animals, cook, listen, classify, and, in general, "discover" the world around them. In the developmentally inappropriate classroom setting the emphasis is on memorization, drill, and pencil and paper testing that a teacher feels is important for the acquisition of academic knowledge for the next grade level. In this setting the early childhood classroom is totally teacher-directed.

With these contrasting descriptions of developmentally appropriate practice versus inappropriate practices it is not difficult to recognize what are optimal activities and learning situations for young children. The ideas and caveats we have presented here are not stunningly new information to those who work with young children. The importance of an emergent literacy perspective coupled with a redefinition of play, the centrality of Piagetian theory, and the popularity of the British Primary School approach, have been discussed. Prominent early childhood educators have known about and utilized developmentally appropriate practice for a very long time. What is *different* at the close of the twentieth century, what is striking, innovative, and essential is the recognition and incorporation of ethnic, gender, and social class diversity into developmentally appropriate practice in the early childhood curriculum.

During the latter part of this century, educators have learned that an effective multicultural curriculum is achieved when teachers at all grade levels change the basic assumptions of the curriculum so that we enable students to view concepts, themes, issues, and problems from differing perspectives. We now know that it is imperative to infuse throughout the curriculum, frames of reference—history, cultures, and perspectives of many groups—and not teach solely about majority Anglo history and culture. This infusion should begin in early childhood, long before students reach the high school level.

Further we have come to realize that all curriculum decisions are not made by curriculum planners or curriculum specialists. When the teacher actually closes the classroom door, frequently it is *intent* rather than *content* that truly impacts the curriculum. Therefore it should be the *intention* of every early childhood teacher to infuse the classroom with an appreciation of diversity and a recognition of the multicultural nature of American society.

For too long the study of any ethnic group was usually included only in those schools where the ethnic group was dominant. That is, in Hispanic communities early childhood programs were urged to celebrate Cinco de Mayo in grand fashion, while programs in African-American communities did many things with Martin Luther King's holiday. A restructuring of the curriculum for living in the twenty-first century will mandate that all schools, including early childhood centers, infuse the heritage, the experiences, and the perspectives of the many diverse ethnic groups throughout the curriculum not just at special times of the year or on unique occasions. Most students in America are surrounded and immersed in the majority, dominant culture. It is necessary for them to learn about other heritages and traditions. This can be accomplished not within the confines of a "unit" on the African-American, the Hispanic American, Native American, or some other ethnic group, but throughout *all* their learning and educational experience. One cannot justify lumping a group's history, customs, art, literature, music, outstanding role models, and their past and present contributions to America into one week or month of study, and then never making reference to the group again during the entire school year.

Today, students from kindergarten through college learn that pluralism is a fact of living in a modern world. Even if one happens to teach or reside in a school district that is predominantly white, the children growing up there need to know that, beyond the classroom walls, everyone may not look like them. Pluralism has replaced assimilationism in this nation, and our schools now must develop in students a cultural consciousness starting in the first years of schooling. Appreciation of diversity must be *taught.*

In an important offering for teachers of young children, *Anti-Bias Curriculum: Tools for Empowering Young Children* (1989), the authors (all teachers and advisers for early childhood programs), write that in most settings for young children there is an abundance of material reflecting white, able-bodied children in traditional gender roles. They note that in classrooms for children of color, the majority culture is the one predominantly reflected in the setting. In addition materials depicting people of color are frequently biased, of a stereotypic and token nature, or absent altogether (see chapter 2).

Rejection comes in many forms. In early childhood classrooms when a teacher notes that a child continually writes his or her name with many letter reversals, that teacher will spend much time and not hesitate to correct these letter reversals before inappropriate writing habits become entrenched and hard to break. If another child, in one-to-one matching activities, continually miscounts and mismatches the items, the concerned teacher will not hesitate to work each day until the errors are rectified. Why, then, do otherwise competent early childhood teachers allow negative stereotypes regarding the abilities and intelligence of children of color to persist and feel few obligations to change these discriminatory attitudes? An appreciation of cultural diversity must be systematically and conscientiously taught.

The formation of attitudes of understanding and acceptance and celebration are not relegated to formal classroom study alone. Appreciation of diversity can be infused and extended through the entire school setting and not just in the curriculum. Classroom climate, teaching strategies, assessments, group interaction, the providing of comparable opportunities, the use of community models from every group, equal status treatment of information regarding all groups, all are components that must be enveloped in the microcosm called the early childhood classroom. Only in this way can *all* children enter the twenty-first century prepared to live in a diverse society.

The following anecdote was written by a woman of African descent:

My daughter and I were exhilarated as we marched in the Martin Luther King, Jr., Parade in the city of Denver. I noticed the wide array of tee shirts with all types of slogans and sayings printed on them, all celebrating the sheer beauty of being black. But there was one particular tee shirt that caught my attention. It read "BLACK BY NATURE— PROUD BY CHOICE."

I thought, "How can we ensure that our children make that conscious choice to be proud? There is so much talk about self-esteem. If they have the self-respect that arises from the knowledge of their foreparents and their great accomplishments, and from knowing that they also can be strong, capable, and accepted as they are, then they can and will be PROUD BY CHOICE.

Teachers of young children can help. They are called upon to make an honest assessment of their attitudes and values, and how these are reflected in their teaching. They are called upon to evaluate their own feelings regarding their own ethnocentricities, and to make a conscious decision to infuse their classrooms with culturally sensitive curriculum materials. Every school program may not have appropriate materials, but teachers can be conscientious enough to begin collecting their own, making games or buying bulletin board displays through their own initiative.

One cannot say "Next year's teacher will do it." Here the words of poet and educator Gabriela Mistral ring very clear: "To the child we cannot answer 'tomorrow,' the child's name is TODAY." Curriculum decisions for our young children should reflect the knowledge that the child's name is TODAY.

To demonstrate what is meant by incorporating *diversity* into activities and lessons for young children, we present the following unit, "Apples: A Multicultural Cooking Activity for Children at Preschool, Kindergarten, and First Grade Levels."[3] Through this series of activities young children are involved with ethnic, gender, and social class (including interaction with senior citizens) experiences embedded in a philosophy of developmentally appropriate practice. More information and examples of developmentally appropriate practice in classrooms of young children are provided to highlight the awareness serving youngsters from widely diverse populations. This is the reality of American society and of worldwide culture.

APPLES   A Multicultural Cooking Activity for Preschool, K, 1

Most of today's preschool and kindergarten classrooms incorporate some type of cooking in their curriculum on a fairly regular basis. It may range from merely popping corn to the grating and frying of potatoes for latkes in celebration of Hanukkah. Some teachers prefer strictly "no-cook cookery," which still has the same basic teaching tools and end result.

In whatever manner it is done, cooking is a delightful learning experience for youngsters. It is a cooperative effort with almost immediate, almost always satisfying rewards for the whole group.

All of the main areas of primary-level development can be approached in cooking. Consider these examples:

Perceptual—sequencing; sorting; sense of smell, taste, and touch

Language development—following directions, describing, reviewing steps

Cognitive—measurement, counting, predicting, transforming of shape

Fine Motor—sifting, pouring, stirring, kneading

Social-emotional—waiting for turn, sharing utensils, manners

In "Apples," the children experience multicultural cookery. These activities and recipes can be used individually or in conjunction with other activities. Actually, however, they are written for sequential use as a short unit.

Continued

APPLES   *Continued*

The outset of school in the fall of the year is the best time for establishing an atmosphere of acceptance of all diversity. Ethnic awareness should permeate the classroom yearlong, not just on special days. This small activity can serve as one of many ways to do this. As it so happens, in the fall of the year apples are at their delicious best, just harvested and crisp and juicy. They are plentiful and also inexpensive.

Some school districts allow the teachers to use petty cash for their expenditures for art and cooking materials. In other cases, a group of mothers may, together, maintain an available supply of odds and ends for miscellaneous projects. In this instance, if funds present a problem, asking each child to bring one apple should result in plenty of apples.

Senior Citizen Volunteers

All primary-level teachers know the value of an extra pair of hands in the classroom. Before school begins, or at Back to School Night, the teacher should attempt to establish a base of volunteers. Among the contacts could be housing complexes for active senior citizens. Seniors there, male or female, may willingly give one or two hours a week of their time for directed volunteering in the classroom. Seniors can bring another cultural dimension to the students' awareness. Seniors are a valuable resource and should not be overlooked as potential sources of enthusiastic help.

Introductory Session

Teacher Materials:

Apples of several kinds and sizes, hidden in a basket covered with a cloth. Purchase Rome, pippin, Winesap, Golden Delicious, and any others.

Knife

Paper plate

Napkins

Damp cloth

Begin by asking the children to guess what's in the basket:

Clue #1: They may be different colors and different sizes.

Clue #2: We can group them by color and size, but they still are known by one name despite those differences.

Clue #3: They have many different uses, and that makes us like them even better.

(Do not use clues such as "they grow on a tree.")

Show the apples and review the emphasis of each clue.

Have the children sit in a large circle:

APPLES *Continued*

A. Pass around the different kinds of apples. Let the children feel and smell them. Discuss what likenesses and differences they see.

B. Wash apples or wipe them off with a damp cloth. Cut each apple in half and put on paper plate. Discuss the *inside*. Sameness of texture, color, seeds, core.

C. Slice apples into wedges and put on napkins. Let children taste a wedge of each color.

D. Discuss similarity of taste and of function (to satisfy a hungry spot). Discuss the many different ways to eat apples (raw, caramel, in salads, pie, jelly, baked, boiled, etc.).

E. *Relate to people*, referring back to the original clues. We have different colors of hair, skin, and eyes. We are different sizes. There are different names by which we can be grouped, but we are still called by one name: . . . *people*. We have different uses (talents), and that makes us even better (special personality). Like the apples, all of us are good, useful, wonderful. We are different, yet the same inside with a heart of love (core) and seeds of friendship that we want to plant.

The Cooking Center

Parent helpers, paraprofessionals, senior volunteers can oversee the cooking centers. They can let the children serve as both participants and spectators as the recipe progresses. Actual cooking time is short so the class can eat and enjoy the warm "fruit of their labor." (The stove in the teachers' lounge may have to be used if the physical setting does not include one in proximity.)

Additional Centers

Using the apple theme and motif, activities can be set up in appropriate language, fine motor, perceptual, cognitive, art, social studies centers, health and nutrition centers. A great deal of social interaction will take place as these content areas are integrated.

An excellent bulletin board display could feature snapshots of the children at the cooking centers with the volunteers.

Culminating Session

A. Review the initial exercise in which the apples were cut open. Discuss the beneficial samenesses and differences in all of us as people in the classroom and in the world.

B. Discuss the different apple treats cooked and enjoyed by all. Show the ethnic prints and banners previously displayed at the cooking centers, and ask which apple treat was prepared as being representative of that group.

C. Be sure to have the senior and other volunteers comment regarding their involvement with the children. Let the children respond to them as well.

MORE IDEAS FOR INCORPORATING DIVERSITY INTO DEVELOPMENTALLY APPROPRIATE PRACTICE

The preceding unit, "Apples: A Multicultural Cooking Activity," provided a model for the type of learning experiences advocated for early childhood classrooms. In our pluralistic society the learning environment for young children must be reflective of our cultural diversity. Moreover, the approach must be one of *infusion,* not merely adding on an ethnic holiday here or an ethnic hero there. Well-planned activities contribute to establishing a multicultural and gender-aware atmosphere that will permeate all areas of the curriculum. It has been said that the curriculum must be a mirror in which the children can see themselves reflected. If children never see images of themselves or of people like them, then the curriculum is not a mirror but a wall. The valuing of diversity can begin early in a child's life. For the whole class, as well as in activities planned for individuals or small groups such as learning centers, an appreciation of diversity can be readily incorporated. The teacher who is aware and willing can plan learning experiences that are both developmentally appropriate and inclusive of all cultures, ethnic as well as dominant.

The following are ideas, lessons, exercises, and suggestions organized by the aspects of the early childhood curriculum presented previously.

Language Activities that Encompass Diversity

In the book *Literacy Development in the Early Years* (1993) Morrow notes the importance of recognizing language differences in young children as a major instructional concept in early childhood literacy programs. Activities and experiences for emerging literacy immediately evoke the fine collections of young children's stories and poems currently available to teachers and parents alike. It is important to include stories and poetry that are both *by* and *about* people of color. The idealized versions of the American home is not experienced by everyone. Children should see and hear stories depicting their backgrounds as well as others and should be familiarized with central characters with whom they can identify.

An Important Project by a Teacher Concerned with Multicultural Education

Recognizing the need for teachers of young children to have ready access to multicultural authors and their exciting and inspirational children's books, Frances Day of the Cherry Creek School District, Colorado, embarked on a project of several years duration to compile a teacher's guide to multicultural authors. In 1992 she completed the teacher's guide titled *Multicultural Authors: An Interdisciplinary Approach to Multicultural Education*. Day asserts that she takes a proactive approach in dealing with the institutionalized bias present in all aspects of schooling. She wrote her teacher's guide with the hope that it would be a catalyst for similar projects and that it would inspire other teachers to take a stand against bias and discrimination.

Day not only catalogued and developed in-depth descriptions of multicultural stories and books, but also sought out the authors and illustrators of these children's books and interviewed them, either in person or by telephone contacts. Her guide lists books for children by specific themes in the social studies, such as tradition and change, participatory citizenship, organization of societies, cultural diversity, and global perspectives. The books are also listed by ethnicity or nationality of their content (pp. 14–15). A unique feature of this singular and outstanding teacher's curriculum guide is a list of authors (and how to contact them) who are available to make visits to schools and libraries and the fees they charge for such presentations (p. 17). Each of the fifty-two authors, some of them also gifted artists and illustrators of children's books, is presented and discussed with inclusion of home address, birth date, speaker information, and a brief biographical sketch, followed by an annotated bibliography of the author's most distinguished offerings for children and the age level for which the story is appropriate. This material also includes the themes of the book or story and any awards that the book has garnered. Suggested activities for the teacher when using the book or story with a group of children provide valuable support and guidelines. A list of additional multicultural authors and illustrators not covered in detail in *Multicultural Authors* is included. Further, this guide is exceptionally well indexed with sections that list all titles of books in the volume and a subject index by categories that facilitate coordination with curriculum topics in both the social studies and the language arts.

Two examples of the types of storybooks for young children that are found in Frances Day's *Multicultural Authors* are as follows:

From Sharon Bell Mathis, *The Hundred Penny Box* (New York: Puffin Books, 1975). In this story of African-American heritage, Michael's great-great-aunt, Dew, celebrates her one hundredth birthday. She has an old box filled with pennies, one for each birthday. Michael knows the importance of saving the hundred penny box that contains all the stories of Aunt Dew's life. This story is a touching affirmation of love and loyalty. Another story by Sharon Bell Mathis for young children with African-American perspectives is *Sidewalk Story* (1971). It is a Children's Award Winner of the Council on Interracial Books and tells the heart-warming story of Lilly Etta who decides to help her best friend's family when they are evicted from their apartment.

Illustrated by Mai Vo-Dinh, the story written by Michele Surat, *Angel Child, Dragon Child* (Carnival Press, 1983) is a tale about a young Vietnamese girl who has just arrived in the United States. A book for children of all ages, it brings out empathy for this young girl who deeply misses her mother, who is still in Vietnam and unable to join her daughter in the United States because of a lack of funds to make the trip. Frances Day notes in her description of the book that the lovely illustrations by Mai Vo-Dihn, along with the text, depict the sensitive, determined spirits of newcomers (p. 241).

Other outstanding children's books with multicultural content that have long been favorites of children and teachers are the following:

A beautiful story for young children from the Navajo tradition is *Annie and the Old One* by Miska Miles (Little, Brown, 1971). This touching story of a young girl's attempts to delay her beloved grandmother's impending death is a Newbury Honor Book.

A famous and well-known book many teachers enjoy reading to young children is *Crow Boy* by Taro Yashima (Puffin Books, 1983). A Caldecott Honor Book, the story captures the pain of being different and being excluded. Chibi, of Japanese ethnicity, is rejected until, after six long years, he demonstrates his special talent for imitating the voices of crows in the school's talent show. This makes all his classmates realize how cruel they have been to Chibi for so long.

Jane Yolen, the author of *Owl Moon* (Philomel Books, 1987), has created a gentle, poetic story that lovingly depicts the special companionship of a young child and a father as well as humankind's close relationship to the natural world. The gender of the child is never revealed and so leads to insightful discussions with children about relationships with their own parents.

Teachers should not overlook the exciting and vital resources of local storytellers brought right into the classroom. Both men and women of majority heritage and of color can be tapped in most communities as storytellers for early childhood programs. Often they are available for a small honorarium or will come to tell stories for the children without expecting any remuneration.

Social/Emotional Aspects

In chapter 2 we discussed in detail the importance of the housekeeping corner for the social/emotional aspects of developmentally appropriate practices in the early childhood curriculum. Role-playing with favorite toys, dolls, or with one's peers enriches the young child's social and emotional experiences. It is important for young children to have available in their environment a variety of dolls of various ethnicities, as well as dolls of each gender. The "dress-up clothing" that is procured for their imaginative play can include items such as dashikis of Africa, kimonos from Japan, dishdasha of the Arabic Gulf states, as well as dresses, suits, hats and other items of the traditional American outfits. One early childhood teacher told us she prefers a wide variety of scarfs of various lengths and colors for children's imaginative play because of their non-specific nature.

An alternative technique for projective and imaginary play is the creation of an ethnic dollhouse. Young children delight in observing, collecting, and playing with dollhouses and doll-sized furniture. An exciting variation on the traditional housekeeping corner is to create a multiethnic dollhouse, made up of rooms representing differing ethnic heritages and traditions. One early childhood teacher was able to interest various parents and resource persons in putting together a dollhouse with rooms representing differing cultures. One room of Oriental tradition had gold paper on the walls, mirrors, model Japanese furniture, and dolls dressed in Kabuki robes. Another room was outfitted in Polish tradition with wall decorations, paper cutouts, and hand-painted ornaments. Mexican-American culture was represented by clay and tin dolls in costumes of the Hispanic tradition. The possibilities for heritage rooms are manifold and very intriguing to young children. Further, the gender-related customs of these various heritages can be depicted in the rooms of the ethnic dollhouse.

Cognitive/Perceptual Activities

Cognitive and perceptual skills can be taught with diversity as an integral part of the planned activities. For instance, sorting materials can include the colorful beads that are worn in the braided hair of hundreds of African-American girls. Cooking center activities have already been extensively detailed in our "Apple" unit, but many other possibilities exist for a creative teacher. Some puzzles are now available that include depictions of children of differing heritages. Even the posters on the wall and the bulletin boards around the room should be filled with representations of children of all colors, in many settings, rather than only of animals or cartoon characters.

Songs and musical games bring together both the cognitive and perceptual aspects and the social/emotional aspects of developmentally appropriately practice. Diversity can be intertwined by choosing music, songs, and dances from many cultures and traditions for the early childhood classroom. Here is an example of such an exemplary activity. We call it "Beating the Drum and Passing the Flowers." After a number of months in the classroom setting where young children have been exposed to stories, songs, games, and dances from a variety of traditions and heritages, they will be excited about participating in this innovative multicultural/gender-neutral activity.

Direct the children to sit in a circle, taking care that boys and girls are interspersed so that boys do not sit all together on one side of the circle with only girls grouped on the other. Give one child a small drum and show the children how one beats rhythmically on this instrument with fingers or a drumstick. Place this child, who is to beat on the drum, with back to the circle of children. Next chose one child in the circle to hold a bunch of flowers (artificial or real). Tell the drummer to beat the drum for some time before stopping. Inform the children that once the drummer begins to beat the drum, they must pass the bunch of flowers from child to child around the circle. Once the drummer stops beating, the children should stop passing the bunch of flowers. The one who is left holding the flowers when the drummer stops must tell a story, sing a song, or say a poem from an ethnic tradition or heritage that has been presented sometime during past sessions. With very young children, the teacher or other adults present may have to assist the "flower holder" in this activity. The flower holder then takes the drummer's position and this multicultural activity continues.

SUMMARY

The voices of well-meaning parents, politicians, social reformers, and others cry for increased academic content in early childhood education. Still, research continues to support the insightful theories of Piaget and Montessori, the British Primary School approach, and outstanding American child psychologists, who contend that play and concrete learning experiences are the best means of educating the young child. The National Association for the Education of Young Children has indicated that the quality of an early childhood program is directly related to the extent to which developmentally appropriate practice is followed.

Most patterns of growth and development are predictable in the lives of children from birth through the early years. Within this normal range, individual differences also exist. Therefore, activities that reflect both age-appropriateness and individual-appropriateness must be planned and integrated across the content areas of the early childhood curriculum. The teacher serves as enabler and facilitator of discovery-oriented learning. Additionally, by intentional design, the curriculum must include an appreciation of cultural diversity and gender awareness. This is not difficult to do in contemporary America. An infusion of materials and activities that are relative to ethnicity and gender leads young children to a natural awareness that cultures other than their own exist and are of equal worth.

KEY CONCEPTS

Developmentally Appropriate Practice This term refers to curricula for young children that is planned and carried out with the principles of *child growth* and *development* as guidelines. Developmental appropriateness in based on the crucial factors of *age* and *individual differences.*

Emergent Literacy This is the perspective on early childhood language learning and development that views early reading and writing behavior as integral parts of a process that emerges from the child as a result of environmental stimulation and, therefore, is intimately intertwined with cultural and social factors.

Major Areas of Developmentally Appropriate Practice These are defined in this chapter as acquisition of oral language, gross and fine motor skills, social/emotional aspects of the curriculum, and cognitive/perceptual aspects of the curriculum.

The Role of Play in Early Childhood Education Through play young children learn not only about their society and the people around them, but also the cognitive and perceptual aspects of intellectual growth so essential to life in the modern world. "Play is the child's work."

Piagetian Theory of Cognitive Development Piaget conceived of the child as an action-oriented, seeking, continually adapting organism that learns through the interactions of spontaneous, active play with the environment and with other people. The child is an active rather than a passive learner. The Piagetian theory of child growth posits that the child develops in *stages* from infancy to adulthood. These stages are sensorimotor, preoperational, concrete operational, and formal.

British Primary School Approach Based in Piagetian theory of child growth and development, the British Primary School approach is a philosophy that regards all children as active learners. The daily program for young children is structured into large blocks of time to allow children to explore and investigate. The classroom is arranged in "interest" centers, where activities can flow from indoors to the outdoors. The curriculum is developed around topics drawn from community interests and the local environment, including frequent field trips that utilize parents and local citizens as well as teachers.

Age-Related Changes in Growth and Development   Early childhood educators, researchers, and child psychologists stress that in planning early childhood programs the basic developmental needs of children predicated on age-related factors—long documented by research and program evaluations—should be foremost and central in all activities and lessons and in the total learning environment.

Individual Difference in Growth and Development   Although age-related aspects are vital to planning the early childhood curriculum, we should also recognize the crucial nature of individual differences among children that include gender, ethnicity, and social class, as well as uniqueness of an individual's physical and intellectual abilities.

Incorporating Diversity into Developmentally Appropriate Practice   Based on developmentally appropriate practice, this is the infusion of multicultural awareness into the learning environment of young children. This does not mean the occasional addition of an ethnic or gender-neutral activity or lesson, but the continual, ongoing inclusion of the pluralistic nature of our society in all aspects of the curriculum.

ISSUES AND ACTIONS

1. A parent tells you that for too long children in this neighborhood have not been given the lessons taught in those "ritzy" areas of town, because the school considered the children "disadvantaged" and not ready to learn the things that the privileged children on the other side of town get in their classrooms. The irate parent quotes a passage from a book describing children in disadvantaged families as not having access to such enrichment as classical fairytales and accurate descriptions of the world's geography. These children, it asserts, start school already behind and fall further back as they continue through the grades. Therefore, says this concerned parent, it is essential that teachers start in kindergarten to press children to learn academic facts and general information of cultural significance. The parent wants to know when you and the others will begin to revise your curriculum and take up "better" methods for the first graders in this school. How would you respond to this request and what would you do?

2. Find other ways to have children "line up" than by forming a boys' line and a girls' line. Hold a contest among your colleagues or fellow students to design and create new ways for organizing children in their movements from one place to another. Vote on the most clever and unique techniques. Think up an unusual and appropriate prize for the winner, too.

   In recent years numerous creative children's writers have written and illustrated exciting, innovative, and touching books for young children based on themes of ethnic affiliation, gender awareness, and social class membership. After looking over some of the titles listed and described in this chapter, visit your local or school library and find additional titles for use in your teaching and work with young children. Make a bibliography for your personal use and keep adding to it as new books are published that fulfill the criteria for developmentally appropriate practice that includes both ethnic and gender diversity. Share your bibliography of these books with others; they may help you in adding even more titles to increase your resources for oral language areas of developmentally appropriate practice with young children.

3. After reading the section on "More Ideas for Incorporating Diversity into Developmentally Appropriate Practice" in this chapter, think about and then write down some activities, lessons, or units that you develop on emergent literacy for young children. We particularly refer you to some seminal resource materials cited in the References and Suggested Readings that follow. Please note the book by Lloyd Ollila and Margie Mayfield on the emerging literacy movement in preschool, kindergarten and the primary grades, as well as Lesley Morrow's extensive coverage of literacy development in the early years of schooling.

ENDNOTES

1. The literature on Piagetian theory as well as the writings and research of Piaget and his students is immense. If one wishes to learn more about the theories of child growth and development, espoused by Piaget both in the cognitive and in the social realm, we encourage you find the section of the library containing these materials and just start reading!

2. During the 1960s and into the 1970s much was written and promulgated in educational circles extolling British Primary Schools and the British "infant school" method. The interest and attention that these schools and the British Primary Method were given has waned considerably. Currently, very little is being written featuring the once-innovative "integrated day" learning centers and the "project approach" to young children's education that were the hallmarks of this curriculum.

3. All of the classroom activities, units, and lessons described in this chapter have been developed by early childhood teachers and implemented in their classrooms. These are teacher-tried-and-tested projects that proved successful with young children.

REFERENCES AND SUGGESTED READINGS

Aries, P. *Centuries of Childhood: A Social History of Family Life*. New York: Vintage Books, 1962.

Bredenkamp, Sue (Ed.). *Developmentally Appropriate Practice in Early Childhood Programs Serving Children from Birth through Age 8*. Washington, DC: National Association for the Education of Young Children, 1987.

Day, Barbara. *Early Childhood Education: Creative Learning Activities*. New York: Macmillan, 1988.

Day, Frances. *Multicultural Authors: An Interdisciplinary Approach to Multicultural Education*. Cherry Creek School District, Colorado, 1992.

Derman-Sparks, Louise, and the Anti-Bias Curriculum Task Force. *Anit-Bias Curriculum: Tools for Empowering Young Children*. Washington, DC: National Association for the Education of Young Children, 1989.

Elkind, David. *Children and Adolescents: Interpretive Essays on Jean Piaget*. New York: Oxford University Press, 1970.

Elkind, David. *Child Development and Education: A Piagetian Perspective*. New York: Oxford University Press, 1976.

Gammage, Philip. Children Don't Get Taller by Being Measured. *Education Now*, Spring 1991; 12:22–24.

Hildebrand, Verna. *Guiding Young Children*. New York: Macmillan Publishing Co. 1985.

Hildebrand, Verna. *Introduction to Early Childhood Education* (5th edition). New York: Macmillan, 1991.

Hodges, Carol Ann. Instruction and Assessment of Emergent Literacy. In Lois Weis et al. (Eds.), *Critical Perspectives on Early Childhood Education*. Albany: State University of New York Press, 1991:153–168.

King, Edith W. *Teaching Ethnic and Gender Awareness*. Dubuque, IA: Kendall/Hunt, 1990.

Lavatelli, Celia. *Piaget's Theory Applied to an Early Childhood Curriculum*. Boston: American Science and Engineering, 1970.

Lawton, Denis. *Social Change, Educational Theory and Curriculum Planning*. London: University of London Press, 1973.

Morrow, Lesley M. *Literacy Development in the Early Years*. (2nd edition). Needham Heights, MA: Allyn and Bacon, 1993.

Ollila, L. O., and Margie Mayfield (Eds.). *Emerging Literacy*. Needham Heights, MA: Allyn and Bacon, 1992.

Seefelt, Carol, and Nita Barbour. *Early Childhood Education: An Introduction*. Columbus, OH: Merrill Publishing, 1990.

Stevens, Joseph H. Jr., and Edith W. King. *Administering Early Childhood Education Programs*. Boston: Little, Brown, 1976.

Teale, W., and Elizabeth Sulzby (Eds.). *Emergent Literacy: Writing and Reading*. Norwood, NJ: Ablex, 1986.

Wadsworth, Barry J. *Piaget's Theory of Cognitive and Affective Development* (4th edition) New York: Longman Press, 1989.

Weber, Lillian. *The English Infant School and Informal Education*. Englewood Cliffs, NJ: Prentice Hall, 1971.

4

THE YOUNG CHILD'S CURRICULUM AND MULTICULTURALISM

In this chapter we examine different approaches or theoretical positions in child growth and development that underlie specific curriculum models. Our discussion of these curriculum models in early childhood education stems from a review of standard texts for teachers of young children that present various theories of learning. However, what has been strikingly missing in these authoritative presentations of the curriculum in early childhood education is attention to, concern for, or inclusion of ethnic, social class, and gender differences among young children. After presenting three major views of early childhood curricula—the stimulus-response view, the cognitive-interactionist view, and the maturationist view—we go on to discuss the relationship of curriculum materials with the philosophy of the program. Throughout the material that follows, the reader will be made aware of the disregard of diversity in groups of young children that theorists have traditionally displayed. In this volume, we assert and pose ideas that infuse a concern for gender, social class, and ethnic diversity in the young child's curriculum.

THREE MAJOR VIEWS OF THE
YOUNG CHILD'S CURRICULUM

Some General Comments

Educational psychologists, learning theorists, child development specialists, and other social scientists who have focused their work on human growth and development are in consensus that human beings develop gradually in small increments that evolve from one to the next. No child development and learning theory advocates the position that an individual arrives full-blown, mature, and filled with wisdom about the world, as the Greek myth claims Athena was created from the head of Zeus. Within the broad field of psychology a welter of theories has been produced to describe human growth and development. Often the theories have foundations drawn from other social sciences—philosophy, sociology, anthropology, even history—and certainly from the biological sciences as well.

To present these general approaches to early childhood curricula in the most meaningful and concise way, we have categorized them into three major views or philosophies on how learning and human growth and development take place. Each of the three major views has its strengths and contributions to make to any early childhood program. Yet, the reader must keep in mind that these are idealized versions of the actual curricula that one would observe in practice in classrooms. Keep in mind that these descriptions are limited in their ability to represent reality. Further, with the heightened awareness of gender and ethnic diversity that we bring now to the literature in educational research and development, we can examine these three main approaches to early childhood curricula with new perspectives.

The three views are: the stimulus-response view; the cognitive-interactionist view; and the maturationist or classic view.

The Stimulus-Response View

The terms *stimulus* and *response* have become synonymous with behaviorism, "S-R bond" psychology, and especially the work of B. F. Skinner (1959). This view pictures the individual as a receptive organism whose behavior is shaped mainly by the environment. It is assumed that each person is born with a repertoire of response capabilities and the ability to learn. Children learn that when they behave in certain ways, given particular environmental circumstances, specific consequences are produced. The nature and the timing of these consequences determine whether the child will continue to manifest that behavior. If rewarding or positive consequences follow immediately, then the child will probably behave similarly in like situations. Should adverse consequences or nothing distinctive follow, the child will not tend to repeat that behavior. Complex behavior patterns are built by combining simpler behaviors. Again, environmental consequences will determine which combinations are sustained in the child's behavioral repertoire.

The stimulus-response view is deeply rooted in an environmentalist approach to learning. Early childhood educators who base programs on this theory argue that those skills and attitudes necessary for competence in our culture should be the focus. A technological society such as ours selects those individuals who manifest achievement motivation, persistence, internal control, and internal evaluation; who have mastered basic skills; and who manifest sound intellectual abilities. Learning to read, to do arithmetic, and to be able to understand science concepts would be central in such programs, as it is thought that success in school helps to ensure success in society. The learner moves from simpler to more complex and abstract concepts. The learner would first need to acquire prerequisite and component skills before complex tasks can be mastered.

Learning in the behavioral view of the curriculum involves an observable change in behavior, something that can be measured. Teachers of young children specify the target behavior that they are interested in helping the children acquire. Through an analysis of the types of prerequisite and component skills needed to perform the task, a skill sequence is devised. This sequence specifies the learning steps that the child must follow to move from no skill to fully developed skills. Thus, to count ten objects the child must first learn to count to ten by rote; to touch one object, moving it as the object is counted; and to remember the number that was designated. Consequently, the steps that the teacher has logically determined could be tested with a number of children to verify the skill sequence. Researchers and educators such as Bereiter and Englemann (1966) have built their programs for young children around this view and conception of the early childhood curriculum. Wolfgang and Wolfgang (1992) characterize this approach as "teacher-centered."

Those embracing the stimulus-response behavior analysis view of learning advocate a strongly teacher-centered, teacher-directed classroom structure. The learner is passive, imitating the behavior modeled by the teacher. The teacher diagnoses and then prescribes the learning tasks, structures the environment, instructs, and reassesses the learner's skill level to determine whether the instructional procedures have been effective. The teacher matches the difficulty of the task to the child's level of skills and abilities. One of the strengths of this approach is the clarity of the steps in the teaching process. The teacher has specific direction for engineering an environment that will help the child acquire the desired behavior. Whether the child learns becomes the teacher's responsibility. Likewise if the child does not learn, the conditions for learning need to be systematically altered.

Critics of this approach raise questions about the ability of the child to apply the skills learned to new situations and problems in this teacher-directed manner. Some have also questioned whether such procedures can be applied as effectively to the learning of more complex concepts, such as seeing that no matter how a group of objects is arranged its number remains invariant. However, the behaviorists criticize the inability of others to specify clearly the target behavior desired. If such behavior can be clearly defined, they argue, the principles of behavior analysis can be systematically and effectively applied.

To teach the academic skills—reading, mathematics, science—the stimulus-response approach calls for designing systemic reinforcement procedures. Rewards can range from smiles and praise to more tangible items such as candies, desirable snacks, opportunities to go out on the playground, hearing a story, or doing an art activity. Rewards are awarded only for improved academic or social behavior and as soon as possible after the desired behavior has been manifested. In the DISTAR model developed by Beireiter and Englemann in the 1960s, the teacher works with small groups of children on carefully programmed learning materials that grow more difficult as the school year progresses. In each lesson or group of lessons the teacher must assess whether the children have acquired the lesson objective, because success in later lessons depends on mastery of earlier skills before more complex ones are undertaken. To facilitate the acquisition of generalized responses, children have an opportunity to practice applying the skill across several lessons. The DISTAR materials must be used almost precisely as the developers have set forth in the teacher's guides and manuals.

The acquisition of generalized responses to broad categories of concepts and labels is a most powerful technique for verbal acquisition and verbal facility manifested by this learning approach. For example, four-year-olds learn to identify objects such as cars, trucks, and bicycles as "vehicles," objects that are used to transport people. They then are encouraged to transfer the broader concept of "vehicle" to all types of objects that transport people and goods. In the area of labels for clothing, for example, a group of four-year-olds could tell a visitor to the classroom that this is Maria's jacket with a yellow collar and blue pockets and yellow and blue trim on the sleeves and on the zipper. Such attention to detail can astound an adult interacting with these four-year-olds, the products of the stimulus-response (DISTAR) curriculum. The extent of the children's abilities to categorize, generalize, and display their verbalization and language facility is impressive. However, this intensive language development component in the DISTAR program concentrates on teaching concepts used in logical thinking rather than focusing on the social and interpersonal aspects of language usage. It is assumed that children will develop positive self-concepts and self-esteem through their mastery and achievement in the cognitive, academic domain.

A Critique of the Stimulus-Response View from the Diversity Perspective

In most volumes the discussions of the stimulus-response view, this teacher-directed, behaviorally oriented curricular model for young children, make the assumption that the reader envisions the learner as a four- to five-year-old white, middle-class boy of normal health and ability. No efforts are made in these traditional descriptions to differentiate children by ethnicity, social class, or gender. For example, in the description above of the stimulus-response view—a composite of several such scholarly presentations—it is noted that the teacher diagnoses and prescribes the learning tasks, structures the environment, assesses the student's progress, and hence evaluates the learning outcomes. Yet no mention is made of the pressures on a teacher of young children to understand and empathize with the wide range of diverse cultures that could be represented in the classroom (Ogbu, 1992).

Can a teacher know the values, attitudes, and customs that preschoolers have already internalized in their family setting about reading, counting, science concepts, and even uttering specific words or phrases? The rhetoric of learning in the behavioral framework seldom refers to ethnic or gender variations in learning styles or openness or closedness to the teaching methods proposed. The child is a passive, receptive organism awaiting a teacher's inputs, totally void of individuality or uniqueness, as well as bereft of family or ethnic group identity.

Although in the past some attempts have been made to promote behaviorist methods for economically and socially "disadvantaged" children, little attention has been given to these concerns recently. We go on to point out that when a curriculum model assumes that the values of the majority society are internalized by all members of the society—values such as the high worth of mathematics and science expertise (especially when girls and women have been dissuaded from such achievements until very recently)—that model is an errant one. The developers of the stimulus-response view based their theoretical positions on the white middle-class children they knew and saw around them in families and schools. The widely diverse populations of young children that have entered the public schools of the United States since the 1950s and 1960s, when the behaviorist scholars where at their zenith, have not benefited from the philosophical and social science tenets on which this curricular theory is based.

To underscore the deterioration of the learning environment for many of our children through this stimulus-response approach, Jonathan Kozol has chronicled the decline of education in America in his book, *Savage Inequalities: Children in American Schools* (1991). He visited P.S. 79, an elementary school in New York City. This badly overcrowded school was built to hold one thousand children, but housed 1,550. The school enrollment was 29 percent African-American and 70 percent Hispanic. Kozol anguishes:

> *In a very small room on the fourth floor, 52 people in two classes do their best to teach and learn. Both are first grade classes. . . . "The room is barely large enough for one class," says the principal. The room is 25 by 50 feet. There are 26 first graders and two adults on the left, 22 others and two adults on the right. On the wall is the picture of a small white child, circled by a valentine. . . . (p. 90)*

The behaviorist curricular philosophy, which places the major emphasis on teacher-centered methods, was not designed for classroom conditions such as those described above.

The Cognitive-Interactionist View

The cognitive-interactionist view, based in cognitive developmental theory and often labeled the child-centered approach, has evolved from the theories of Jean Piaget and his followers. We discussed Piagetian theory in some detail in chapter 2; therefore, we will merely reiterate here that this view characterizes child development in broad stages. In contrast to the stimulus-response, behavioristic, teacher-centered curriculum where the child is seen as a passive, receptive entity, the cognitive-interactionist view sees the individual as an action-oriented, searching, seeking, continually adapting organism. Children learn through the interaction of spontaneous, active play with the environment and people around them. Emphasis is placed on the individual as an active rather than a passive learner.

Advocates of the cognitive-interactionist approach in early childhood education emphasize a classroom that is child-centered and designed for self-teaching and discovery learning. The teacher structures the environment by setting up learning centers that stimulate the child's interest and arouse the child's curiosity and desire to learn. Each child is seen as an active experimenter who explores his or her environment and selects from it the materials and topics that stimulate his or her interest. The child provides his or her own match with the help of the teacher as a facilitator of the learning situation.

Learning is an active process, and the outcome of the process may not be directly observable. The result of learning is the internalizing of constructions of the child's external actions. New activities are optimally attractive to the child when they incorporate a bit more novelty or complexity than previous activities. The child attempts to make sense of the world and his or her encounters with it. The teacher's task is to assist the child in organizing what he or she knows.

A teacher operating from this view of learning has a significantly different purpose from one operating from the stimulus-response framework. For example, in helping children learn to classify, the teacher's goal is to help the child learn to make groups in any logically consistent manner and to justify verbally the construction. A teacher operating from the stimulus-response view would systematically help the child learn to classify first by physical characteristics (shape, color, size, etc.), by function, and finally by category. Learning would have occurred when the child could reliably utilize each of these criteria. From the cognitive-interactionist view the teacher attempts to help the child sort, justify, shift criteria to sort another way, justify, and perhaps shift again. In the cognitive-interactionist view, the child is encouraged to construct his or her own logical relationships among phenomena.

The cognitive-interactionist teacher adopts both a directive and a less directive role. The teacher may choose to diagnose and then prescribe particular activities for the child. However, much of the time the teacher observes and questions. Through questioning the child's view is expanded, and sufficient disequilibrium is triggered so that further explorative inquiry can occur. The teacher also gathers sufficient data from observations and these encounters to guide the selection of additional learning materials and activities that will expand the child's interest and skills. The case study in chapter 2 provides an in-depth and detailed description of an early childhood program that exemplifies the cognitive-interactionist, child-centered curriculum in action.

A Critique of the Cognitive-Interactionist View from the Diversity Perspective

It can be readily assumed that the more obvious thrust and preference of the authors of this book will be expressed for the child-centered, cognitive-interactionist, discovery learning environment curriculum. In this view of the curriculum for young children the focus is on the individual child as a unique and active learner, while the role of teacher is that of facilitator who structures the learning environment. In the cognitive-interactionist program the teacher and the child adopt more balanced roles; both initiate activities and respond to themes and ideas developed by others. These others can be parents, care givers, classroom aides, family members, and the local community. This brings opportunities for the teacher and the school to incorporate aspects of a child's ethnicity—the heritage, tradition, language, and family setting—into daily activities, as well as into the broader curriculum. Because the child-centered curriculum derives the applications of the body of knowledge to be taught from the child's own environment and past experiences (grounded in Piagetian theory of accommodation and assimilation), the teacher has ample opportunity to include relevant ethnic, gender, and social class elements in the lessons.

Yet, it would be naive not to recognize that this child-centered, cognitive-interactionist, Piagetian theoretical model also was developed, normed, and tested on white, middle-class children. As trainers of early childhood teachers continue to promulgate the cognitive-interactionist, Piagetian-based curriculum in teacher education, this methodology and the research supporting this approach only reflect and reiterate the majority society values, attitudes, and customs (Ogbu, 1992). It is incumbent on teachers of young children to realize this fact and to utilize child-centered learning experiences with a new awareness of the implications for ethnicity, gender, and social class of the children in the program. It is the teacher in the early childhood classroom who must interpret, and then apply, what the child-centered curriculum really means in multicultural America at the close of the twentieth century. Wolfgang and Wolfgang in their espousal of the child-centered, "play-activity based" curriculum as supportive of developmentally appropriate practice note that:

> *Even when there is an agreement on what is developmentally appropriate and that play-activities are the central method of learning for young children, early childhood teachers will vary dramatically as they set out to implement a play curriculum. They will differ on what is put into the classrooms, on materials arrangement, on how discipline is done, and on a multitude of other practical decisions. (1992, p. 18)*

In other words, a multicultural curriculum for young children that incorporates diverse ethnic heritages and attention to gender issues and social class affiliation is directly the responsibility of the early childhood teacher.

The Maturationist or Classic View

It is important to include this third approach or view of the early childhood curriculum because of its historical basis. It has its origins in the European nineteenth century movements for the recognition that very young children have different needs and learning styles from older children and adults. One of the earliest advocates of the maturationist or classic approach was the Swiss educator Johann Pestalozzi. He stressed that the head, the hand, and the heart must all be integral elements in the child's curriculum. Children were to be taught not solely intellectual facts, but the practical arts as well, by loving teachers that cared and were attentive to their needs and wants. Pestalozzi advocated teaching children in groups. His educational theories included the concept of moving from the concrete to the abstract, using objects and materials to help children learn rather than requiring them to learn by rote and memorize information.

The major influence in the 1800s on early childhood education, though, came from the German educator Friedrich Froebel, commonly labeled the "Father of the kindergarten." Froebel was deeply affected by the German philosophers and religious thinkers of his time. Froebel's approach led him to advocate the use of play and specially designed toys for toddlers and children under six years of age in classes that Froebel named the "kindergarten" or "child's garden." He also called for the training of women as teachers in these kindergartens. The kindergarten curriculum included building with large wooden blocks; creative activities using natural materials such as pebbles, leaves, and shells; finger-plays and activity games, bringing pets into the classroom, and using mothers as aides. All of these practices are still central to early childhood education.

Moving into the twentieth century, the maturationist approach, which is most often associated with Arnold Gesell and the work that he has done with France's Ilg and Louise Ames in the 1930s and 1940s (Gesell and Ilg, 1949), influenced the traditional curriculum of nursery schools, kindergartens, and preschools across the nation in the decades just before and during World War II. The familiar concept of "readiness" has been most closely identified with this maturationist or traditional curriculum model. This view is postulated on the belief that the human being is primarily the product of genetic inheritance, whereas environmental influences play only a minor role in development. In this view a child is thought to be born with a full set of genes to guide development. Given the proper nourishment and psychological setting children will achieve each stage of growth and development on a predetermined schedule. Therefore, environmental experiences influence only the relative ease with which each developmental stage unfolds and the fullness to which it unfolds. In this view one allows each child to develop his or her own innate capabilities. The process is seen as one of unfolding and of developing the "whole" child. The "plant" analogy is often cited here—that of the acorn which eventually grows to be a "mighty oak."

The nursery school or preschool provides a rich, relatively nonrestrictive environment, and each child will develop his or her own unique abilities and talents, with which he or she has been endowed by genetic inheritance. The concept of "readiness" dictates that the teacher be knowledgeable about these readiness periods and provide the appropriate activities and materials to activate the state of learning. Curriculum experiences are often organized by units. These consist of a series of activities organized around a central theme, such as the family, community helpers, the seasons, and animals, among others. The teacher creates a warm, positive, but organized environment and waits for the child to show the signs of readiness to read, to write, or to desire mathematical knowledge. The role of the teacher is to guide children's behavior and development and to allow children to reach their potential at their own rate. Concerns about intellectual stimulation are not so pressing or central in this view. The child's activities are self-selected and self-directed, so, in a sense, this view also advocates developmentally appropriate practice and a child-centered approach, but with a crucial difference which we discuss below.

Programs for four-year-olds may have a paraprofessional or parent helper, and the size of the group could be fifteen to twenty children. The public school kindergarten may have only one teacher, and the size of the group could range from twenty-five to forty children. However, activities are usually undertaken in the total-group setting rather than small-group arrangements, since classic or traditional early childhood programs advocate everyone doing the same thing at the same time in a self-contained classroom. Routines are set up early in the school year, with the classroom schedule firmly established by the teacher. The daily schedule for a typical maturationist, traditional early childhood program would be similar everywhere and would be carried out each day of the entire school year with only exceptional instances of change. This type of schedule would have an opening from about 8:30 to 9:00 a.m. with time slots for arrival, informal conversation, and greetings. From 9:00 to 9:15 a.m. there would be "Show and Tell," marking the calendar, and a greeting song. Next would come a "work" period, including activities with paint, clay, crayons; play in the housekeeping corner; looking at books, working puzzles, block building, play with trucks; closing with a cleanup at 10:00 a.m. Then would be snacks and rest, toileting, followed by a playtime outdoors if the weather permitted. These activities would cover another hour of the three-hour session. In the last hour of the morning session the teacher would undertake activities in language arts, including listening to stories and poems; dramatization; discussions on health, safety, and social subjects; and possibly ending with music and rhythms. Closure by 11:30 to 11:45 a.m. would bring "getting ready for dismissal" and then dismissal. An afternoon time schedule would be the only variation in this program.

Critique of the Maturationist or Classic View
from a Diversity Perspective

The major and most serious objections to the maturationist, classic curriculum for educators committed to the recognition of diversity, are:

1. The grounding and philosophy, which are based in Western European culture and tradition, leaving no regard for those children and their families whose traditions, heritage, language, and customs stem from the many other cultures now represented in American schools.
2. The outmoded conception that heredity is the crucial force shaping the individual's growth and development and that environmental

influences have little effect. In this curriculum the teacher plays a passive role, while waiting for the child to develop physically and intellectually, without awareness or concern for what may have happened to the individual in the family setting or the broader society. Given the crises and traumas in our modern world, this is naive and inappropriate. We no longer exist in an unchanging and safe society.

3. The stereotype that the teacher of young children must be a woman. The maturationist, classic view, grounded in the nineteenth century Western European, patriarchal culture perpetuates the myths that assign lesser roles to females while the males grow up to fulfill their destined role in society to be those in power.

4. The deterrent this model creates to individualizing learning and the teacher's role in prescribing optimum teaching situations. The maturationist, by organizing the curriculum into blocks of time and "classic" units of content, does not allow the teacher to utilize the differences in gender, social class, ethnicity, and background that each child brings to the classroom, and that also are represented in the wider society.

However, the maturationist, classic curriculum has contributed to early childhood education the important recognition that the child learns in different ways from the adult. The very young child needs hands-on, active learning. Teaching methods and strategies that eschew active learning and call for rote memorization with punishments and negative effects are not appropriate in childhood. As was pointed out, some elements and aspects of the maturationist, classic early childhood curriculum are still found in practice today in preschools and kindergarten. These contributions, such as using firsthand experiences with hands-on materials and encouraging active learning, are worthwhile and should not be disregarded.

We now go on to examine the relationship of curriculum materials to the curricular view or approach.

CURRICULUM MATERIALS AND THE THREE VIEWS OF THE CURRICULUM

Curriculum materials reveal the underlying philosophy for teaching and learning being implemented in the classroom. It is helpful to examine the selection and use of materials to bring perspectives to the various approaches to the curriculum in early childhood education and the implications this has for acknowledging multiculturalism and diversity.

Curriculum materials can be categorized as those that are resources for the teacher (instructor's manual, films, kits, and the like), and those for use by the pupils.

The Relationship of Curriculum Materials to the Program

Each of the three curriculum views discussed in this chapter has an underlying philosophy or theoretical framework from which decision-making stems. These decisions pertain to the kinds of materials used as well as to the daily schedule of activities, the ratio of adults to children, the arrangement of the physical facilities, and many other aspects of the program. We now focus on how the curricular view influences the curriculum materials chosen and used in the daily program.

Materials for the Stimulus-Response, Behaviorist Curriculum

The curriculum materials that most exemplify the behaviorist curriculum are the DISTAR kits developed by Siegfried Englemann and his associates, published by Science Research Associates of Chicago, Illinois, in the 1960s. The DISTAR kits contain a number of spiral-bound presentation manuals with a maximum of 180 lessons for small groups of children. Materials include student workbooks, take-home exercises, a teacher's guide, and supplementary student materials in the form of a large storybook and a "color book." The kits were divided into programmed learning sets titled "Reading I and II," "Arithmetic I and II," and "Language I and II." The materials advocated a built-in testing procedure beginning with a base-rate examination for the children. This enabled the teacher to know where the children were in relation to what was to be taught during the programmed learning set, for example, in the Language I Program.

According to the behaviorist approach, to teach something new one begins with what the child already knows and proceeds by taking small steps until the desired goal is reached. An example of this type of teaching would be the following:

> *The children are shown a picture of a boy. The teacher asks the group of five children, "What is this?" (pointing to the picture of the boy). A child responds, "Boy." The teacher says, "A boy." Another child states, "A boy." The teacher then goes on to model the statement desired, the full sentence, "This is a boy." The children are then encouraged to repeat after the teacher, "This is a boy," and are rewarded when they can say the full sentence. (Derived from Englemann, 1969.)*

Curriculum materials in the behaviorist, stimulus-response curriculum stem from the view that children learn in small increments building on former learning. The materials are devised in a highly programmed, static, regulated format in keeping with this approach to human development and learning. This contrasts greatly with the cognitive-interactionist approach to curriculum in which children are encouraged to be creative and free ranging in their thinking, activities, and learning.

Materials for the Cognitive-Interactionist Curriculum

A kit of materials inspired by the cognitive-interactionist approach and characteristic of this curriculum was developed in the 1970s by Dr. Celia Stendler Lavatelli and labeled "The Early Childhood Curriculum: A Piaget Program." The kit consisted of three sets of toys that appealed to young children such as beads, puzzles, toy trucks, planes, animals, various containers, doll pictures, and so on. A teacher's guide and a hardback text titled *Piaget's Theory Applied to an Early Childhood Curriculum* (Lavatelli, 1971) completed the kit. The three materials kits were titled "Classification," "Number, Measurement and Space," and "Seriation." They contained sufficient manipulative materials for groups of four children to work together under the guidance of an adult. Statements from the Early Childhood Curriculum guide describing the materials indicate how these materials clearly stem from a cognitive-interactionist approach to child growth and development. The guide informs the teacher that the program is designed to lay a foundation for the emergence of concrete operations. Piaget held that it is the action of the subject on objects or events in the environment that leads to the assimilation of new ideas. Therefore, these kits were designed as a sequential series of short small-group activities, each requiring interaction with concrete materials and each producing assimilation of new concepts. The activities provided children with the opportunity to assimilate these concepts and accommodate the concepts into past experiences.

Materials for the Maturationist, Classic Curriculum

The traditional kindergarten and nursery school, which usually are associated with the maturationist view, has promoted the wide range of materials that are labeled "readiness" curriculum materials. We discussed how vital the concept of readiness is to the maturationist philosophy. Still, in some early childhood circles much argument can ensue around the question of providing dittoed papers and coloring books for young children to learn to color within the lines or learn to hold a crayon or pencil properly. Much of the early childhood materials for the preschool and kindergarten found in publisher's catalogues is based on a readiness and maturational philosophy. One clear-cut and easily recognized example is puzzles. Most catalogues of materials for the young student contain several pages devoted to puzzles in a wide range of types, sizes, materials, and prices. Usually these puzzles are grouped in developmental or readiness stages. They start for the youngest child with puzzles to manipulate with little wooden knobs on each piece and a limited number of pieces to be put together. Next are more complex puzzles that contain more pieces and no knobs, and finally there are quite intricate and more advanced puzzles that recreate scenes and contain many objects or attempt to teach facts, such as a puzzle of the United States or Europe. The attempts at age grading of equipment is closely related to a maturationist view.

CURRICULUM MATERIALS FROM THE MULTICULTURAL PERSPECTIVE

Until recently, ethnic and gender awareness has been almost totally lacking in the selection of curriculum materials for all three of the curricula—behaviorist, cognitive-interactionist, and maturationist. For example, when equipping the housekeeping corner and the dress-up area, the traditional implements, objects, and garments of the majority, middle-class American society were the only types of materials found there. In the past most teachers of young children (and their parents) gave little thought to the skin color and facial features of the dolls they chose for the housekeeping corner, when most dolls were manufactured mirroring only the white populace. Today there is an awareness that to build a positive self-image for all children, the representations used by children must reflect all the groups in a population. Toy makers have responded to the demand for a positive self-image and to the reality of our multicultural society. They now offer a wider variety of skin colors and features for dolls for young children. Not only do dolls come in various combinations of hair types and colors, eye styles and colors, and skin tones of a range of hues, but also in various builds, statures, and sizes. The 1980s saw the advent of all types of toys and books for young children that reflect the wide range of ethnic diversity in the United States and in the world.

Gender awareness is another area to consider in the selection of curriculum materials. Recent investigations into the portrayal of male and female roles, images, and occupations in picture books and first readers for young children turned up startling evidence that stereo-typed sex-role behavior—(passive, dependent, quiet, shy, obedient lit-tle girls and active, aggressive, independent, boisterous little boys)—is the traditional image found in many curriculum materials and books. In the past several years strong pressures has been put on developers and publishers of picture books and story books for children to correct these stereotypes, but teachers must be constantly alert and sensitized to subtle gender biases and prejudice in curriculum materials for young children. In the taken-for-granted practices of the early child-hood setting, girls are unquestioningly directed to the dolls, pots, pans, and dishes, to play with, while boys are urged toward the trucks, cars, and big blocks.

The implications of sexism, racism, and stereotyping should enter into considerations for every selection of curriculum materials. The influence of toys, games, picture books and photos, study prints, and illustrations that fill preschools and kindergartens are of great impor-tance in the individual's early socialization. The impressions children receive in these first years of school life are crucial. This applies not only for what is expected and accepted practice (i.e., girls play with dolls and boys play with trucks, Asians and Hispanics are servants and menials, Chinese people run restaurants, African-Americans are ath-letes), but also for what is omitted (e.g., women are never seen doing heavy physical labor, people of color are never portrayed as doctors and lawyers).

Some curriculum material developers, publishers, and authors of children's books have tried to dodge the entire issue of sexism and racism by using neutral objects such as animals or inanimate objects as the central characters in their publications. This ploy is neither honest nor realistic. It does not come to grips with the issues that are at stake. Omissions and negations are as damaging to the learning situation and to the curriculum, generally, as is the imposition of stereotypes and discriminatory practices. Honest, forthright, authentic curriculum mate-rial is difficult to locate and identify. Choices in curriculum materials cannot be made lightly or only on the basis of one or two factors, such as cost and durability. The ramifications of ethnic diversity and gender awareness are of major importance in American society today and will be with us in the decades to come now that heightened ethnic, gender, and social class consciousness abounds. Furthermore, now that the problems have been identified, it is time to develop appropriate curricu-lum materials to fulfill our new awareness and desires to present Ameri-can culture and world society to young children in realistic, accurate, and authentic ways. Examples of such multicultural, curriculum materi-als are discussed throughout the pages of this book.

DEFINING A MULTICULTURAL ATMOSPHERE IN THE CLASSROOM

Stepping forward, teachers may say: "All this information and discussion about the urgency for a multicultural perspective in the early childhood curriculum is well and good. Tell us *how* an educator knows exactly what the conditions of multiculturalism for classrooms of young children should be? "How *does* one define a multicultural atmosphere?" "How does a teacher recognize and begin to evaluate the efforts expended to develop sensitivity to diversity?"

One way to answer these questions is to use some of the techniques that are employed in teacher education seminars and courses. These strategies can be adopted by both pre-service and in-service teachers to observe and record the extent—or lack of—ethnic and gender awareness in classrooms of young children. A typical assignment for students in teacher training programs is to observe a classroom for a daily block of time, several times a week, for a period of several weeks. Using the same technique, a teacher can keep a record, notes, or journal on the interactions of children and adults that focuses on ethnicity and gender aspects. This will often suffice to document the quality of ongoing multiculturalism. To provide some examples of such projects we offer excerpts from one student-teacher's journal and from the records of an experienced teacher on leave.

Notes from a Student-Teacher's Journal on the Multicultural Atmosphere: For the past month I have been an observer in Ms. T's combination first-second grade and in Ms. G's English-as-a-Second Language (ESL) classes because both classes serve many of the same children in this early elementary school with a widely diverse student population. By going to the school several times a week, for periods during both the morning and afternoon sessions, I have had opportunities to observe examples of ethnic and gender awareness and involvement. One striking example I want to relate occurred during a particular classroom activity. This involved the children sitting at tables drawing items in the "rainforests" of South America that they have been studying in a unit on the environment. On the whole the children arranged themselves in ethnically integrated groups with both boys and girls in each group. However, one non-English speaking boy, who had recently arrived from Russia, was isolated by the children. He sat on the side by two girls and no interaction took place except for the sharing of crayons which was initiated by the teacher. In contrast, to demonstrate that the children were not necessarily prejudiced, there is another new boy in the class. He is from Palestine and also speaks no English. He, however, has been more readily accepted into the group of children. During this art activity he sat within a group of girls and boys sharing crayons and comparing drawings. The two boys are in a similar situation, yet are affected differently. Perhaps this is because the Russian boy alienates himself from the children by playing alone and disrupting lessons from time to time with loud outbursts that distracted the teacher. The Palestinian boy does not act on his own without being told what to do and so never appears disruptive.

This thought made me more aware when I had the opportunity to observe a new girl, a black child from Zambia, who just arrived in Ms. G's class. Her female classmates came up to me to tell me all about her and were most protective of her. The children told me that their new classmate did not speak English and so was not yet able to state everything she wanted. They said that they would try to help her. I observed that she was never left alone—someone was continually playing or talking with her. She did not appear lonely. . . .

. . . I will comment on another observation in Ms. G's ESL class. She has students from various countries and cultures and they bring with them many different skills and abilities. For instance, making a "cat's cradle," a children's game using one's hands and string to do tricks, was a group activity one morning. Two Southeast Asian students, one a boy and the other a girl, were more skilled in using their hands, doing intricate maneuvers with the string. They wound up teaching the teacher, me, and the other students many of the tricks. This exercise gave the Southeast Asian students new status with their classmates and an opportunity to increase their self-esteem. I must admit everyone, myself included, laughed a lot, learned, and had a good time during this lesson.

From these anecdotes of this student-teacher we vicariously experience the dynamics of classrooms where young children and their teachers cope with highly diverse cultural and linguistic backgrounds. Awareness of gender influences as well as cultural differences is displayed. In this atmosphere, multicultural education is taking place.

Next, the perceptive observations and then teaching activities of an experienced teacher, sharing a second grade classroom with her associate, describe what constitutes an atmosphere of multiculturalism:

Records of an Experienced Elementary School Teacher on the Multicultural Atmosphere: Mrs. R's second grade room is large, sunny, and busy. Rabbits and hamsters munch away in cages in the center of the room, while bright new computers gleam in a corner. The room is creatively disorganized and Mrs. R's desk is located by searching for a larger piece of furniture heaped with student papers, broken shoe laces, chewed pencils, teachers' manuals, and possibly a hair ribbon. Tote trays are stacked in another area with papers poking out from half-finished student projects. The students in Mrs. R's class come from a variety of ethnic backgrounds, including Hispanic, Asian, and Caucasian. Of the twenty four children enrolled in the class, nine are "special education," two are considered gifted, and the remaining 13 are "regular"—as Mrs. R explains (obviously frustrated by the lack of a better word). Mrs. R. has been a classroom teacher for about fifteen years, and is one of the finest teachers I have know in my twenty years of teaching.

During my professional leave time I agreed to observe in several early elementary level classrooms and record examples of interactions of gender, ethnicity, and social class affiliations. If possible, I was also to seek opportunities to assist the classroom teacher through modeling and teaching some activities involving multicultural awareness. Since one of the classrooms I had chosen was Mrs. R's, I was welcomed as a colleague and long-time friend. This provided the opening to suggest and implement an activity from Teaching Ethnic and Gender Awareness: Methods and Material for the Elementary School *by Edith W. King (1990), called "It's Me!: Self Portrait Collages" (p. 104). King points out that this activity will prove a meaningful classroom experience that has subtle ethnic and gender implications, allowing children a means to express their inner feelings about themselves, and assisting the teacher and other adults involved to gain new insights into personality development, and self-identity.*

The second-graders were instructed how to make their self-portraits collages: each child received a large sheet of manila-colored construction paper as a neutral background paper; the students were also supplied with a number of differing colors of construction paper scraps. They were urged to use only scissors and glue; but no pencils, crayons, or markers were allowed to create their self-portraits. I told them that this is your portrait so make it however you think is best. Mrs. R and I moved about the room encouraging the individual students, suggesting that they design their features, body parts, and clothing by using scissors and then pasting the parts together, rather than trying to draw themselves.

The next day when I returned I was greeted by a smiling Mrs. R and a proud class. The portraits were absolutely wonderful. Mrs. R selected a few portraits that she had special comments about, and we discussed these portraits when her children had left the room for their music class. She had carefully coded the backs of the self-portraits with information about the ethnicity, gender, and educational classification of each student. Mrs. R told me how interesting it was for her to observe her own students doing this activity, noting that using various colored construction paper scraps, and not letting the children use crayons to actually draw themselves, forced them to make some hard and fast decisions about which colors to use for their skin. She remarked that some children discussed the self-portrait activity at length with their classmates before making a decision on which colors to chose. She assured me that this is an activity she wanted to use again with other classes because it gave her much insight and new understandings about each of her students.

Here is another example of how informed observation and then participation in the classroom program by a perceptive professional can create a multicultural atmosphere for the young child's curriculum.

SUMMARY

This chapter contains discussions of three categories of curricular models for the early childhood program. We have called them the stimulus-response, behaviorist curriculum; the cognitive-interactionist (Piagetian) curriculum; and the maturationist, classic curriculum. These early childhood program models were developed and implemented in preschools, kindergartens, and the early elementary grades before educators and the public became so aware of multicultural education, the diversity perspective, and the more recent viewpoint of emergent literacy. From our vantage point at the close of the twentieth century we now can critique these curriculum models from a multicultural and diversity perspective.

Curriculum materials to fit each of the three types of programs were described and discussed in depth. The need for more awareness of ethnicity, social class, and gender perspectives for both early childhood models and their supportive curriculum materials was addressed. One promising direction toward meeting this need is through teacher education for both beginning and experienced teachers. The chapter closed with two accounts, those of a student-teacher and of an experienced teacher, who observed and participated in early elementary school multicultural classrooms. Their efforts to define and describe the multicultural atmosphere in the classroom was the focus of these reports.

KEY CONCEPTS

Stimulus-Response, Behaviorist View of the Curriculum Based in behaviorist psychological theory, this model of the early childhood curriculum asserts that the young child learns in small, succinct increments, building from simpler behaviors to more complex learning. This view pictures the individual as a receptive organism whose behavior is shaped mainly by the environment. It is assumed that each child is born with a repertoire of response capabilities and the ability to learn. Learning in the behaviorist view of the curriculum involves observable, measurable changes and is teacher-centered.

Cognitive-Interactionist (Piagetian) View of the Curriculum This view is based in cognitive developmental learning theory. It has evolved from the theory of Jean Piaget and his followers, featuring a child-centered, active learner approach. Interaction with people and the environment surrounding the child is essential in the learning process. The teacher is characterized as a facilitator, who structures the learning environment for the young child.

Maturationist, Classic View of the Curriculum Also referred to as the traditional approach to early childhood education, this view has its origins in the kindergarten philosophy of Froebel. This includes the concept of using actual objects and materials rather than making children learn by rote and memorization. This approach also encourages active learning and a child-centered program. However, it is closely identified with the concept of "readiness," which holds that the individual is primarily the product of genetic inheritance. Hence, the teacher's role is a passive one, allowing the child's inner time clock to dictate the learning program.

Subjects of the Early Childhood Education Curriculum Generally accepted as traditional subjects taught in the curriculum for young children are: literacy and language arts; expressive arts; mathematics; science or nature studies; social studies (the family, neighborhood, community); motor skills; and health and safety. Integration of content areas is of importance in developmentally appropriate classrooms.

The Diversity Perspective As used in this text, a diversity perspective includes the gender, ethnic, and social class aspects in the analysis of an issue, problem, viewpoint, program, or theory.

Curriculum Materials Concrete objects used in teaching and learning in early childhood classrooms are classified into three categories: pupil materials; curriculum kits and sets; and teacher resources.

A Multicultural Atmosphere This is the milieu of a school or classroom where awareness and concern for ethnic, gender, and social class diversity permeate the ongoing program of teaching and learning.

ISSUES AND ACTIONS

1. Presented in this chapter were excerpts from two teachers' journals on their observations and experiences in classrooms of young children. Design and carry out such a project. Plan a series of observations in a school in one particular classroom or with a group of children. Observe and record examples of interactions of ethnic affiliation including language or dialect spoken and of gender and social class. Describe your experiences in detail.

   From your notes, prepare a commentary on your conclusions and the implications for developing an atmosphere supportive of diversity and multiculturalism in the classroom.

2. Another aspect of observations and participation in classrooms of young children is an analysis of the curriculum materials used in the program. Examine the different types of curriculum materials you find in the room and that are used by the teacher. Try to decide if the curriculum materials reveal the underlying philosophy and view of the ongoing curriculum. How difficult is it to determine what view of the curriculum is being followed by the teacher? Ask the classroom teacher what theory or theories are being implemented in the program. Record the explanations and comments and compare this information with your notes and journal entries. What does this reveal about defining the atmosphere of multiculturalism in the young child's classroom?

3. While in the school or classroom ask to examine, (or obtain elswhere), several recent textbooks or teacher's manuals on the curriculum for young children. Analyze these materials from a diversity perspective. Do these professional guides and texts for teachers of young children discuss ethnic, gender, and social class issues and aspects of teaching? How many pages or sections are devoted to multicultural topics and crosscultural aspects such as concerns for linguistically diverse students, and international families?

REFERENCES AND SUGGESTED READINGS

Bereiter, C., and Englemann, E. *Teaching Disadvantaged Children in the Preschool.* Englewood Cliffs, NJ: Prentice-Hall, 1966.

Elkind, David. *Miseducation: Preschoolers at Risk.* New York: Knopf. 1988.

Engelmann, E., et al. *DISTAR: An Instructional System.* Chicago: Science Research Associates, 1969.

Gesell, A. L., and Ilg, F. L. *Child Development: An Introduction to the Study of Human Growth.* New York: Harper and Row, 1949.

King, E. *Teaching Ethnic and Gender Awareness: Methods and Materials for the Elementary School.* Dubuque, IA: Kendall/Hunt, 1990.

Kozol, Jonathan. *Savage Inequalities: Children in America's Schools.* New York: Crown, 1991.

Lavatelli, C. *Piaget's Theory Applied to an Early Childhood Curriculum.* Boston: Center for Media Development, 1970.

Ogbu, John. Understanding Cultural Diversity and Learning. *Educational Researcher,* November 1992; 21(8), pp. 5–14.

Skinner, B. F. *The Cumulative Record.* New York: Appleton Century-Crofts, 1959.

Stevens, Joseph, and King, Edith. *Administering Early Childhood Education Programs.* Boston: Little, Brown, 1976.

Weis, Lois, P. Altbach, Gail P. Kelly, and Hugh G. Petrie (Eds.). Critical Perspectives on Early Childhood Education. Albany, NY: State University of New York, 1991.

Wolfgang, C. H., and Wolfgang, M. E. *School of Young Children: Developmentally Appropriate Practice.* Needham Heights, MA: Allyn and Bacon, 1992.

5

THE SIGNIFICANCE OF ETHNIC AND GENDER IDENTITY IN CHILDHOOD

Every person has an ethnic identity, a heritage that shapes his or her attitudes, values, tastes, habits, language or dialect, and choices in everyday life. Everyone also has a gender identity. People differ in the degree to which they recognize their own ethnic identity and in their awareness of how their ethnicity and gender affects their day-to-day lives. Many do not realize that their ethnic identification can change with the passage of time, with geographic location, with upward or downward social mobility, from the impact of international events, and with their professional and social contacts. Social constructions are so taken for granted and unexamined that people do not realize that gender identification and social class affiliation subtly affect how they view themselves.

Ethnic and Gender Identity: Some Definitions

It is useful to examine the definitions of these social science concepts: ethnicity, ethnic identity, ethnic group, gender, socioeconomic class, and socialization.

Ethnicity is the sense of peoplehood derived from distinct commonalities. King (1990) has delineated seven specific "aspects of ethnicity." These are:

- the *historical* aspects of cultures and ethnic enclaves
- the *geographic* aspects of cultures, nationalities and ethnic enclaves
- the *linguistic* variations between peoples and across language groups
- the *religious* aspects that include the customs, ceremonies, and traditions associated with different belief systems
- the *social class* aspects and their economic implications
- the *political* aspects including international or transnational ties
- the *moral* aspects or stereotyping, prejudice and racism—the negative aspects of ethnicity

Ethnic identity is defined as the personal dimension of ethnicity or how one identifies oneself. There are instances when an individual may choose among ethnic preferences. These ethnic affiliations can be inherited or acquired through marriage. For example, it is not unusual for a woman in American society to acquire an ethnic family name through marriage and discard her birth name. If she makes a concerted effort to become familiar with the customs, foods, traditions, festivals, and holidays of that heritage, she may surprise her friends and acquaintances one day when they find out by accident that she was not born into, but married into, her current ethnic group.

An *ethnic group* is a group of people within a larger, dominant society that has a common ancestry and history, may speak a native tongue other than English, and may practice customs and traditions that reflect their ancestry.

An *ethnic minority group* is an ethnic group that has unique characteristics that make its members easily identifiable and may subject them to discrimination and prejudice in the broader society. (Banks, 1991; Barth, 1969.)

Gender identity is encased in sex-appropriate behaviors. Primarily biologically based, gender also includes the statuses, roles, appearances, and activities that distinguish males from females in a society.

Socioeconomic class is a measure that combines a person's education, occupation, and income to derive that individual's ranking in the social structure.

Socialization is the dynamic process that brings human beings into the human group, causing an individual to internalize the values, mores, traditions, language, and attitudes of the culture in which they live.

Ethnicity, gender, and socioeconomic class are factors that influence an individual's socialization. Thus, an individual's specific affiliation and heritage often are carried on through the family tradition from generation to generation. True, the customs and folkways may undergo variation, but the core of ethnic identity is still recognizable. Ethnic scholars, particularly sociologists, have noted this not only in examining American ethnicity but in transnational contexts as well. Often it is useful to draw examples and accounts from a crosscultural, international context to more clearly determine and understand the significance of ethnic and gender identity in early childhood. The following excerpt from one American educator's story of his family's experiences during their two-year assignment in Germany in the 1980s brings out many of the subtle and overt aspects of ethnic affiliation and childhood socialization.

ROSA'S SCHOOL SOCIALIZATION: ON BEING BLACK AND AMERICAN IN A GERMAN KINDERGARTEN[1]

After much negotiation and months of waiting we were finally winging our way across the Atlantic to Germany. We, my family and I, consisted of my wife, a Milwaukee German American with the Hawaiian name of Leilani (flowers from heaven), as well as Miguel, our adopted five-year-old Cuban American son; Rosa, our adopted four-

year-old Mexican–African American daughter; and Casey, a "home-made" two-year-old.

On the airplane I described Germany in glowing terms to my excited family. I gave them pictures of forests of stately oaks and towering pines, the glistening lakes of Bavaria, the green countrysides of middle Germany, and the quaint towns of timbered medieval houses. Warm thoughts of my childhood, growing up near Heidelberg where my father had been serving as a visiting professor on the faculty of the famous university there, came back to me. But when we arrived in Wiesbaden and began our search for living quarters—a family of five, with three children under six years of age—my joy and delight at returning to Germany, the scenes of my childhood, soon faded.

After days of searching we finally located a townhouse, small by American standards, with a tiny, fenced backyard in the town of Taunusstein, a short distance from Wiesbaden. But, at least, we now had a roof over our heads and could live with other Germans, learning the culture and language. Lani and I had nurtured the ideal of immersing our family in the local culture, so that the roots of a multicultural tree might take hold and the fruits of multiculturalism might someday blossom. With this in mind, we sent our girls, Casey and Rosa, out to play in the local park, just across the street from our new home. The two girls had been playing in the park for just a short while when I thought to take a look from the upstairs balcony, which had a commanding view of the entire park.

What I saw was most interesting. Our little blond Casey was happily playing in the sandbox with a brood of German toddlers, being watched solicitously by a gaggle of German mommies sitting on nearby benches. Rosa, on the other hand, was five yards away, playing with a group of dark-skinned children who looked quite distinct from German kids. The girls in that group wore colorful head scarves, and some wore pants underneath their heavy skirts. The boys, anywhere from two to ten years old, had ruddy complexions, jet black hair, and sported heavy-knit sweaters. The dark-skinned group I observed, which now included Rosa, carefully avoided the sandbox area. The fair-skinned sandbox crowd also paid no attention to the brown children playing nearby. "Curiouser and curiouser," I thought to myself (like Alice) and went to the park to solve this riddle.

I didn't immediately go to my kids, but chose to sit with the German moms on one of the three benches. I had brought a German newspaper and had dressed casually, wearing shorts and German sandals. I greeted the ladies in perfect German. That I was a newcomer to the neighborhood was obvious, but the mothers did not *suspect I was American or father to the two new little girls. A moment's hesitation went by, smoothed over by the inevitable small talk about the weather. A few minutes later I was accepted, or, perhaps more accurately, graciously ignored by the moms. However, I was able to listen in on their conversations, while pretending to be absorbed in my newspaper. What I heard explained the invisible barriers between the two groups of children.*

The moms were discussing Turks, both in specifics and in general terms. Mom #1 made the comment that Turks were getting out of hand, simply by their numbers. I thought about this for a moment and intellectually agreed that it was odd that the third largest Turkish city in the world should happen to be in the Kreuzberg district of West Berlin. In terms of inhabitants, Kreuzberg ranked right after Istanbul and Ankara. Mom #2 commented favorably that Germany needed the Turks, as well as the Italians, Yugoslavians, Greeks, Spanish, and other foreigners who had made Germany's economic miracle possible. Mom #3 chimed in and agreed, but added that it was a shame how Turks had abused the welfare system, bringing in kids by the truckload, who could be claimed as dependents and receive social subsidies. Mom #3 continued that she knew one Turk, who lived in her apartment complex, who had imported eight children—who may or may not have all been his. All she knew was that all eight were now in German public school, gobbling up medical and social benefits, and that Ali's wife now received fistfuls of D-marks every month in children's subsidies. It wasn't fair. The other two moms clucked in agreement and continued their disparaging observations about Turks.

After a compendium of sins was duly noted, discussed, and elaborated, it became clear that Turks were: noisy, dirty, sometimes lazy, primitive, smelly, odd, exceedingly religious in the wrong faith, too dark, too strange, and too unwilling to adapt to the German way of life. Mom #1 observed that Turkish cooking smelled up the hallways in her complex and that, besides, the drumbeat of their music drove her to distraction. Moms #2 and #3 agreed and added they couldn't understand why older Turkish women wore coats in the summer and up to three petticoats at a time.

I lowered my newspaper and asked why the ladies were so concerned about Turks in the first place. They examined me with an air of suspicion and Mom #1 explained that most of the six-story housing complexes surrounding the park were public housing shared by Turks and Germans. It had once been a purely German area, but not anymore. It was common knowledge, the mom continued, that Turks have a herd instinct. This means that once the door is opened to even a single Turkish family, a neighborhood's fate is sealed and the floodgates are lowered to admit wave after wave of Turkish newcomers. Germans move out and Turks move in, and so it goes. Mom #1 commented that not all Germans could afford to move and, thus, many were tied down by economic circumstances. The three women seemed to sigh in unison, in tacit agreement that the vagaries of fate had conspired to keep them bound to these tenement buildings.

I nodded in what they must have thought was a sign of agreement. I asked whether the children always played in separate groups. The moms said yes, that it was better that way. The moms feared that the Turkish kids were too wild and harbored secret aggressions, based on jealousy, toward their German peers. The Turkish kids couldn't be trusted, sometimes played with knives, and had different ideas about right and wrong. Turkish kids fought more often and were latch-key kids who lacked proper supervision. Mom #2 added that Turkish kids were terribly clannish, preferring to speak their own language, instead of learning proper German. "I don't know one Turk who can speak a correct sentence of German," Mom #2 announced in a voice tinged with sorrow and pity. "It's a crying shame."

Armed with new sociological insights, the playground dynamics made more sense. Rosa, being dark-skinned from her Hispanic and African-American heritage, was without a doubt a person of color, who neatly fit into the Turkish children's world view of safe and acceptable people. In contrast, the German children saw Rosa as "different" and not belonging to their in group. Luckily, Rosa was oblivious to this distinction and sorting out, for she was having a great time with her Turkish playmates. It was equally clear that Casey, with her blond hair and Germanic looks, belonged with the Teutonic tribe playing in the sandbox. Though she couldn't say a word, Casey was giggling and laughing with little Trudy, Analiese, and Marla. There almost seemed to be an incontestable, natural order to this sandbox world, which I didn't want to disturb. Casey, herself, by getting up and joining her sister, toppled the psychological apple cart.

Like marionettes whose strings had been pulled, the moms came to attention and watched Casey's every move. One of the moms wondered out loud where Casey's own mother might be. At this point, I let the ladies know I was Casey's father, though I didn't volunteer that Rosa also belonged to our family. The ladies watched to see what I would do, which was—nothing! I let Casey join the Turkish kids, who seemed a bit taken aback at first. One of the Turkish girls helped Casey swing, and afterwards, a little Turkish boy of three led her around by the hand, trying to give her pretend kisses while stroking her blond hair. In broken German, the little boy told Casey, "Hubsches

Madchen. . . !" ("pretty girl"). The Turkish kids were gentle with Casey and the play continued for another hour. After awhile, Mom #1 looked at me and her glance seemed to say, "Are you going to let this continue?"

I thought it a shame that the moms didn't give the Turkish kids more of a chance to dismantle their value-laden, preconceived notions and ideas. I mused that with such deeply rooted ideas and expectations in place, the German moms were perhaps unwittingly providing the fuel and stoking the fires of self-fulfilling prophecies. After all, what came first? A German mother's expectations of how a Turkish child would necessarily behave or the behavior itself? I kept reading my newspaper and watched the children play.

Gordon Allport (1954) taught me that perceptions are often more powerful than facts in fanning the flames of prejudice. When it was time for Rosa to go to the German, church sponsored-kindergarten, I came along to observe. Francis Bacon (in Burtt, 1944) had long ago spoken of community and individual prejudices as the "idols of the tribe" and the "idols of the cave." I had a suspicion that little had changed since then and wanted to be sure Rosa did not stand alone. I was able to observe without being seen by the children and soon spotted a familiar pattern of segregation. Kids, in general, didn't play with Rosa, though they interacted with her when told to do so. Rosa kept to herself, when not involved in group activity, and didn't pair off during recess. On the playground, I asked a little girl in Rosa's class what she thought of the "new girl." "Oh, she's all right, I guess," the girl replied. "But she looks Turkish."

Rosa's integration into kindergarten went so-so, though the teacher mentioned that Rosa had temper tantrums and shied away from group activities. I was pondering what to do when Shakespeare's words from "As You Like It" came to mind: "All the world's a stage, And all the men and women merely players. . . ."

It seemed that children were not seeing Rosa as she really was. Rosa had already been tried, convicted, and hung as a second-class world citizen, and it was high time to correct the kindergarten tykes' ideas of Rosa's heritage. I thought that what might be needed here was a bit of theater and drama to fine-tune some faulty perceptions. I explained to the classroom instructor that Rosa had a fascinating cultural background, complete with fame and glory.

Playing fairy godmother, I transformed Rosa into someone with a glorious past, much more glamorous than just another non–German-speaking brown girl. Rosa had become an Aztec Indian with a golden-bronzed complexion, who had a mysterious biological father from the Sugar Islands. The kindergarten teacher was excited by my offer to share Rosa's cultural legacy with the rest of the class. Arrangements were quickly made for a cultural show and tell.

On the appointed day, we were ready and heavily armed. Rosa was decked out in a flurry of colorful petticoats, layered to look like a flamenco dancer. Her hair was graced with bows. Bronze necklaces, arm bracelets, and rings gave her the festive air of Brazilian carnival. A bright golden kerchief completed her attire, which drew "oooooh's" and "aaaaah's" from the kindergarten crowd. Rosa was all smiles, prancing in front of her appreciative audience. In simple German, I explained the proud legacy of the Aztec empire, whose people had built tremendous cities, invented astrological calendars of great precision, and had peopled a land mass many times the size of Germany. I brought along artwork from Mexico and passed around jewelry, clay figurines, pottery, and hand-painted parchment scrolls. We shared pictures of Guadalajara and mariachi bands in full regalia. Turning to Rosa's black heritage, we spoke of mysterious islands in the Caribbean Sea, where sun-drenched beaches gave way to clear, blue, shark-infested waters.

When all was said and done, the whole kindergarten was ready to buy one-way tickets to Mexico City, the old capital of the Nahua. Rosa had gained, in an hour's time, the status and prestige she couldn't have earned in a year of perfect behavior. Her skin color was seen in a new light and her inability to speak German yet was forgiven. Kids wanted to touch her dress and be close to her. The glory reaped during our cultural presentation lasted for most of the year, though there would be ups and downs. Rosa gained a new self-confidence, which made it possible for her to shrug off the occasional thoughtless comment or gesture that still came her way.

The Commitment to Our World Society

This forthright account of one American family's concerted attempts to imbue their children with a multilingual, multicultural, international perspective, starting in their early childhood years, is unique and enlightening. It demonstrates that some parents are deeply committed to preparing their children for the world of the twenty-first century, where multilingualism and cross-cultural experience will be essential not only for education, but also for business, politics, and world peace. Additionally, this father's story of his young daughters' socialization in a small German village and in that village's kindergarten exemplifies the important influence of ethnic identity and ethnic minority group membership.

THE SIGNIFICANCE OF EARLY SCHOOL EXPERIENCE IN CHILDHOOD SOCIALIZATION

The persistence of ethnic identification in contemporary pluralistic societies is due to both negative and positive factors. When the primary reason for group affiliation is hostility from the majority group, it is inevitable that ethnicity seems more to confine and constrict the individual than to provide opportunities and enhance the quality of life. Yet people usually hold to ethnic identification because of the advantages it offers. The ethnic group can be a buffer between the individual and the broader society; individuals use ethnicity as a filter for forming their opinions, tastes, values, and habit patterns. Ethnic affiliations also help organize social, economic, political, and religious interaction, both between individuals and among groups.

The Social Construction of Ethnic and Gender Identity

In exploring the concept of ethnic identity, we inevitably encounter questions about the "reality" of the social world in which the individual exists. It seems appropriate, then, to introduce the theory of the social construction of reality and to apply it to the meaning of ethnicity and of ethnic and gender identity. The leading theorists on the topic of the social construction of reality are Peter Berger and Thomas Luckmann, whose ideas and insights will help clarify the significance of the social construction of ethnic and gender identity.

Berger and Luckmann contend that the reality of everyday life presents itself to us as a world we share with others. We share a common sense about what is reality and, therefore, our everyday life is characterized by a taken-for-granted reality. However, human beings are unique among living creatures, for they can experience and exist in several provinces of meaning or taken-for-granted realities. These can be enclaves within the paramount reality. The theater provides an excellent metaphor for coexisting realities. To this point Berger and Luckmann tell us:

> *The transition between realities is marked by the rising and falling of the curtain. As the curtain rises, the spectator is "transported into another world," with its own meanings and an order that may or may not have much to do with the order of everyday life. As the curtain falls, the spectator "returns to reality." (Berger and Luckmann, 1966, p. 25)*

So it can be with an individual's ethnic identity. Within the ethnic group, the taken-for-granted world calls for conduct, use of language, referents, mutual affinities, and antipathies that are implicit and unspoken. These ways are shared with others of the same ethnic and racial affiliations. Yet, the same individual can function within the majority society in the taken-for-granted reality of the supermarket, the street traffic, or the daily newspaper. Common habit patterns take over to guide conduct. A person pays the price posted and does not bargain with the cashier at the supermarket; goes on the green light and halts on the red light, not chancing the traffic just because no cars are in sight; and comprehends the news story on the front page. We accept and function within cultural continuities even from childhood.

Our view of reality and of the world helps us to make sense of our experiences. We interpret social events in light of the social meanings we attach to them. Here our ethnic identification and ethnic affiliation come forth to interpret the meaning of everyday occurrences. Additionally the individual is socialized into assuming the roles and behavior of the society that are considered proper by internalizing behavior that is considered appropriate for one's gender.

In the story that follows, "Girlhood in Puerto Rico," which chronicles one woman's remembrances of her childhood experiences in what is now a suburb of San Juan, Puerto Rico, the ethnic, gender, and social class assertions stated above come into a more meaningful reality. This account is presented in its original telling to provide readers with an authentic rendition.

GIRLHOOD IN PUERTO RICO[2]

Unfortunately, as adults, we often cannot recall those forces in our childhood experiences (social, academic, cultural, gender) that have had a strong impact on our lives. I have had the great fortune of having grown up in a social and cultural system that reinforced my beliefs in myself and provided the backbone for a very productive life. With that strength I have been able to experience and examine the American social, cultural, and educational systems. I have seen how diversity and pluralism are not a valued and integral part of children's lives, particularly within an increasingly pluralistic society. "Minority" children are frequently denied access to the richness of their heritage as well as to opportunities; but "majority" children suffer a much greater loss: they do not learn the potential possibilities for mutual support, growth, enrichment, and general social betterment.

All children can be encouraged to grow both as individuals and as members of society—a society of nations and of people from diverse backgrounds.

I was born in Puerto Rico and spent most of my early childhood years in Rio Piedras, a suburb of the capital city of San Juan. I grew up used to the bustling metropolitan area where I attended large, modern schools. However, when I was in fourth grade my parents moved to a town located about twenty miles west.

The Town

In spite of my parent's excitement, at the time it seemed to me like a long distance and an awful place for our family to live. It was a small underdeveloped town with unkept roads and public buildings. The "plaza" or public square was small, ungroomed and the buildings surrounding it were in serious need of painting and refurbishing. The only building which appeared cared for was the cathedral, also located in the "plaza." Majestic and splendorous, this structure ironically accentuated the vast deprivation around it. It was a growing town and our house was one of the first to be built in this new "booming town" outside of San Juan. To my father the town was in the path of progress; to my mother it represented the small, communal living she had been raised in and wanted her children to experience. I remember initially hating that town where it rained all the time or was always overcast, even when the vegetation was lush and green and bright flowers were ever in full bloom. You never left the house without an umbrella even when the sun was shining brightly. It took time, but the town eventually grew on me and I became quite fond of it.

We were literally surrounded by new housing developments. The houses were coming up fast and people kept moving in. We enjoyed comparing new house models and meeting new neighbors. The houses were built out of concrete with marbleized floors, glass windows, terraces, carports, gardens, yards, etc. and were considered "state of the art."

We did not have a lawn when we moved in. Red, sticky clay soil stuck to our shoes and dragged into our new house. My younger sister and I mopped the floors constantly until we finally planted a lawn. The house did not have screens on the windows and we fought a never ending battle with the flies and mosquitoes. Memories of the "Mosquito and Fly Patrols" we formed as the children marched around the house armed with "swappers" made out of rolled newspapers bring laughter to us now. Mother paid us a penny for each exterminated fly or mosquito. Finally we got window and door screens. With all the *construction also came air saturated with chalky dust. The girls cleaned and it seemed like we spent an awful lot of time mopping floors, killing flies, and dusting the house.*

There was only one small shopping center with a real supermarket in town. Most of the time we had to shop at the public market which was always crowded, hot, and very unsanitary. Public buses too were old, hot, and usually crowded. Back in the metropolitan area, some of the women drove or rode the modern public buses. Yet, overall, many of the adult women, especially in this small town, did not drive and either waited to be taken places by their husbands or took "public cars" to get around rather than ride the buses. Father often took us places and then came back to pick us up at an agreed time. Women rarely wore pants, even around the house, and were not permitted to ride the buses or go to public places wearing them. Girls wore pants to play and work around the house but had to wear skirts to go to town.

My father was right about the growth potential of the town. The town continued to grow and now the distance to San Juan is not quite as apparent. The open fields and farms are gone and today the town is a big city continuous with San Juan—the metropolitan area. The small, sleepy town was swallowed by a growing giant. It is now full of skyscrapers, condominiums, and yes!—shopping malls. It has the same traffic and people congestions that are prevalent throughout the rest of the metropolitan area. Unfortunately, its provincial sleepy innocence is also gone.

Family Life

When we moved into our new house mother never closed the doors to the house. As a matter of fact, all the doors in the neighborhood remained wide open all day. The children went about the neighborhood all day long, going in and out of each other's houses freely. The community was very conservative and believed in unquestionable respect for all adults. Neighbors looked after the community children and there was always more than a handful of children to feed during meals—your own and a few others! Whenever one got hungry you just went in the nearest house and sat yourself at the table with the rest of the children. You could always expect to get a good reprimand, and an occasional spanking from any neighbor who caught you doing something wrong. Then they told your parents and you "got it" from your parents, aunts, grandparents, cousins. Between close-knit comunities and extended families being bad just didn't pay.

Our family is interracial: father is black and mother is white. Father owned a successful business with a white Jewish-American partner, who had just migrated from the mainland. The business had several employees, too. As such, we enjoyed social and economic status. I played with the partner's two daughters regularly. Although they spoke little Spanish, and I little English, we seemed to understand each other quite well. I liked their mother with her blonde hair which was always dyed the same color as her dress. I liked their less rigid lifestyle which included the children. At their house adults and children sat together and talked to each other freely. Children could express their ideas and even disagree openly. At our home children only spoke to adults when adults spoke to them; children kept their heads down and only answered what was asked of them; children never stared adults eye to eye. To volunteer conversation or opinions around adults was a serious offense. Children never disagreed with adults because "adults (are) never wrong." Mother always complained about her children going to "that house where the wife (is) always out of the house and serves the children cold sandwiches." Mother bragged that the partner's daughters loved coming to our house just so they "could eat good hot meals and be treated properly." Meanwhile, I visited their house whenever I could because I enjoyed being treated almost like an adult and sharing my ideas without fear. Father wanted to appear progressive, particularly to his American partner. Yet unknowingly, he was exposing me to another education that was radically opposite to his real values and expectations. This new mode of gender and social interactions slowly chipped away at some of the traditional ideas that I had been taught. I began to question the status quo. During my rare moments of open defiance, Father lashed out at me in indignation: "Perhaps the Americans are here, but I don't have to live with them in my own house!"

Our entire neighborhood was integrated and race was not an apparent concern. Our nextdoor neighbor was from Galicia, Spain, and loved to sing old Spanish songs. Everyone in the area could hear him. Each evening we awaited his singing even more than people wait for their favorite television shows today. We had a lot of friends and playmates were never lacking. We had television and telephones, but our lives centered around outdoor and community activities. Children always had a lot of games: Escondite, La Cebollita, Doña Ana, Carbonerita. Children made a circle, rotated and sang: "Doña Ana no está aquí, está en su vergel. . . ," while a child in the center tried to escape the circle. On rainy days we had plenty of indoor activities. My favorite was paper dolls and make believe. A favorite outdoors activity was just lying on the grass to look at the clouds and discovering the different shapes they made—dragons, castles, mountains. Playing in the warm rain was a treat. We took large leaves from the plantain (green banana) trees called "jaguas" and used them as sleds. They were very slippery against the wet grass. Our best toys were those we created ourselves. At mealtime, the females set the table but no one sat down until Father did. Sometimes Father wished to eat alone, and no one ate until he was done. Often Mother served everyone and ate last. During meals Father spoke at length about his business while the children only listened and answered his questions. Father read a lot, especially electronics materials, and enjoyed talking about new discoveries and technology. He asked the children a lot of questions about school and expected a full report from each of us. He specifically wanted to know what we had learned. He also wanted to know what we each had taught our younger siblings—we were expected to teach our younger brothers and sisters. He expected us to know current local and world events and often asked what was in the newspaper's headlines for that day. We children had to be quick with the answer.

Father questioned Mother about her activities, particularly household management. Mother often told him about things we needed, such as shoes or notebooks, because Father managed the family budget. He rarely refused us anything we needed, especially for school, but Mother had to ask him for money first. Most of the time, though, we shopped and he paid the bill when we were done. Sometimes Mother encouraged us to ask Father for things she really wanted, like the new stereo and washing machine. Quite frankly, we all detested this drilling. Meals and conversation with Father frequently were not welcomed times.

It was not uncommon, from time to time, to also have other children and/or relatives living with us. They, too, were expected to accept the sovereign rule of our father and the other males in the family. After eating, the males left the room while the females cleaned the table and dishes. Any child needing disciplining also left the room with the males. Those were the only times I truly enjoyed housework.

The School in the Community

We walked about five miles each way to get to our neighborhood school because none had been built in the new housing developments. When we lived in Rio Piedras, Mother could walk to the school and visited there often. Not so in the new town. We walked in groups and collected other children along the way. The neighborhood immediately surrounding the school was a lower socioeconomic one. The houses were made out of wood and were old and small. Many of the streets were unpaved (and remained muddy with red clay soil). Some houses had no indoor sanitary facilities. I made many friends along the school route and enjoyed visiting the "fighting rooster" farms near the school. There, families raised roosters for "cock fights." They were beautiful animals and I never understood why anybody would entice them to fight to the death. Anyway, people kept chickens and other farm animals.

All students attending both private and public schools in Puerto Rico wear uniforms. A student better never "get caught anywhere else" (but school grounds) wearing a school uniform—particularly the girls. Any adult could ask for your "pass" or letter from parent or teacher giving you permission to be out of school. If you were out of school without your uniform during school hours you had better be accompanied by an adult and/or be ready to produce your "pass." Girls were not permitted to wear pants to school although we often wore shorts under our skirts.

Classes were grouped by ability and achievement. Therefore, competition was always tough. All my brothers and sisters were in the top classes so I always felt in competition with them too. Even though classes were so separated, achievement was valued and respected. Other students admired us and sought our help with school work. Humility is part of our culture and we were taught that helping others was our obligation—to share with others our good fortune and talents.

The students in my class, and the school, were of various racial and ethnic backgrounds. There were children of Arabic ancestry, Italians, Chinese, Germans, Irish, etc. Puerto Rico has always been a land of immigrants and just about every world nationality is represented. There were many "mulatto" children, or of mixed black–white parentage as myself. I was considered "trigueña" (brown-skinned) but was never made to feel inferior because of it. I loved some of my friends' blonde hair and blue eyes, or straight black hair and almond-shaped eyes. I enjoyed visiting my "Abuelita Negra" (Black Grandma) because she and my aunts always styled my hair in fancy ways that the other girls at school admired. We visited Abuelita Negra often and I learned much about my African ancestry through those visits. We also visited our white grandmother, nicknamed "Mother." I was never ashamed to share my heritage with my peers at school.

Although I was not conscious of racial differences, as such, at that time, I do remember that the class was fully integrated. I knew who and what I was but that was never a major concern. Eri, my toughest contender (and boyfriend) for first place, was mulatto or of mixed parentage as I was. He had been the boyfriend of another contender, Judi, who was blonde with blue eyes. Eri, Judi, and I always managed

*to attain the same grade point average and always shared the honor
of being number one.*

The Hidden Social Agenda

*The "hidden agenda" of gender inequities was very much in place in
Puerto Rican schools and society. On our first Sunday at the new
house, my brother and I walked miles through swampy fields where
tall bamboo grew, and "arrabales" (shanty towns) to buy bread and
milk for the family breakfast. As head of the household when our
father was away, it was my brother's responsibility to care for the
family. My mother, or the girls, were not permitted to go to town or
the store alone. Although I was expected to stay home and help out
with my four younger siblings I insisted on going with him. My
brother, although only a year older than I, was expected to make
decisions for the rest of us, including my mother when father was
away. I often envied and resented his higher status.*

*I wondered what it felt like to have that much power and be so
privileged at such an early age. We were close and he often let me go
with him, even on "dangerous missions" such as this one. Sometimes
he said no and that was that! It was his duty to demonstrate that he
could lead and protect the family. My brother's quick decision could
free me from the drudgery of housework and send me on the road to
discovery and adventure. Luckily for me, we grew almost inseparable,
except when he went with our father. When I turned twelve and was
told that a "woman's place is in the house with other women" and
"respectable women do not mingle with men." After that I was not
permitted to follow my brother and his friends.*

*When not in school, my brother spent increasing periods of time
with our father helping with the business, while I stayed home with
Mother and the younger children. Father would teach my brother
about his career and business. Mother took care of the cooking and
laundry and the girls cleaned the house and cared for the younger
ones. We were told that when my brother was born—first son—Father
celebrated for three days. I was the second child and was followed by
three other girls. Father referred to us as "chancletas" (old slippers).
Father kept wanting another son but kept getting "chancletas." When
the youngest child was born, a boy, Father celebrated again and
showed his son off to his friends. I remember that Father was visibly
happy with Mother for giving him another son.*

*My father and brother did not have any household responsibili-
ties. All the females in the family were expected to serve them. They
sat while the females did household work, removed their shoes, and*

fetched them their food and water. Since education was a priority in our family and other work was secondary, I developed a strong love for school and school activities which took me away from the dreaded housework and indoor life.

Education in Puerto Rico was valued and was seen as the social equalizer. Through education, opportunities were open to anyone willing to work hard; and the opportunities were endless. Regardless of race you could aspire to achieve any goal. Although society relegated women to a lower status, pioneering role models such as Doña Felisa Rincon de Gautier, the mayoress of San Juan, opened doors of hope and dreams for many aspiring young girls. I studied her biography and adopted her as my role model. Doña Fela was famous for her fans and I learned how to handle one with skill and grace. Overall, though, women were encouraged to go into "traditionally female" careers, marry and give support to their husbands and their careers, and build their lives around their husbands' choices and decisions.

Although education was important to my father, the emphasis was on the boys' education. After all, they would be the "breadwinners" and "men of the house" someday. Girls became educated enough to be "marriageable." The emphasis for girls was to learn homemaking skills in order to be cooks and hostesses, and to be able to sew for their family. I remember Father's proud celebration around his friends when I sewed my first dress at age ten. He bought me shoes and a purse to match and would have me wear it to go out with him. It was his way of showing that he was raising his daughters properly, meaning marriageable.

Somehow I grew up knowing that I wanted other things for myself. I wanted a college education—in the mainland—and equal rights as a woman and human being. It is hard to say just what it was that imprinted that message in my very young mind. It started early in my life and became solidified over time. Perhaps it was exposure to options and different ways of interpreting the world. Perhaps it was role models and the development of a positive self-esteem. Perhaps it was my search for answers to the contradictions I found so apparent in my world. I still search for those answers as I look at today's education systems and realize that we really have not changed that much.

A Portrait of the Construction of Gender Identity

This frank and intimate portrait of "a girlhood in Puerto Rico" informs us how the social construction of ethnic and gender identity takes place. It reiterates that every person is born into a human group that shapes or socializes him or her during childhood. Through socialization, social constructions (in other words, social reality) are internalized by the individual. Hence, the individual's self-perceptions and identity are being formed through his or her encounters with everyday life. In this perceptive account of childhood we learn that others interpret the meanings of experience in the social world for the child. Further we see how this applies not only to social class membership, but also to ethnic affiliation and gender roles as well. Ethnic identity helps explain the wide differences in people's perceptions of the social world across class lines. Ethnic identity also gives us a more accurate understanding of why an individual might interpret social reality in so many diverse ways. Primary socialization during the years of childhood, the internalizing of values, attitudes, preferences, and habit patterns in the early years of life, has the greatest impact on the individual. All secondary socialization, in adulthood, must be filtered and made to fit within the social construction of reality internalized during primary socialization.

ETHNICITY, GENDER AND SOCIAL CLASS: IMPORTANT AWARENESS FOR TEACHERS

Often, growing up in the ethnic enclave, ghetto, or barrio socializes children into the belief that all the world is Mexican-American or Jewish or Italian or Puerto Rican. Teachers must realize that children hold these conceptions quite naturally and logically. Recognizing the value of lifestyles and constructing teaching and learning experiences that broaden and expand children's conceptions of the social world is vital in a pluralistic society. Biographies and personal histories reveal how the chance factors of everyday life can affect people's conceptions of the ethnic and social world that surrounds them. Socialization can lull a child into believing that most of the existing society that she or he will ever encounter is made of people of the same ethnicity or race as the child. Examples of this are seen in the following statements compiled from experienced teachers' accounts of their childhood socialization:[3]

On Ethnicity

As a young child I had limited contact with people of color. I knew that they existed because I would see them on the buses, or at the shopping malls, or at the movies when I would go. I never really thought too much about them, though, because I never met a person of color, nor did I ever have an opportunity to speak with one.

An ethnic experience that I remember was when we went out to eat once at a Chinese restaurant. I was totally amazed to see a room full of Chinese people. The food was totally weird to me, and watching the people using chopsticks, kept me mesmerized during the entire meal.

Looking back I understand why there were not any blacks in my town. Even though Newark, New Jersey, a major city, was only a fifteen-minute drive away, we were isolated. I remember when a black man just walking in the streets of our town caused great concern. Everybody was convinced that he was up to no good and the police were called. The cops would pick the guy up, whether or not he was innocent did not matter, and bring him down to the police station for questioning. To this day I do not think that there is a black police officer employed in my home town.

I am a product of the South. In the 1950s my town was a racially segregated city. It was two cities in one. The blacks lived in an area referred to as "colored" town and rarely mingled with the white population except when catching the bus. In "colored" town were churches, schools, small stores—all the essentials to keep the blacks from mingling with the whites. On Saturdays on Main Street there were no blacks doing their weekly shopping, only crowds of white people. Blacks did not buy their shoes at Thompson's or ice cream at the Dairy Queen. Although my neighborhood was only three blocks from "colored" town, I never visited that area of town nor did any of my friends. It was off limits to us. Sometimes our parents would drive blacks home from their jobs cleaning our houses or yards, but we were never invited to ride along.

On Gender

When it came to gender awareness, both of my parents encouraged me to be a secretary, school teacher, or a nurse. They said that I needed to get a good education so that if my husband ever died in a war, then I would be able to support my family. They encouraged me to participate in traditionally female activities. I played piano for several years, took ballet lessons, and was a Girl Scout. My female role models were Donna Reed, Loretta Young, June Cleaver, Wilma Flintstone, Betty Rubble, Jackie Kennedy, and the most incredible woman of them all—Marilyn Monroe!

I remember my younger brother had a doll he called Suzie Q. He must have been around five years old then, and I was around eight years old. Even at that early age I used to make fun of him and called him a girl because he carried this doll around. He hated being called a girl. It was probably the worst thing that could have happened to him. He had no sisters, so being a girl must have been something he imagined to be absolutely horrible. I thought so, too, or I would not have called him one. That was the last doll to come into our house.

Every summer until we were in high school, my father would take me and my brothers on a camping experience. It was a place where fathers and sons would go for a week of camping, fishing, shooting guns, and watching sports films. There were never any women. The men were allowed to be men and the boys to be boys. One of the fathers owned a restaurant and cooked all the meals, so we ate like kings. We, the young boys, were never asked to help clean the dishes or anything that resembled a chore. I think the men thought that this was women's work and they did not want to ask their sons to get involved in it.

On Social Class

When it came to social class, I thought that we were average, just like the neighbors. It never dawned on me that my family probably had more wealth than others because both my mother and my father worked. I just thought that we were all the same. When we took our family vacations we would fly to California. Back in those days, flying was reserved for the very wealthy. The rest of the neighborhood families would go on vacations to local spots just a car ride away. It never occurred to me that my vacations were special; the difference in transportation was meaningless to me.

When I was very young, my early childhood years, I was unaware of any class differences at all. I spent most of my time playing in the backyard sandbox, on the swings, or in my toy-filled room. I first began to notice a difference between myself and my peers in the third grade when I was old enough to visit my friends' houses. I noticed that their homes did not sit back, away from all the others on their street; and their backyards, if they had any yard at all, were much smaller than mine. Most did not have a dog. I wondered how these kids could be happy living in what seemed to me to be terrible conditions. Though their homes were always very clean, they were smaller than mine, and I think size makes a big impression on children.

These anecdotes are adult reminiscences. All the participants were teachers, who were encouraged to remember their childhood aware-nesses of ethnicity, of gender, and of social class and its impact on their self-perceptions and their self-identity. Teachers need to be aware of these dynamics because of the implications they have on behavior in their classrooms. Too often, a teacher just reproduces the attitudes and values of the majority culture, unthinkingly and unwittingly, thereby reinforcing the primary socialization of the majority society.

SUMMARY

In this chapter we have explored meaning inherent in belonging to an ethnic group or an ethnic minority group. The conception of the social construction of ethnic and gender identity, understood as the repertoire of acts and statuses recognized as valid by a social group, has also contributed to our understanding of the significance of these dynamics in childhood.

In recent years much more attention has been focused on intergroup relations and prejudice reduction. We know that ethnic group affiliation and gender identity are decisively influenced by what happens in the schools and in the home. Yet, by the time a child comes to school, he or she has already been socialized into a set of language patterns, values, attitudes, habits, and customs that are determined by ethnicity and gender. If the school, however subtly, devalues these characteristics, the child will inevitably have less self-esteem and pride. Since there is a direct relationship between a child's self-esteem (or lack of it) and the ability to learn, children who have been made to feel inferior because of their ethnicity or gender find the learning process more difficult. Teach-ers can call on the concepts of the social construction of ethnic and gender identity and primary and secondary socialization to bring a new awareness to their classrooms and revitalize their teaching.

KEY CONCEPTS

Ethnicity A sense of peoplehood; the sense of a shared historical past, geography, kinship patterns, religion, language, social class, political appeals, attitudes, values, and folkways held by a group.

Ethnic Identity Defined as the personal dimension of ethnicity, or how one identifies oneself.

Ethnic Group A group of people within a larger society who has a common ancestry and history, may speak a language other than English, and practices customs and traditions that reflect their ancestry.

Ethnic Minority Group An ethnic group that has unique characteristics that make its members easily identifiable and may subject them to discrimination in the broader society.

Social Construction of Ethnic Identity How we view social reality and interpret the meanings of experience by filtering these experiences through our ethnic identity.

Social Construction of Gender Identity How we view social reality and interpret the meanings of experience by comparing these experiences with the roles, statuses, and behavior that society considers proper for one's sex.

Socialization The dynamic process that brings human beings into the group, causing an individual to internalize the values, mores, traditions, language, and attitudes of the culture in which they live.

Socioeconomic Class The measure that combines a person's education, occupation, and income to derive that person's ranking in the social structure.

ISSUES AND ACTIONS

1. This chapter featured some concepts and theories from the social sciences, particularly from sociology. Teacher education, especially in the area of early childhood education, does not always draw heavily on the disciplines of sociology and social psychology.
   A. Of what use to teachers of young children is a knowledge of sociology and social psychology?
   B. Why should teachers of young children know about the concepts of ethnicity, ethnic group, and ethnic minority group?
   C. Think about someone that you know well. Try to characterize their social construction of ethnic identity and their social construction of gender identity.
   D. What is your own social construction of ethnic identity? What is your social construction of gender identity? Find opportunities to discuss these questions with your classmates or other teachers at your school.

   View a film or video that presents the lives of young children and their families from differing ethnic backgrounds, or find a recent novel or story about an ethnic, refugee, or immigrant family with young children and read about their experiences. In your group discuss the various aspects of the family's existence as portrayed in the film, video, or book. Talk about the role of the mother, the father, or main care givers, the children, other relatives, and friends. Describe and analyze the setting, geographically and locally. Analyze and discuss the various attitudes, interpretations, and feelings about American society. Particularly emphasize the experiences of the young children in the family and the impact on their childhood socialization.

3. Role playing is a useful activity to help people emphathize with others. Bring together several of your classmates or fellow teachers and plan a role-playing session that focuses on gender issues and gender awareness. Create some scenarios that illustrate gender situations involving families with young children. How do the dynamics of gender and social class affiliation work to produce highly complex and ambiguous experiences for adults and for children? Discuss this with the others in your group, as well.

4. In this chapter we pointed out that in every school, in every classroom, are young children who come from a number of diverse ethnic groups in American society. Too often teachers are prone to think that since all the children in their class appear to be Anglo or "white" there is no differing ethnic representation among their students. In addition to the families of the children in your classroom, the school's local community presents a rich source of ethnic heritage and multicultural backgrounds for investigation and as resources for multicultural education. Explore and discover the different ethnic groups that exist in the neighborhood surrounding the school where you teach or where you student-teach. Prepare a questionnaire or an informal set of questions and go into the neighborhood of your school to obtain the answers. You can use your telephone directory to help you, too. Be sure to include such information as:
   A. What different ethnic and cultural groups exist in the neighborhood of your school?
   B. What languages are spoken in the school's neighborhood? Is there evidence of written languages other than English, such as signs or advertisements, being used in the school's neighborhood?
   C. What holidays, festivals, or special events are celebrated?
   D. Are there ethnic restaurants in the neighborhood or businesses that reflect ethnic traditions or practices?
   E. Are there individuals representing differing ethnic groups working or owning businesses in the neighborhood?

5. In recent years the general public has been alerted to and is becoming sensitive to the stereotyping of ethnic groups, particularly African Americans, Hispanics, and Native Americans, in our daily newspapers. Yet how often do reporters, editors, and politicians guard against the stereotyping of gender issues, expectations, and traditional roles in reporting events and statements in the local press? (An example: A politican running for national office was quoted in the daily papers as saying, "The vagrants on our city

streets pose a terrible danger to *women* and people.") Take some time to examine how free of gender prejudice and stereotyping the local daily newspapers actually are in their reporting of daily events and activities.

ENDNOTES

1. Robin Glaser. Unpublished manuscript. Denver, CO: University of Denver. "Rosa's School Socialization: or All the World's a Stage." 1991. Permission has been granted the authors to reprint this material.
2. Marta Cruz-Janzen. Unpublished manuscript. Denver, CO: University of Denver. "My Elementary School Experience." 1991.
3. These excerpts were taken from student papers written on personal socialization and the impact of ethnicity, gender, and social class for the graduate-level course, "Race, Class and Gender in Education," Fall, 1991. Denver, CO: School of Education, University of Denver.

REFERENCES AND SUGGESTED READINGS

Allport, Gordon. *The Nature of Prejudice.* Garden City: Doubleday, 1954.
Aries, Philippe. *Centuries of Childhood.* New York: Random House, 1962.
Banks, James A. *Teaching Strategies for Ethnic Studies,* 5th ed. Needham Heights, MA: Allyn and Bacon, 1991.
Barth, Frederick (Ed.) *Ethnic Groups and Boundaries.* Boston: Little, Brown, 1969.
Berger, Peter, and Luckmann, Thomas. *The Social Construction of Reality.* New York: Anchor Books, 1966.
Bulka, H., and Lucking, S. *Facts about Germany.* Gutersloh, Germany: Bertelsmann Lexikothek Verlag, 1984.
Burtt, E. A. (Ed.) *From Bacon to Mill.* New York: Modern Library, 1944.
Cuzzort, R. P., and King, E. W. *20th Century Social Thought* (4th ed.). Ft. Worth, TX: Holt, Rinehart and Winston, 1989.
Glaser, Nathan, and Moynihan, Daniel P. *Beyond the Melting Pot* (2nd ed.) Cambridge, MA: M.I.T. Press, 1970.
King, Edith. *Teaching Ethnic and Gender Awareness.* Dubuque, IA: Kendall/Hunt, 1990.
Laws, Judith, and Schwartz, Pepper. *Sexual Scripts: The Social Construction of Female Sexuality.* Hinsdale, IL: Dryden Press, 1977.
Mindel, Charles, and Habenstein, Robert. *Ethnic Families in America: Patterns and Variations.* New York: Elsevier, 1976.
Postman, Neil. *The Disappearance of Childhood.* New York: Delcorte Press, 1982.

6

THE CONCEPT OF CULTURE AND EARLY CHILDHOOD EDUCATION

To this point we have urged teachers to begin early in the formal education of young children to prepare them to live in our multicultural society. Early schooling can play a major role in reducing stereotypes and the feelings of fear that young children hold about those who seem different or strange to them. Early childhood education can help children develop an appreciation and understanding of the rich cultural and linguistic heritage that exists in America—a multicultural heritage that reflects the wide variety of cultures throughout the world. Within the *diversity perspective* delineated in chapter 1 is an assumption about the centrality of culture and the pluralistic nature of American society. How does cultural pluralism in this country affect early childhood education?

THE CONCEPT OF CULTURE

This chapter presents information and background on the concept of culture and its importance for teaching, for developing the multicultural dimension in early childhood education, and for the implications in programs for young children. For anthropologists and social scientists in allied fields, the concept of culture is a fascinating study with many ramifications, characteristics, and subtleties of meaning and viewpoints. We will not pursue in depth the numerous and fine points of the study of this concept. Yet, a fundamental understanding of the term is essential for the teacher of young children. With a grasp of the concept of culture, one develops new insights into education and students' interactions in classrooms which are useful in one's teaching, and everyday encounters with colleagues, parents, and other professionals in the community.

The classical definition of the concept of culture was promulgated over one hundred years ago by the British anthropologist E. B. Tylor in his writings on the social science discipline of anthropology. Tylor proposed that culture was the complex whole, which includes knowledge, belief, art, morals, law, custom, and any other capabilities and habits acquired by people as members in a society (Tylor, 1871). In the 1950s, two famous American anthropologists, Alfred Kroeber and Clyde Kluckhohn, published a comprehensive study of 160 different definitions of culture. They concluded that culture consists of patterns of behavior acquired and transmitted by "symbols," constituting the distinctive achievements of human groups; this includes artifacts as well as written language. Kroeber and Kluckhohn noted that the essential core of culture consists of traditional ideas and, especially, common values held by a group of people (Kroeber and Kluckhohn, 1952).

However, the term *culture* is succinctly defined in the writings of the eminent anthropologist Leslie White (1959), a major authority on the culture concept. He holds that only humans can be the possessors of culture and that culture is an integrated whole composed of capacities and habits that humans have adopted as a result of their membership in a society. Knowledge, religion, art, folkways, laws and legal codes, among other elements, comprise culture. White underscores the point that all of humanity's development of culture is based on the human ability to "symbol," or in more common parlance, the human ability to use language. Because humans have language, they can hold ideas, thoughts, theories, and concepts in time—from the past into the present and on to the future. Human beings create or produce culture, and then by language or symboling they keep and pass it on. This in essence is the dynamic concept of culture.

To understand, apply, and use the culture concept, one needs, in addition to its definition, some basic facts about its nature. What does the concept of culture signify? What are the elements of culture? According to Goldschmidt, culture is:

> *Learned behavior acquired by each organism in the process of growing up; shared behavior characteristic of a population; based upon customs. Culture is not merely a bag of customs; it is an orientation to life. (1962, p. 14)*

Culture is made up of configurations. It is patterned and has an internal consistency. Therefore, the behavior of a group of people reflects the fundamental attitudes and beliefs of their culture. Anthropologists use the classic example of the acquisition of the horse by the Plains Indians to illustrate what is meant by a cultural configuration. The Plains Indians developed their culture around horsemanship. They created mores and folkways related to the use of the horse in their daily lives. Techniques for hunting, for waging war, for exchange and trade, and for estimating economic standards of wealth all revolved around the horse.

Several other terms related to the concept of culture help amplify its meaning and validity. These are socialization, acculturation, and cultural diffusion. We already have discussed socialization in depth in previous chapters. This is the dynamic process that brings the individual into the human group. *Socialization* causes people to internalize the ways of their group; the values, attitudes, the language, the traditions, and mores. We learn to eat certain foods, wear specific types of clothing, speak the language that we do as a result of our socialization. *Acculturation* is the process of incorporating the folkways of other groups as one encounters different ways. So we come to enjoy eating enchiladas, wearing a kimono, and punctuate our speech with French or Yiddish phrases as we become acculturated. *Cultural diffusion* is the spreading of cultural traits and patterns, folkways, and mores to groups of people other than the group where the practice originated. With cultural diffusion, practices and traits are varied and subtly changed as they are spread about the world. Classic examples of cultural diffusion are MacDonald's hamburger stands and Coca-Cola bottles found the world over. *Assimilation* involves giving up one's unique and particular ways to practice the traditions and mores of another group.

The concept of culture has been elaborated on by generations of anthropologists (Tylor, 1871; White, 1959; Goldschmidt, 1962; Kneller, 1965). Our discussion here permits only a brief paraphrasing of some of these positions, terms, and theories. Some anthropologists speak of cultures as being "organic," or deeply rooted in human beings. People act, speak, feel, and make artifacts that create culture. But culture is also supraorganic, living on from generation to generation. Culture is "overt" in that it can be manifested in such things as houses, clothing, and other concrete objects. Yet culture is also "covert," manifesting itself in attitudes, values, and the ethos of a people. Culture is described as "explicit," such as the rules for playing football or baseball, driving one's car from the left side or from the right side of the vehicle, and so forth. Culture is also "implicit," in a whole host of taken-for-granted expectations in the ways that people interact with one another. A major portion of the culture of the school is the implicit, taken-for-granted traditions where the student remains passive while the teacher has the power to determine the learning situation.

Culture is thought to be a very stable phenomenon because tradition and heritage dictate the ways of a people over the centuries. Yet, culture is ever changing, especially in modern, technological nations with worldwide affiliations and trade agreements. Finally, culture has been called a force that is "sui generis;" an entity that has a life unto itself, evolving and changing beyond human control (White, 1959). For those who work with young children, an understanding of the concept of culture brings renewed importance to multicultural education.

Culture and Language

We pointed out that the concept of culture is intimately bound up with the language one speaks. One views the world, organizes experience, and rationalizes and communicates one's thoughts through the language learned from earliest childhood. How do young children view their language in relation to the languages spoken by others that sound foreign or strange? Some perceptive researchers have done studies that involved interviewing children at various ages to assess their attitudes toward "foreign" people and the languages they speak. When asked how people in other countries are different, one eight-year-old responded that "most talk different from us; most talk Mexican." The interviewer then went on to inquire if the child thought it would be better if everyone in the world were American. The child's response to this was, "Yes, because I want them to talk normal, the way we do." This eight-year-old displayed the type of ethnocentric thinking that takes the stance that the language of one's own group is the only "normal" language. However, some young children recognized that when focusing on the language people speak there could be a variety of reasons for diversity. Some children understood that people were born into their linguistic systems and would resent being forced to speak another language if English was not their mother tongue. They noted that it really did not matter what language people spoke because it could always be translated (Torney-Purta and Morris, 1972).

Traditionally, young children that come to an American school speaking a language other than English are seen as struggling against an impediment that needs to be eradicated before they can successfully acquire the English language and advance in the graded system. In more recent years, since waves of non-English speaking children have entered American classrooms, a shift in thinking has been under way. Instead of regarding the mother tongue as a barrier to learning English, more early childhood educators are coming to see bilingualism as providing children with a valuable foundation of confidence in using and understanding how language helps us think and reason. Some teachers have discovered, through their efforts to incorporate aspects of their students' home cultures into the day-to-day work of the classroom, just how inseparable language is from the culture in which it is embedded. Gradually teachers are recognizing that the multicultural curriculum should also be a multilingual one, and the development of relevant classroom strategies and curriculum materials is becoming a major priority to meet the needs of our ethnically diverse school population.

THE STUDY OF A NATIVE AMERICAN PRESCHOOL PROGRAM: THE CONCEPT OF CULTURE AS APPLIED IN EARLY CHILDHOOD EDUCATION[1]

It is important for teachers to understand the concept of culture in working with young children. An in-depth research study was carried out over several years in a unique preschool program for low socioeconomic, Native American preschoolers and their families from widely diverse tribes. The purpose of this research was to describe and document "The Circle Never Ends" program, based in a culturally thematic curriculum developed by Native American early childhood educators. It also investigated the impact and effectiveness of this unique approach in early childhood education on the later success of culturally different, minority group children in the public school kindergarten.

This study involved the use of the continuous observation, microethnographic method to collect information on the use of time and space, the use of materials, and the interactions of children and adults in the program. Opinions of parents and teachers about "The Circle Never Ends" preschool curriculum were assessed as part of this study, as well. The study was carried out at the Denver Indian Center, which offers a three-year program called the "Circle of Learning Education Program for Native American Children." The Circle of Learning Preschool has been in existence for almost a decade. Some of its former students are now enrolled in or completing their classes in Denver-area middle schools. The Denver Indian Center, itself, serves an intertribal community of approximately 18,000 Native Americans, representing fifty different tribes or Native peoples' language and cultural subgroups.

In the initial years of growth for the Denver Indian Center's early childhood program, the director and the staff, Native Americans themselves, developed the culturally thematic curriculum and labeled it "The Circle Never Ends." The program is designed to be intercultural, fitting the multitribal urban setting of the preschool and the larger center where it is housed. Native American legends are used as the center of the curriculum "web." Each unit presents a tribal legend through the use of oral tradition, transmitting, in a cultural manner, traditional knowledge to the children. The children are first taught about themselves, then their awareness is increased toward the broader world around them. The developers of The Circle Never Ends curriculum felt that the problem facing all Native Americans was how to provide their children with the knowledge and skills that would fit their developmental needs and provide for optimum learning in the majority white society. The Circle Never Ends program addresses this problem by building positive self-esteem and strong roots in a proud heritage, that of the indigenous peoples of North America.

This study is valuable because it provides insight into the effectiveness of a culturally thematic curriculum, "The Circle Never Ends." The results are based on qualitative and quantitative research methods and give information that can be used to formulate similar preschool programs for other cultural groups who are preparing children to enter the public school kindergarten.

Since World War II, an ever-increasing number of Native Americans are leaving the reservations and seeking greater economic opportunities in the metropolitan areas. Ethnic minorities look to the schools to help them attain equality and social mobility. The Native Americans in the metropolitan Denver area, as elsewhere, are keenly interested in the education of their young children. They realize that an ethnic group identification is necessary before a national identification can develop, that the cultural contact between two groups produces a third culture, and that the culture and language of a child are interwoven. For a cultural group to continue and not disintegrate, be assimilated, or become totally extinguished, its heritage and traditions, language, and mores must be transmitted to each new generation of children. Therefore, this particular study of very young Native American children is important because it focuses on and examines the efforts of a group of Native American educators to use the early childhood program as a vehicle to transmit and perpetuate its heritage while preparing its children for the public schools of the broader society.

The Setting

The Morrison Road Community
The Denver Indian Center is located in what is known as the Westwood neighborhood of Denver. The population mix is closely divided between Hispanic and Anglo, with a smattering of Native Americans and Asians.

The street front is composed largely of automotive businesses, car lots, garages, bars, a carpet store, and a funeral home. The businesses of the area are generally single designation enterprises that serve the local area. Many billboards line the street. One of these advertisements is written in Spanish.

A fairly large number of senior citizens on fixed incomes live in the neighborhood. Many of the families are single-parent. The incomes of the families in the Westwood neighborhood range from low to low-moderate (moderate being a $13,000 to $15,000 annual income for a family of two).*

The Denver Indian Center, Inc.
The Denver Indian Center provides an array of services for Denver's ever-growing Native American population. Many Native-American families are relocating to the Denver urban area; the majority are coming directly from reservations.

The Denver Indian Center was established and incorporated October 11, 1983, as a nonprofit corporation under the laws of the State of Colorado. The purpose of the Denver Indian Center is:

---

*The information for this section was obtained from the office of Ramona Martinez, City Council, District 3.

To engage in such activities which will expand opportunities and elevate the quality of life in the areas of health, education, employment, and social self-sufficiency for all American Indians within the Denver metropolitan area in the State of Colorado. (Denver Indian Center Annual Report, 1988)

The center provides services for Native Americans who reside in a six-county area. A diverse group of tribes are served, the majority of which represent the Sioux, the Navajo, and tribes from the Southwest and the Northern and Southern Plains. These people have moved to the Denver area for specific reasons, that is, economic stability and security for their families. To enhance this transition from reservation to urban life, the Denver Indian Center provides educational, social, cultural, and employment assistance.

The following are programs that are designed to meet the specific needs of the individuals and families of Native Americans in the Denver metropolitan area:

Adult Education
Early Childhood Education
Family Literacy
Employment and Training (JTPA)
Senior Citizens
Social and Human Services
Vision Quest (Substance Abuse Prevention)

Because of the wide range of available services, the Denver Indian Center serves as a major resource for Native Americans who are in need of direct assistance, counseling, and referral services, and who want to successfully complete their adjustment to urban life.

The Denver Indian Center is housed in an old school building. After purchasing the building the center put an addition on the gym and remodeled the classroom area. The facility has 22,000 square feet, used for offices and classrooms, with a kitchen and a gymnasium located at the rear of the building, to serve as a dining area for the preschool children and senior citizens.

Early Childhood Education Program

The Circle of Learning is an early childhood preschool program for the children aged 3 to 5 years of the Native American families served by the Denver Indian Center. The program focuses on nurturing the child, parents, and family. The program has three basic components:

Preschool
Home-Based Instruction
Parent Education

The home-based program provides opportunities for parents of at-risk children to assist in the development of their own children and enhance the quality of their homes as learning environments. The home-base representative works in the community with parent-education classes, and deals with any subject that would empower and benefit parents.

The Early Childhood Education program is guided by a curriculum that allows for the development of literacy, pre-math, and other cognitive skills; fine and gross motor skills; and social-emotional growth in a Native-American cultural setting. Fully licensed by the state of Colorado, this child care facility provides three classrooms for two half-day (morning and afternoon) sessions of educational opportunities and nutritional services. Van service to and from school is available to children in need. Transportation is also provided for field trips, parent education, and special events.

There is an enrollment of forty five intertribal students in the program, and a waiting list of more than twenty five children. The students represent fifty different Native-American tribes. Many of the students reflect integrated backgrounds, representing two or more tribes (e.g., father Sioux and mother Hidatsa/Ute).

The preschool occupies four rooms in the building's east wing. This wing was shared with the Social Services Department. One of the rooms was acquired during the school year and was being used as a faculty workroom and resource room and for parent conferences. The three classrooms are separated by folding partitions. In this way, the children could be regrouped among the teachers and classrooms.

Native-American legends are used in a thematic approach. This theme is integrated throughout the curriculum, evidenced in lessons, centers, materials, and activities. Field trips and special events enhance cultural enrichment opportunities.

The Circle of Learning philosophy is that fostering of positive parent and child partnerships and communication promotes strengthened families and healthy environments for children.

The atmosphere in the Denver Indian Center preschool is very warm and friendly. A great deal of care and concern is shown by each teacher for the children. Many of the children are younger siblings of former students. In many cases, a bond had been established between teacher, school, child, home, and extended family.

Parents are encouraged to visit the preschool and participate in the Parents Association. One of the preschool administrative goals is to establish a positive "partnership" with the parents. This familiarity through parent conferences, committees, and extracurricular activities enhances interpersonal skills, enabling parents to communicate needs and desires for their child, themselves, and their culture, while reinforcing their involvement with their child's education.

Enrollment is on a first-come, first-served basis. The only criterion is tribal enrollment which required documentation. Generally, a tribe required one-quarter Native American ancestry. Priority is also given to court-assigned cases. A needs assessment is used in determining tuition and food services.

Funding for the Early Childhood Education program comes from Title V; the Bernard van Leer Foundation, Hague, Netherlands; Mile High United Way and the Hogan Foundation of Denver, Colorado; State of Colorado Food and Nutrition Program; Title XX, Department of Social Services for low-income families; parent fees; and donations. The ECE program receives food assistance from the state Community Food and Nutrition Program and is subject to the state's guidelines on child care.

Population

The population for this study was the four- to five-year-old classroom during the school year 1989–90. The class was composed of seventeen Native-American children, one teacher, and one teacher's aide. Table 6-1 presents demographics of the families of these children. The information was compiled from the admission packet forms filled out by the parents at the beginning of the school year. Over half of the children came from single-parent homes.

"The Circle Never Ends" Curriculum

"The Circle Never Ends" curriculum guide presented nine units that could be used during a nine- or twelve-month cycle. Each unit contained at least one sample legend story and a teaching model. The first units began with learning about oneself, and then progressed to include the rest of the world. The units were: The Beginning, The Self, A Member of a Family and Tribe, A Member of a Community, A Cultural Being, A Member of the Physical World, A Member of the Living World, An Inhabitant of a Region, and A Member of the Wide, Wide World.

Each unit was developed around a Native-American legend from the region being studied (Table 6-2 on page 124). Nine regions were

Table 6-1   Family Demographics of the Seventeen Four- to Five-Year-Old Children of the Circle of Learning Preschool, School Year 1989–90.

Demographic Information	Number	Percentage
Family Members:		
Both Parents	5.00	29%
Mother Only	9.00	53%
Mother and Stepfather	2.00	12%
Aunt and Uncle	1.00	6%
Average Number of Children	3.12	
Education:		
GED or HS Diploma:		
Fathers with	11	73%
without	4	27%
Mothers: with	13	76%
without	4	24%
Both Parents:		
with	8	47%
without	1	6%
Income:		
Source of Income:		
Father	4	24%
Mother	9	53%
AFDC/Welfare	4	24%
Average Family Income:	$709.71 monthly	
Tuition:		
Waivers:		
with	13	76%
without	4	24%
Average Tuition Paid:	$79.41 monthly	
Lunch Program:		
Free	14	82%
Reduced	2	12%
Full Price	1	6%

studied: Far North, Northwest, Far West, Southwest, Northern Plains, Southern Plains, Northeast, Southeast, and the region of the preschool. Since the curriculum was developed in an intertribal urban setting, a wide variety of tribal legends were used. Oral tradition was employed in the initial telling of a legend, transmitting traditional knowledge in a cultural manner.

The overriding philosophy of the curriculum was that we are all unique human beings. This was reflected in the three major goals of the curriculum: to give Native-American children a positive self-concept,

Table 6-2   Regional Overlays by Unit

Region	Unit
Far North	Unit 1, Unit 2
Northwest	Unit 2
Far West	Unit 3
Southwest	Unit 3, Unit 4
Northern Plains	Unit 6
Southern Plains	Unit 7
Northeast	Unit 9
Southeast	Unit 9

*All regions were studied in Unit five as part of a cultural celebration. [Unit five coincided with March's Regional Powwow in Denver.] Unit eight, the region or tribes that were local to the school, were studied.

knowledge of their cultural heritage, and an academic foundation for success in the public schools.

The series of nine units began with a unit on change. The premise for the curriculum was that the only real constant in our world is change. It is an individual's keen sense of identity and his or her adaptation to change that provides two of the basic skills needed for survival in this modern world.

Unit One explored the home/school transition. The concepts presented were to prepare children for lifelong changes. Unit Two focused on the self, a study of each unique child, the body, its parts and movements, feelings and emotions, and flows into the basic tribe and family unit. Unit Three's emphasis was placed on knowledge regarding family members, relationships, roles, and then tribal membership, culture, clothing, ceremony, and language.

The fourth unit presented the community. Once children know who they are, what relationship they share with their families and tribe, and something about their culture, they can enjoy and participate actively in their communities. The unit provided for active participation in local communities, helping the children to learn about themselves, their families, and friends, and their respective roles in each, working together for common good. This continued the development of a positive cultural identity.

The next three units looked at the world—physical, living, and regional—and the child's role in small and large natural life cycles. Unit

Nine addressed the wide world. The children were encouraged to see themselves as world citizens, thus completing the cycle. The children were ready to identify themselves and recognize their responsibilities in a changing world.

Knowledge of themselves, their families, tribes, the physical and living world, and the region allowed the children to develop self-confidence and the ability to maintain self in the midst of change and to become productive members of the wide world. With these skills, it is hoped that children can succeed in lifelong learning and education and in bringing harmony and peace to the world.

Each unit had a regional overlay. The legend used in a unit was from a tribe located in that region. Unit One drew its legend from the Far North region and dealt with change: the transition from home to school. An Inuit legend was used, *The Very Last First Time.* After looking for food with her mother many times, a young Inuit girl goes out for the first time by herself. This was easily compared with visiting school with one's parents, then coming to school the first day as a student. Unit Two used a Chinook legend from the Northwest region.

A unit was not restricted to only one legend nor to the use of legends alone. Several legends could be used as well as other stories, nursery

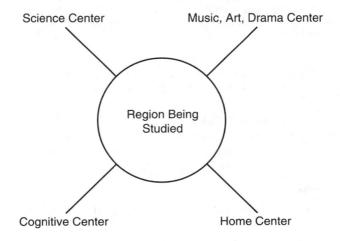

FIGURE 6-1   The Use of Centers in the "Circle Never Ends" Curriculum

Source: Lisa Harjo and Irma Russell, *The Circle Never Ends. A Multicultural Preschool Curriculum Model.* Denver, CO: Circle of Learning Denver Indian Center, Inc. and the Bernard Van Leer Foundation, 1990.

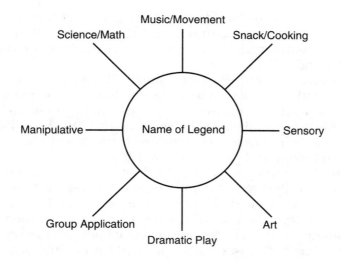

FIGURE 6-2 The Use of Legends in the "Circle Never Ends" Curriculum

Source: Lisa Harjo and Irma Russell, *The Circle Never Ends. A Multicultural Preschool Curriculum Model.* Denver, CO: Circle of Learning Denver Indian Center, Inc. and the Bernard Van Leer Foundation, 1990.

rhymes, and traditional fairy tales. Examples are "Little Red Feather," "Mary Had a Little Lamb," and "Little Red Riding Hood."

Organization of Curriculum Guide
The outline for each of the nine units is given below. Details from Unit One are presented as an example:

Generalization

A brief statement about the philosophy and content of the unit.

Unit One

When children leave home, especially for the first time, they experience feelings of loss and adventure. They are exposed to environments that are new and unfamiliar. Change can be confusing. Building links to things that are familiar and guidance through the unknown helps make this a successful experience.

Purpose: Unit One

The overall purpose is the goal for the teacher: To actively engage children in experiences that build a broad base of knowledge about the new environment.

Learning Goal: Unit One

The learning goal is the child-oriented goal for each unit. Upon completion of this unit, children will be familiar with their new environment, know new safety rules, proper location of learning materials, classroom management procedures, and will have positive feelings about themselves.

Topic List: Unit One

A topics list is an expanded list of topics appropriate to be covered in the context of each unit. It can be expanded as needed. Transition from home to school, change is natural, class rules and scheduling, safety rules, tours of school, introduction to people in school and their roles, introduction to each other, sight, sense, new surroundings.

Sample Legend Development

Illustrates the use of a legend to transmit unit generalizations to students and sample activities that relate to the legend, unit purpose and learning goals.

Concept: Unit One

There is always change in our lives. Our survival depends on our adaptation to change.

Presentation: Unit One

One aspect of life that is constant is that there is always change. Native-American people believe that our survival is dependent on how we view change and how we feel about ourselves. Change can be positive. Feelings of loss and confusion can be transformed into contentment and awareness.

Native Americans also believe that there are certain ways of living that are sacred and are given to the people by the creator.

Adherence to these ways increases chances of survival and benefits all living things. We all live on the earth together. Application of these ideas in the classroom will help children in their home/school transition. Parents and teachers help guide children through the unknown, making it become familiar. *The Very Last First Time,* by Jan Andrews is a story about an Inuit girl from the Far North who was taught by her mother about new experiences. When she finally tried it on her own she mastered feelings of loss, change and uncertainty. The book is full of beautiful pictures and is available commercially. Light a candle and tell the children the story. Blow out the candle when you finish.

(Harjo and Russell, 1990)

Method of Implementing the Curriculum
The curriculum framework was organized in a style called "centered" learning. Within a week's time, the children rotated between four different learning centers: the science center; the music, art, and drama center; the cognitive center; and the home center. Here the children were offered planned lessons and activities in music/movement, snack/cooking, sensory, art, dramatic play, group applications, manipulatives, and science/math. These lessons and activities were to integrate the legend and unit theme in the various centers.

One day each week was set aside for a culturally oriented circle activity, bringing all three age levels together: three-, four-, and five-year-olds. The children were guided through activities—music, songs, stories, and dances—that enhanced the children's knowledge of their heritage and complemented and supported the development of a positive self-identity.

For each lesson the teacher was required to prepare an activity record. These activity records were to assist in organizing goals, content, methods, materials, and the evaluation of the lesson or activity. Each was related to the unit theme, generalization, cultural legend, and specific skills and/or objectives.

Evaluation of Students
Students were evaluated through the teacher's observation. A record of each student's attention, participation, or product from a lesson or activity was an indication of that student's growth and learning.

A checklist was developed to document the progress of each student. The overall goals of the curriculum were divided into specific areas for the teacher's observation of skills: personal-social, gross-fine motor, cognitive, multicultural, and language. The checklist was organized by labeling Levels 1 and 2. Skills that took longer to master were included on both levels. Color coding was used to indicate which quarter of the year a skill was mastered. This checklist was used in planning lessons and activities, and when writing reports for parents.

Observing "The Circle Never Ends" Curriculum

Lesson Preparation
Prior to initiating each unit, the teacher developed two culturally thematic webs for the region and the legend to be studied. The first web was to give the teacher ideas for lessons, centers, and activities. These were used to introduce and to give knowledge, experience, or practice in the developmental areas of language, cognitive, social, motor, and multicultural.

The second web drew ideas from the first to help organize lessons and activities for the centers. From these two webs each teacher wrote her activity record plans, appropriate for each group of children to be taught, during the coming week. The plans were then turned in to the head teacher.

Preschool Staff
The preschool employed four teachers; three were Native American. The head teacher was non-Native American. One full-time and one part-time aide were Native American. The director, office staff (3), cook, van driver, and janitor were Native American. The total staff came together biweekly to discuss the mechanics of operating the preschool. The teachers also met weekly to work on the curriculum. The last Friday of each month was reserved for teacher training. Issues addressed at this time included center activities, discipline, testing, and development of a unit. This planning day could also be used to visit other preschool centers.

All but three members of the teaching and office staff were single parents. The head teacher was not only a single parent but also was raising her granddaughter. The teachers' employments ranged from three to thirteen years with the preschool, and the head teacher had been there the longest time. A close relationship had developed among the staff. They shared problems and offered each other encouragement. The head teacher was viewed with respect as a matriarch. She was respected for her knowledge (educational and cultural) acquired from years of service and practice in early childhood education. She was also director-certified by the state and at times was called on to act in a director's capacity.

The Classroom Environment

The sun-filled classrooms were decorated with the children's work, cultural artifacts of Native-American heritage, and posters, creating a warm, nurturing atmosphere. Cooperative work and play among the children were valued and encouraged. Activities were frequently initiated with a cheerful song that the children quickly learned (e.g., "Cleanup Time," "Hold Hands Like Friends"). Disagreements were handled quickly with a teacher-child discussion. In a learning situation the teacher could move a disruptive child by saying, "Francisco, come sit by me, I need your help." In this way, the disturbance was stopped, time was not taken away from the lesson, and the child was given a positive behavioral alternative. Positive comments were frequently make by the teacher about the group: "For the first day I have such good workers," and, about individuals, "David is working so nicely."

The development of a positive feeling in the children about themselves appeared to be the mainstay of the teaching staff. Children were given positive feedback whenever possible about: appearance ("How nice you look today"), responses ("How smart you are; I had not thought of that one"), a product ("How beautiful—I love it").

Tribal membership is highly prized and recognized. The director of the preschool explained, "Tribal membership is the most important thing. You are a member of your tribe before you are even born." A major goal was for each child to know of which tribe or tribes he or she was a member. In the case of some children, there were as many as three contributing tribes (e.g., Mandan, Hidatsa, and Sioux; and Choctaw, Creek, and Seminole) to their heritage.

Involvement with Parents

Another goal was to develop a partnership with the parents. This was not an easy task. Twenty-seven percent of the fathers and 24 percent of the mothers had not completed high school. The staff wanted to make education a positive experience. By getting parents involved at the preschool level, the staff hoped that this would carry over into the public schools. The preschool parent organization met monthly to communicate and advise the preschool staff about their needs and concerns for their children. Open house was well attended by the parents. Parents were also encouraged to visit the classrooms and volunteer to help whenever possible.

Use of Time

Overview of Daily Schedule

The day began early for most of the children. The first van arrived at 7:00 A.M., delivering eight to ten children, who were greeted by the teacher. Three of the children were brought to school by their families. The second van arrived about 8:00 A.M., in time for these children to join the others for breakfast. During this free time period, all three age groups were together. After breakfast, the children were given recess time. Depending on the weather, recess could be outside or held indoors, either in the gym or individual classrooms.

Home room time began at 9:00 A.M. The children were divided into three groups according to age: three-year-olds, four-year-olds, and five-year-olds. Each group spent this time with their home room teacher. At 9:30 A.M. the children started Centers.

Second recess was called at 11:00 A.M. for all of the preschool children. The children began returning to their home rooms at 11:20, starting with the youngest group, to clean up and prepare for lunch. Lunch, 11:30 A.M. to 12:00 P.M., ended the morning session and began the afternoon session.

Mondays had been designated Cultural Day. At 9:30 A.M., after home room, the children walked to the gym for Cultural Circle. The teachers' team taught at this time, occasionally having a guest give the blessing, teach a lesson, or tell a story.

Monday's Schedule

Free Work	Breakfast and Recess	Home Room	Cultural Circle	Home Room	Recess	Clean Up	Lunch
7:00	8:00	9:00	9:30	10:30	11:00	11:20	11:30

Schedule Tuesday to Friday

Free Work	Breakfast and Recess	Home Room	Centers	Recess	Clean Up	Lunch
7:00	8:00	9:00	9:30	11:00	11:20	11:30

Although the schedule appeared very structured, in reality, it was quite flexible. Because the preschool was held at the Denver Indian Center, many resources (a variety of tribes, age groups, and materials) and influences (cultural occasions and events were available). Frequently, there were visitors, both local and international, such as from

England and China. The needs of the children and the Native-American community influenced how the time was actually used. The children often interacted with the elders who came to the Indian Center. The Denver Indian Center had a senior citizen program that offered meals and activities to the elders of the tribes. Respect and honor given to elders are greatly valued in the Native-American culture.

Breakfast and Recess

At 8:00 A.M. the children walked to the gym for breakfast. They enjoyed seeing their work displayed in the hall. Once in the gym, the children sat with their age group at three tables.

On occasion, the children would arrive in the gym before breakfast was ready. Miss Lori would have the children sing songs with finger play ("A Cabin in the Woods"), review sign language, or discuss a special upcoming event (powwow, field trip). When breakfast was ready, the children would fold their hands and lower their heads to sing a prayer.

Home Room

The children came in from recess and arranged themselves in a circle on the floor in front of the teacher. This ritual was referred to as Morning Circle Time. Seated in a chair, the teacher would initiate a discussion with the children. The discussion would vary. On Mondays, the children might be asked about their weekend or about an upcoming special occasion (holiday, birthday, powwow, a dance or trip). During this time, the children would brush their teeth. Miss Connie, the aide, would send the children to the restrooms with their cups and toothbrushes.

When all the children had returned, role was taken. The teacher would call a child's name and he or she would answer, "Here I am." Complete sentences were encouraged from the children (e.g., if the teacher asked, "What color is the circle?" the child was to answer, "The circle is ____."). They were also encouraged to call objects by name (e.g., if a child said, "I want that," the teacher would respond with, "What is 'that'? It has a name."). Language was an integral part of the curriculum.

A calendar was kept on the wall close to where the children sat for Morning Circle, but it was not always consulted. When the calendar was discussed, the children could easily recall the month and the day of the week. The day of the month would have to be calculated, with sometimes the addition of two or three figures to show the correct day. The calendar would reflect either the unit or region being studied or the season or the holiday of that particular month. The days for October were marked by Killer Whales for the region being studied; January had numbers cut from an old calendar.

The teacher used this time to set the tone for the day. A theme or topic was sometimes reviewed, an activity for the day was shared with the children, or something new was introduced. On occasion, the teacher would do an experiment with the children. The teacher enjoyed and used science. "I like science. It is a natural way for the children to discover things," she said. Any aspect of pre-reading, pre-math, art, science, cooking, geography, and music was discussed at one time or another during this Morning Circle time.

The following protocol is an example of Morning Circle Time (setting described previously):

The teacher referred to the day as Wednesday, when it was actually Thursday. Clint told her, "That's what happens when you're a girl. Forget everything." The teacher asked, "Who told you that?" "My Mom tells me that." Tabatha reminded them, "There was a forgetful boy on *Sesame Street*." Teacher: "Oh, so boys can make mistakes too." The children nodded.

All the children had returned from brushing their teeth so the lesson could begin. The teacher talked about the "Time Out" chair. She preferred to call it the "Thinking" chair. "You can go there and think about things." Clint said he would like to sit in the chair. "Okay, you go and then you can tell me what you thought about."

Role was taken. Clint was called back to the circle. The teacher asked, "What were you thinking about?" Clint said, "A caterpillar." Teacher: "What was he doing?" Zeb suggested, "Turn into a butterfly."

Clint then asked to "read" the book *This Is Me* to the class. (The class was studying about self and this book was about the body parts. There were tabs on each page that moved the part of the body being read about.) Clint got the book and held it up. As the teacher read, Clint pulled the tabs on each page, moving the body parts. The class became excited, moving about the circle and laughing. The teacher did an exercise called "Open Them, Shut Them" to quiet the class.

Next the teacher presented a poster on shapes: circles, squares, rectangles, and triangles. The class discussed differences between the square and the rectangle; the number of sides and their length.

Then the teacher played a game with the children. She pretended to be a mirror, and the children reflected what she did; she gave the sign for love, touched her ears, her nose, and wiggled her fingers. The children mirrored her movements. Zeb was chosen to be the next mirror.

The learning experiences developed by the teacher during the Morning Circle Time included the following: as children sat in a circle in front of the teacher eager to contribute to the discussion, she employed this time to teach several lessons. She used herself to show that everyone makes mistakes (boys, girls, children, and adults), and it is okay. Using the "Thinking Chair," she turned discipline into a thinking process, "We must think about our actions." The researcher never saw the "Thinking Chair" used for disciplinary purposes. The teacher's awareness of Clint's needs helped her be attuned to his energy level and need for attention that particular morning.

By reviewing geometric shapes, the teacher reinforced a previous lesson and assessed the children's learning. The mirror game was a quick and fun way to evaluate motor skills.

Centers

The children from the three classrooms interacted in groups with names of bird: Hummingbirds, Scissortails, Hawks, and Eagles. Appropriate learning activities also taught the children cultural lessons.

Each of the children knew that he or she would progress through four levels and was proud of each group membership. The youngest group was called the Hummingbirds. The hummingbird is a very small bird that flies from flower to flower, not staying long in any one place, much like a busy three-year-old. The scissortail is a larger bird and shows its gracefulness by the beautiful, cutting action of its tail feathers. The children in this group were a little older. They had started refining their motor skills and had a longer attention span. The hawk is a skilled hunter and is able to maneuver through the sky with great ease. These children were becoming skilled learners and avid users of their environment.

The Native American views the eagle as the strongest, most powerful, and wisest of birds. Many of their legends are about the eagle and its strength, wisdom, and kindness toward the other animals. The children in this group were the ones preparing for kindergarten. They were the oldest and most mature children. By being eagles, these children were to be more responsible, help the younger children, and set a good example. When a child was promoted into the Eagle group, there was a small ceremony. Each child made an eagle feather from paper, colored it, and then tied it to his or her hair.

The four centers—Science, Art, Cognitive, and Home—gave the children a lesson and activity related to the unit, legend, cultural region, topic, or senses. An example from October:

Home Center

Hummingbirds: the teacher was reading a story about Eskimos and whale hunting. She had pictures and artifacts from Alaska.

Art Center

Hawks: the children were coloring and putting fur on Eskimo paper dolls.

Science Center

Scissortails: the children were working with orange play-dough, making pumpkins.

Cognitive Center

Eagles: the children were identifying shapes: circles, squares, and triangles.

Each teacher was to present her lesson for a week, Tuesday through Friday. It could be the way Eskimos meet their needs, the type of clothing Eskimos wear, the developing of fine motor skills, or recognition of geometric shapes. Each day the presentation and activity would be different. For each day, the teacher would be working with a different group. Each lesson and activity would vary in the amount of time needed by the different children. As the children completed their activity, they were allowed to choose free work from the Center area. This allowed for interest and ability differences within the four groups. A child was able to complete his or her work and then choose another activity in the related area. This also freed the teacher to spend more time with children who were having difficulties or needed help, or to interact with a child who appeared to be more skilled.

The children were encouraged to help each other. A child who completed the activity early could choose to stay and help another child. Cooperative learning is a natural extension of cooperative living, a Native-American value. Children were praised for their work by the teacher and each other.

Cultural Circle

Mondays were special days. The children were usually very excited and full of energy. Weekends were typically busy times for their families, many of them attending powwows or activities at the Denver Indian

Center. At 9:30 A.M. the children came together for Cultural Circle. This activity usually took place in the gym. The lesson and activities reinforced many of the weekend activities and creatively channeled the abundance of energy.

After home room, the children walked back to the gym and sat in a large circle on the floor. The black circle of the basketball court was used as a guide. No other activities were scheduled in the gym at this time. The lessons and activities were team-taught by two or more of the teachers. The other teachers and aides seated themselves with the circle of children.

The lessons began with a blessing and prayer. The researcher also observed this to be the case at all other functions at the Denver Indian Center; a prayer was always offered. A large abalone shell was used for the burning of sage. Sage was generally used by the teachers. When someone else was asked to give the blessing, he or she would use the plant of choice from their tribe. Mr. Emhoolah, president of the Inter-Tribal Native American Church, was asked on occasions to give the blessing. Mr. Emhoolah is Kiowa and prefered to burn cedar instead of sage. "If I were to be farther north, I would burn sweet grass for the blessing."

Following the blessing was a cultural lesson. This was usually given by the same teacher who gave the blessing. The lesson might deal with any aspect of Native-American culture, past or present, from values (the earth, our elders), behavior, and language to games. Sign language and songs were taught to the children. One of the teachers would play a drum for the children's singing.

At some time during the lesson, the children were given the opportunity to introduce themselves and give the name of their tribe. It was important that each child knew of which tribe or tribes he or she was a member. The teachers were to know the tribal membership of their children and be able to help a child remember and feel proud.

This lesson time was closed with music and dancing. An audio cassette of dancing music was played. The friendship dance was done with all the children together. They held hands and moved to the left in a large circle. For the other dances, the boys and girls danced separately. The girls went to the center of the circle, while the boys danced around the circle. Two or three of the better male dancers were chosen to lead the other boys. Occasionally, one of the teachers would help instruct the boys. If someone from outside the preschool was present, then a teacher would not dance with the boys. One or more of the teachers danced with the girls. Some of the children were very good dancers. Their dances required a great deal of coordination, balance and timing.

The following is a protocol of a cultural lesson:

The older children entered the gym, followed by the two younger classes. The children rearranged themselves. Two sisters chose to sit together.

Everyone was instructed to shake hands. As Miss Rita shook hands with the children, she greeted them with, "Have a good day brother (or sister)." She then told the children, "This is what the older people did. The elders did this in the old days. When they entered a room, they would shake hands with everyone in that room. This shows respect for others. When you meet Mr. Coffey in the hall, he always puts out his hand to shake yours. I want you to be the first to put out your hand to shake hands with others."

Miss Rita then had the children sing "Good Morning," noting that it was not an Indian song but it had a good message.

> *"Good morning to you,*
> *Good morning to you.*
> *Good morning, dear children,*
> *I'm glad to see you."*

Miss Rita then reviewed the field trip of last Friday. (The two younger classes had gone to Lookout Mountain.) "What did we see Friday?" She uses sign language to remind the children. This way the children who did not get to go could join in. She signed for: buffalo, horse, deer, elk, tree, billy goat, bear, snake, fish, bird, butterfly. She then asked, "Who made these things?" The children responded, "God" or "Creator." Miss Rita said, "We are to be thankful."

Miss Rita showed them Indian cook books and told the children what tribes the recipes were from. (Miss Rita taught Home Center and used many of the recipes with the children.) She then went around the circle having the children, individually, tell their tribe. "I am _____."
They went around the circle giving each child an opportunity to speak. If the child could not remember or had not learned yet, one of the teachers would help.

Time was taken for the children to stretch fingers and toes, and wiggle all over. Miss Lori then came to the center of the circle. She pointed out to the children that the drum they were using this week was different, it was a hand drum. They sang:

> *"Inkpata"—Dakota love song, sung in Sioux and English.*
> *"Ala Ala"—Navajo happy song, sung in Navajo.*
> *"Oh Great Eagle"—Sung in Lakota and English.*

Miss Lori told the children, "The sun is still out." Then asked, "Is he sleeping yet?" The children smiled and shook their heads. They sang the bear song, "Che Chio." This song is not to be sung in the winter when the bear is sleeping.

Miss Madaline started the tape recorder and dancing music began. The children and teachers did the Friendship dance.

Some of the elders had arrived early for lunch and saw the children dancing. Some of the elders danced as they came across the gym floor. One lady sat and clapped her hands in time with the music. They all smiled at the children.

Culturally Relevant Activities

The following protocol is a lesson taught in January. The unit is "A Member of a Family and a Tribe." Region is the Southwest.

The teacher shared the book Pictures from Navajo Land *with the children. They reviewed the book; the color of the land, the use of clay, sand dunes, the bear claw symbol, making of baskets and the use of cactus. "Last week we studied about clay. Do you remember why we taste the clay? If it is sweet, then we can use it." She showed the children a picture of a rock formation. "What would be a good name for this rock?" The children suggested, "Rainbow Bridge." It was also the name given in the book.*

They then discussed the importance of blue corn. The teacher held up the book Corn is Maize *(this book would also be added to the shelves). The book showed the grinding of corn with rocks. The corn was ground very fine. The teacher showed the children some finely ground blue corn that had been blessed. She told the children, "Mr. Emhoolah burns cedar for the blessing. A blessing can also be done with blue corn." The bag of blue corn was passed around so the children could feel the corn. The teacher then handed the bag of blue corn to Brian. "Brian, you are our Navajo. Would you put the corn on the desk?" Brian was very proud. He took the blue corn and very carefully placed it on the teacher's desk.*

Field trips were taken during the year to enhance learning experiences. Time was spent before and after a trip to prepare and review. In October, the children traveled to Colorado University, in Boulder, for the blessing of newly constructed hogans. The children enjoyed the trip. They went inside a hogan (always entering to the left) and saw the structural variations developed by the Department of Architecture, University of Colorado, Boulder. The children became a point of interest for many of the other visitors. The children paid the cameras little attention. When asked, the teacher explained, "They have been photographed so much, it is no big deal."

Music was often played during free work time. The children were exposed to a wide spectrum from the classic lullabies and special occasion songs to cultural music of Native-American and other cultures (e.g., French, German). Other cultural activities were also used by the teacher, usually occurring on special occasions (e.g., the Easter egg tree, making May baskets).

Results and Implications of This Study

The intent of this study was to describe and document the culturally thematic early childhood curriculum "The Circle Never Ends" and, further, to ask parents and teachers—of kindergarten and first and second grade pupils—if this program helped in preparing young Native-American children for their elementary school experience that followed. We think this investigation demonstrated that "The Circle Never Ends" curriculum was culturally and developmentally appropriate for early childhood education. The curriculum presented lessons and activities to achieve goals and objectives appropriate for the cognitive, social, and motor skills of preschool age children in the context of cultural relevance. The results of this study underscore the importance of the concept of culture and the need to instill a sense of identity in the culturally different young child.

When the investigator followed the children from the Circle of Learning preschool into the public school kindergarten, she collected data that showed the children were mainly quiet, socially withdrawn, and struggling academically. Over half of the students were below grade level in reading and mathematics readiness. Fifty-six percent did not participate in a sharing or talking time in front of their classmates. Attendance was poor for some of the children. These follow-up data presented the picture that these Native-American children were experiencing "culture shock" on entering the public school kindergarten. It was reasoned that the children had come from a warm, supporting environment, rich in cultural concepts and materials and based in developmentally appropriate methods. They then entered a school environment foreign to them, sterile of their cultural heritage; they were instructed by people who, for the most part, were lacking in cross-cultural techniques or multiethnic teaching strategies. There was an omission of their culture in the environment.

However, the investigator did find that by the time they reached the first and second grades, these Native-American students became more involved in social and classroom interaction. They also engaged in more cultural sharing and showed a marked improvement in reading and mathematics. A larger portion—67 percent—of the Native-American students were at or above grade level in both reading and math by first and second grade. By that time the impact of "The Circle Never Ends" curriculum goals—to give each child a positive self-image, knowledge of cultural heritage, and an academic foundation for success in the public schools—was having a positive effect on school achievement. This study has provided a model for developing other culturally thematic curricula, replete with experiences set in a cultural context, for culturally different groups in American society. Cultural group identification can imbue early learning with more significance for the culturally different child.

SUMMARY

The importance of the recognition of culture for teachers of young children was developed by providing some background and a brief history about this major anthropological concept. The connection between language and culture was noted. To demonstrate the relevancy of the concept of culture and its application to early childhood education, a detailed ethnographic study of the "The Circle Never Ends" curriculum at the Circle of Learning Preschool of the Denver Indian Center was presented.

The background and development of this innovative, culturally thematic early childhood curriculum, "The Circle Never Ends," was described, as well as the setting, the families, the students, and the staff of the preschool. Anecdotes and accounts that highlight the culturally relevant activities were included in the discussion of this unique program for Native-American preschoolers. The results and implications of the micro-ethnography of the Circle of Learning Preschool concluded the chapter.

KEY CONCEPTS

Concept of Culture The complex whole, which includes knowledge, belief, art, morals, law, custom, and any other capabilities and habits acquired by people as members in a society. Culture is not merely a collection of customs; it is an orientation to all living.

Cultural Pluralism The process by which a variety of ethnic cultures are able to share in the common expression of American societal ideals.

Cultural Diversity The condition of wide diversity and differences within and among ethnic groups. Such factors as social class, occupation, and life-style affect cultural diversity.

Acculturation The subtle process of taking on new cultural traits and folkways when interacting with new and different groups of people.

Assimilation Sometimes called the "melting pot" theory, the absorption of a group of people or a person into the major group of the society. This involves the giving up of one's unique and particular ways and mores to practice the ways and traditions of the majority.

Multicultural Dimension in Early Childhood Education The philosophy and approach that recognizes the myriad cross-cultural transactions in classrooms of young children and the structuring of multicultural learning in early childhood.

"The Circle Never Ends" Curriculum A culturally thematic curriculum for preschool Native-American children.

Bilingualism Is the condition under which an individual is exposed to speakers of other languages or dialects so that the person adopts and internalizes the speech patterns of two or more languages.

ISSUES AND ACTIONS

1. You have now read about the culturally thematic early childhood curriculum, "The Circle Never Ends" of the Circle of Learning Preschool in Denver, Colorado. We have described in detail how this culturally relevant curriculum for Native-American young children was carried out in classrooms in Denver over an extended period of time. Are there any such programs for culturally-diverse young children in your local area or in your vicinity? Investigate to find out if such early childhood programs exist in either public or private schools in your area. If such a program with its culturally specialized curriculum is in place, request an opportunity to visit and observe the children, teachers, and other adults at the school site. Take notes about the program, observing such aspects as the setting, the school population, classroom interactions, the use of time, and the type of culturally thematic curriculum employed. Compare them with the same elements of the culturally focused early childhood program we have described in this chapter.

2. If no such culturally different early childhood program or curriculum exists in your area, survey your local school population to see if an ethnic minority group or linguistically different culture is apparent. Try to develop a culturally relevant and thematic curriculum for this group of children. Use the format and the ideas from "The Circle Never Ends" program as a model to guide your work. Make efforts to implement your program and its curriculum with a group of children. If you are not a member of this

particular cultural group or do not have close contact with and knowledge of the customs, traditions, language, and ways of the people, identify resources and "experts" on the culture to help you design and implement your program.

Write a report of the results of your culturally thematic curriculum after it has been implemented with children, teachers, and parents. Perhaps your local newspaper or other media sources will provide coverage for the program to area residents.

3. This chapter featured terms and concepts from the social science discipline of anthropology, with emphasis on the concept of culture. Of what use is knowledge from anthropology for teachers of young children? Why should teachers of young children be concerned about the concept of culture? Examine your own life and that of your family for indications of how culture, cultural traits, traditions, rituals, and folkways affect you daily, monthly, and yearly. Is language difference or linguistic diversity a factor in your daily life? In your family's day-to-day existence? In the school where you teach or student-teach? What implications stem from the view that the acquisition of a second language is detrimental for the young child?

ENDNOTES

1. Dr. Janice Luellen has kindly given the authors permission to reproduce this material from her doctoral dissertation carried out at the University of Denver, School of Education during 1988 to 1991.

2. The developers and authors of *The Circle Never Ends: A Multicultural Preschool Curriculum Model,* Lisa Harjo and Irma Russell, state that this curriculum is the product of years of working together with other professionals, early childhood educators, and children. This project was made possible by a grant from the Bernard Van Leer Foundation, The Hague, Netherlands, and the Circle of Learning Early Childhood Education Program of the Denver Indian Center.

REFERENCES AND SUGGESTED READINGS

Day, Barbara and Drake, Kay. *Early Childhood Education and Curriculum Organization and Classroom Management.* New York: Association for Supervision and Curriculum Development, 1983.

Garcia, Ricardo. *Teaching in a Pluralistic Society* (2nd ed.). New York: HarperCollins, 1991.

Gilliland, H., and Reyner, J. *Teaching the Native American.* Dubuque, IA: Kendall/Hunt Publishing, 1988.

Goldschmidt, A. *Exploring the Ways of Mankind.* New York: Holt, Rinehart, and Winston, 1962.

Goodman, Maryellen. *The Culture of Childhood.* New York: Teachers College Press, 1970.

Grace, George. *The Linguistic Construction of Reality.* London: Croom Helm, 1987.

Harjo, Lisa, and Russel, Irma. *The Circle Never Ends. A Multicultural Preschool Curriculum Model.* Denver, CO: Circle of Learning Denver Indian Center Inc. and the Bernard Van Leer Foundation, 1990.

Harvey, Karen, Harjo, Lisa, and Jackson, Jane. *Teaching About Native Americans.* National Council for the Social Studies, Bulletin No. 84, Waldorf, MD: NCSS Publications, 1990.

Hilliard, Asa, Patyon-Stewart, L. and Obadele, L. *The Infusion of African and African American Content in the School Curriculum.* Morristown, NJ: Aaron Press, 1990.

Hilliard, Asa G. III. Why We Must Pluralize the Curriculum. *Educational Leadership* Dec. 1991/Jan. 1992; 49(4), 12–15.

King, Edith. *Teaching Ethnic and Gender Awareness.* Dubuque, IA: Kendall Hunt, 1990.

Klein, Gillian, and Wilby, Simon. *Scrapbooks.* London: Methuen Children's Books. 1984.

Kneller, George. *Educational Anthropology.* New York: Wiley, 1965.

Kozol, Jonathan. *Savage Inequalities: Children in America's Schools.* New York: Crown Publishers, 1991.

Kroeber, A., and Kluckhohn, C. *Culture: A Critical Review of Concepts and Definitions.* New York: Vintage Books, 1952.

Lareau, Annette. *Home Advantage: Social Class and Parental Intervention in Elementary Education.* Philaldelphia: Falmer Press, 1989.

Lubeck, Sally. *Sandbox Society: Early Education in Black and White America—A Comparative Ethnography.* Philadelphia: Falmer Press, 1985.

Luellen, Janice. *Our Little Town: The Littleton Community Grows Up.* Littleton, CO: Littleton School District, 1988.

Mead, Margaret. *Culture and Commitment.* Garden City, NJ: Doubleday, 1970.

Rieber, R. W., and Carton, Aaron (Eds.). *The Collected Works of L. S. Vygotsky.* New York: Plenum Press, 1987.

Santrock, J. W., and Yussen, Steven. *Child Development* (3rd ed.). Dubuque, IA: Wm. C. Brown, 1987.

Stevens, Joseph, and King, Edith. *Administering Early Childhood Education Programs.* Boston: Little, Brown, 1976.

Torney-Purta, Judith, and Morris, D. *Global Dimensions in U.S. Education: The Elementary School.* New York: Center for War/Peace Studies, 1972.

Tylor, E. B. *Primitive Culture.* London: John-Murray, 1871.

White, Leslie. The Concept of Culture. *American Anthropologist.* 1959; 61, 227–251.

White, Leslie. *The Evolution of Culture.* New York: McGraw-Hill, 1959.

Woods, Peter, Inside Schools: Ethnography in Educational Research. London: Routledge, 1986.

7

FORMS OF BIAS IN THE EARLY CHILDHOOD CLASSROOM

In chapter 2 we examined the socialization of young children and observed their interactions in an early childhood educational setting. We noted that very young children adopt and re-enact the roles and expectations of their immediate surroundings, the home and the neighborhood. Young children learn to model the behavior of the adults in their environment and imitate those adults during their play. When children enter the school setting, they already have been impacted by the forces of socialization ever present in their home environments. The school and other influences, such as peers and the media, continue this socialization process through both implicit and explicit actions.

GENDER SOCIALIZATION

We caution the reader to be sensitive to cultural differences in any examination of broader gender issues. The following account clarifies the subtle, unexamined forces of gender socialization:

> *I sat at the kitchen table waiting for my friend to finish feeding her two youngsters, both under four years of age, before we went out for a shopping trip. For the first fifteen minutes I simply made casual conversation without attending or noticing much out of the ordinary. Pretty soon, though, I began noticing what appeared to be quite different behavior patterns between the mother and her two children and between the two children themselves.*
>
> *I noticed that the girl, just over three years, was dressed from head to toe in a color-coordinated outfit of pink and pastel shades. She wore two satin ribbons tied in bows around her intentionally curled pony-tails. Her earrings were little hearts. She wore a striped pastel soft cotton pullover shirt with ruffled lace at the collar. Further, she wore pink soft cotton pants, white dress shoes, and white nylon socks decorated with embroidery. The boy, a year younger in age, was outfitted in a completely opposite way. He wore a checkered "rugged" thick blue, red, and green cotton pullover shirt, faded hand-me-down blue jeans, tennis shoes with untied laces, and heavy, white athletic socks. The girl was dressed to look very "cute," while the boy was dressed for rough-and-tumble play.*
>
> *As I contemplated the children's appearance I became a bit embarrassed remembering that I praised my friend on how pretty her daughter looked when I came in earlier, but had not even mentioned her son's appearance. I had only stated that I was amazed at how*

much he had grown since I last saw him as a newborn baby. I also noticed that the girl's general appearance was very clean, while the boy had soiled all his clothes during the feeding/eating process. Both children sat on high chairs. My friend had carefully covered her daughter with a clean cloth diaper tied around her neck so she would not soil her clothes but had not covered the boy, except for a small bib. He ate with gusto. There was food all over his mouth and face, all over his hands and arms. He ate with or without the spoon she had provided, stuffing handfuls of food into his mouth. Sometimes he missed his mouth and food landed on his clothes and highchair tray. Meanwhile the mother carefully fed the girl, even though she was older. Yet she did not seem to feel a need to do the same for the boy. As she fed her daughter she constantly wiped her mouth and face with an edge of the cloth diaper.

I began to pay closer attention to the scenario unfolding in front of me. Each time my friend spoke to her daughter, the tone of her voice softened and yet the pitch became higher: "Oh, honey, look at you! Poor baby! Here, let mommy help you." She would then take the spoon out of the girl's hand and feed her while wiping her mouth and hands each time the child attempted to eat without the spoon. She sat directly in front of her daughter, while her son was a short distance away. When she addressed the boy, to whom she paid much less attention, she did not look at him directly, and the pitch lowered: "Are you a mess! Let's hurry up so mommy can change your clothes and we can leave." I also wondered why my friend had not fed her children first, and then dressed them up for our outing.

THE SUBTLE NATURE OF GENDER STEREOTYPING

This scenario, replayed in our homes more often that we realize, carries impressionable messages for young children. From the previous account we can see how the differences in the way the mother dressed her toddlers indicated that, in her thinking, boys are allowed to be untidy and do not need to be concerned with their physical appearance, but girls must be neat and carefully groomed at all times. Females in our culture are more often judged by their physical appearance than are males, and therefore little girls learn at an early age to link their self-worth to their looks. Girls learn to be careful, neat, dainty and meticulous; whereas boys are encouraged to be risk takers even if they make a mess.

By taking the spoon away from her daughter and feeding her each time, the mother unknowingly conveyed the message: "You cannot do it, therefore, I will do it for you." The girl did not need to try challenging new activities for herself or by herself. On the other hand, the message to the boy was also quite clear. It told just the opposite: "You can *do* it and I expect you to do it by yourself." In the mother's estimation, her son could independently initiate and pursue challenging new activities.

Certainly my friend, like most mothers, wants the best in life for her children and does not realize that she is conveying differing, often contradictory messages and expectations to her very young son and daughter. Again, how does this happen? The following anecdote examines the subtle nature of gender socialization that impacts all of us daily:

I sat waiting at a local hospital for my turn to visit a friend who had just become the proud mother of a baby girl. The maternity ward waiting room was decorated in pastel colors with well-known cartoon characters. Painted on the walls were the traditional Mickey Mouse and Donald Duck smiling at me, while Bambi stared big-eyed and Dumbo sat on a circus barrel. Minnie Mouse and Daisy stood in provocative poses with flowers on their hair, and long, flickering eyelashes. The coffee table was heaped with magazines filled with the photos of young mothers, babies, and children. There were coloring books and crayons, as well as readers, for the young visitors waiting with the adults. I searched through the magazines for something that interested me. I settled on a young parents magazine. As I thumbed the pages I was attracted by a beautiful two-page ad for disposable baby diapers featuring six babies. It was not difficult to distinguish the boys from the girls: the girls were all wrapped in pink blankets and the boys in blue ones. The message was that the disposable diapers in the pink box were designed for girls and the ones in the blue box were for boys.

I proceeded to find a picture of a young girl, approximately five years old, sitting at a pink "play vanity" combing her hair and putting on make-up while smiling admiringly at her reflection in the mirror. The vanity held lipsticks and other beauty products. The caption on the picture said: "Simply Beautiful." It was an advertisement from a toy manufacturer. The young girl was dressed in a fluffy sleeping gown with ruffles at the hemline and sleeves. Almost immediately, I turned the page and found an advertisement for children's medicine picturing a slightly older boy, wearing a white laboratory coat, stethoscope, eyeglasses, and what was obviously doctors' attire. The picture's background was blue and the caption read: "Why is [name of product] the most-prescribed children's allergy medication ever? Just ask your doctor." I wondered whether they were really referring to the current family doctor or to the future family doctor? The implication is that the comment referred to the boy in the picture—the future doctor.

Although each picture represented an advertisement for a different product and company, the fact that they were found in close proximity to each other may convey subliminal messages for young parents. Boys are encouraged at young ages, to acquire ambition and career aspirations, whereas girls are motivated to make themselves attractive without needing to develop career aspirations because when they grow up educated males will take care of them.

These images foster stereotypes and expectations established by the broader society, here promoted by advertising. The implication is that good parents would not buy the disposable diapers in the pink box for their sons or vice versa. Girls dressed in blue and other "male" colors such as green are not frowned on as much or as harshly. Advertisers manipulate our tastes, and our tastes are influenced by our needs to belong and to feel normal. These are strong emotional pressures crucial to our feelings of well-being. Many children's products, such as clothing and toys, are marketed to the public in terms of the use of specified colors, mainly pink and blue. The use of certain colors in advertising conveys strong messages about gender appropriateness.

When I asked my friend, described in the earlier anecdote, whether she realized that she was treating her children differently based on gender, she was dismayed and awed. After some thought, she agreed with me. Then she acknowledged that she had not given the situations any consideration before our conversation. It had not been her intention to treat her children disparately based on their gender. She just did what came "naturally" to her. She firmly wanted equal educational and career opportunities for both her daughter and son. She expected them both to succeed in adulthood. It never occurred to her how her gender-based customs were conveying opposing and detrimental messages to each of them. After sharing my observations and the underlying messages of her behaviors, my friend acknowledged that she had been socialized that way and that probably this is what contributed to her lack of awareness. She said that she dressed her daughter first because she was older and could count on her to stay clean, while her son always made a mess. Her daughter would be more patient waiting while she dressed her son. She thought that being passive was just her daughter's nature, while her son was naturally more "rambunctious."

I challenged these assertions by asking my friend whether her daughter had *always* been neat and patient or whether she had been trained to be that way. Had she spent as much time and effort training her son in the same way, or had she assumed that boys are just more careless? When I again shared my observations, my friend began to wonder whether she was, indeed, socializing her children differently according to her unconscious expectations based on the role models to which she had been exposed. She acknowledged that she spent more time and money selecting clothes for her daughter than she did for her son. Her daughter's appearance was a greater concern for her. I asked her what would happen if she allowed her daughter to also make a mess and have fun feeding herself as she did her son? Due to her new awareness of this situation, she wanted to learn more about gender bias and what she could do to reduce it in her home and in the world her children would be facing.

HOW SOCIALIZATION AFFECTS OUR LIVES

The process of identity formation in young children is assured by powerful influences in their immediate personal world. From the moment of our birth we are exposed to experiences that we interpret through our senses. We notice people around us, especially members of our immediate family or closely associated caretakers, and observe their behaviors and interactions. We utilize all of our senses in the process, but hearing and seeing become particularly vital in the initial process of socialization for young children. As a result of these external experiences, we begin to develop internal experiences or mental structures that further serve as the foundation for our perceptions and feelings as well as our beliefs and values. Our biases develop from all these components of our mental structures. Mental structures, in turn, shape the way we continually perceive and interpret the world around us. The socialization process is endless, interactive, and cyclical: our external experiences to a large extent shape our internal mental structures and these in turn shape how we see, hear, and feel about the world around us. Mental structures serve as colored filters through which all our subsequent external experiences are channeled. In many ways they also shape our attitudes and behaviors (Elkin and Handel, 1989).

When children enter school they are immersed in a world that further tends to support and promote the roles and expectations they bring with them. Even before children can read words in books, they receive and interpret the messages provided by the schools and society. The schools' environments, materials and textbooks, curriculum content, teachers' interactions, and role models serve to reinforce traditional gender attitudes and behaviors (King, 1990).

SOCIALIZATION AGENTS

Research has shown that adults in schools—teachers, student teachers, administrators, paraprofessionals and parent-assistants—reward girls for their neatness, patience, and helping "nature," whereas boys are encouraged to be independent thinkers and risk takers. Boys still receive the majority of teachers' or other adults' time and attention (Sadker and Sadker, 1986; Grayson and Miller, 1990).

Within the same classroom, boys and girls do not receive the same quantity and quality of educational experiences because of unconscious biases, differing expectations, and hence unequal interactions from adults. Here is just one account as an example of how it happens:

> On a visit to a kindergarten classroom, we were invited to wait for the children to return from the playground and prepare for the daily scheduled activity of "storytime," during which the children were encouraged to become more familiar with books and learning to read. We were invited to model the value of reading by joining the children in this activity. The kindergarteners always came in from the playground and sat or rested on the carpeted floor in an open area of the room. The kindergarten teacher used this rest time as an occasion for the children to look through picture books and primary readers, alone or in small groups, before an adult read a story to the entire class. One of us was called on to sit in the "reader's chair" and present the story of the day. Our colleague was honored and most anxious to participate in the activity.
>
> We watched as the kindergarten teacher's aide gave the signal that it was now time to leave the playground. She readied the children and had them line up, boys in one line and girls in another. Then she led the group to the door of the kindergarten room. As their kindergarten teacher, now inside the classroom, played the piano for their entrance, the girls were ushered in first and marched in an orderly line one behind the next. It was apparent that this was a regular routine and an activity the children enjoyed. The music was happy, fast, and high-pitched. Some of the girls walked or tiptoed quickly to the music. Some danced, skipped, and waved their hands happily. They remained in line and were not boisterous. The girls quickly settled in the places of their choice and waited for the boys to come in. When it was the boys' turn to enter the room, the music suddenly changed. It became slower, louder, and rumbling. Some of the boys came in with slow, long steps as if imitating giants. Their hands hung low and they slumped into their places. Some made grumbling noises and rolled on the floor or over each other. The boys were reprimanded and asked to

settle down. The girls found this bustle an amusing situation and giggled. Some of the girls acted embarrassed by the situation. From the teacher's remarks, it was apparent that the boys behaved in this manner frequently. The teacher again reprimanded the boys for their "excessive" behavior, but excused them by saying that they "knew better and had just gotten overly excited by the unexpected visitors." We wondered why the girls had not reacted in the same manner or what the teacher would have done if they had.

Parents and teachers are crucial socializing agents because they serve as young children's major role models. They provide the foundation for appropriate or inappropriate behaviors either through their own actions or by their acceptance or rejection of children's behaviors. The major socialization agents in our society are the home, the community, the school, peers, the church, and the media. Before the pre-eminence of the media, especially television, initially the home and next the school were the main agents of socialization. The rise of the media has been felt by every institution in our society. Children now spend increasing amounts of time watching television, often without adult supervision or clear and accurate information about what they are viewing. This often causes children to exert pressure on adults to buy products and services they see advertised on television. Advertising is a powerful force in our culture. American media personnel, such as children's television programmers, join with manufacturers of products and services through advertisement conglomerates to capture audiences and sell their products. It is not uncommon, for example, for programmers to integrate advertisements of products, such as cereals or toys, right into the story line of a television show. Regardless of a program's content, when viewers buy the sponsor's products the show is deemed a success. If viewers fail to buy the products, the television show is usually considered a failure and is quickly moved off the air. American children grow up in the culture of Coca-Cola and Pepsi, Keds and Nikes, Guess and Levi Jeans, and foods from MacDonald's and Burger King (Elkin and Handel, 1989; Elkind, 1981; Kilbourne, 1989).

Children in our society also have money to spend. They are heavily targeted by manufacturers and advertising conglomerates as potential consumers for their products. In another vein, teachers often purchase materials for children's use in classroom activities or for decorations and displays that also are reflective of media programming and advertising. We have visited many classrooms displaying "The Little Mermaid," and "Peter Pan," along with more contemporary children's cartoon and video characters. Student peer pressure to conform and wear or do certain things to be "in" also adds to this increasing reliance on the media as a major determinant of our cultural values and preferences.

Television has become a major socialization agent in our society, and children's television programming is dominated by male characters. The highest rated shows feature men in "action-packed," settings. Sadly, this often means that they are full of violence. Many shows do not include any strong and positive female role models at all. Female characters tend to be either weak, vain, malicious, or simply boy crazy. In stereotypic fashion, women are often portrayed as spending their time shopping and squandering men's money or wasting their lives away talking on the telephone about their children or gossiping about their neighbors. Male characters tend to be strong, courageous, adventurous, and usually coming to the rescue of a helpless female. Personal physical attractiveness is not emphasized necessarily in the roles for men.

More girls watch male characters on television and videos (such as adventurous and rebellious "Peter Pan") than boys watch female characters (such as "Miss Piggy" or "Corduroy"). Apparently girls admire male roles and traits more than boys admire generally stereotypic "female" attributes. We now realized that American television programming for young children tends to promote the images created by the biases and stereotypes of the major culture. Unfortunately, the media does not portray the realities present in the homes of most young children today, where either both parents work full-time or the mother works at least part-time to help support the family. Few television programs aimed at young children refer to the increasing number of households headed by single parents, mainly women. Television programming does not reflect the increasingly diverse array of roles and professions that both men and women fill in our contemporary society.

PERPETUATION OF BIASES AND STEREOTYPES

The anecdote that follows describes how very young children, early in their lives, internalize these gender biases and stereotypes:

One morning during a visit to an early childhood education classroom, I approached a boy who was playing alone on the jungle gym. He was dressed in jeans, sporting a large silver buckle, and fancy cowboy boots. I observed that he was very popular with the other boys and girls and tended to be a leader in the boys' groups. He quickly shared with me that he liked his outfit because it was just like dad's and that he wanted to grow up to be strong like his father. He told me that his father often took him to his construction job. This boy rarely played

*in the "house corner" and when he did it was only to be a "father,"
or the naughty pet, or to disrupt the girls' play. I asked what he wanted
to do when he grew up and he answered that he wanted to be a
cowboy, cop, or construction worker like his father.*

*Returning to the topic of his solitary play on the jungle gym, I
asked what he was doing there all alone. He informed me that he had
been "sent away" ("Me acecharon para acá") by the teacher. I realized
that this child had just been involved in another incident of disruptive
behavior. He often had fights with other boys and girls and sometimes
struck children. This time he had been relegated to play alone for a
while.*

*I asked if he knew why he had been "sent away," and he re-
sponded, "How should I know?"/("¿Y yo que sé?") His look gave him
away though. We both knew why he was there. Since I knew that he
often fought with the other children in class, I asked if perhaps he had
been sent away for hitting someone. He shrugged his shoulders without answering.*

*I pressed on asking why he had been fighting, and he answered
that he had been instructed by his father and mother to strike anyone
who bothered him. I asked if he thought that hurting other children
was the right thing to do or could there be another, better way of
resolving problems. The child gave me a scornful look and responded
that he was a boy and boys fought. ("I am a man and men fight."/"Yo
soy hombre y los hombres pelean.")*

*Once again, I asked him whether he felt lonely here playing by
himself and if he would prefer to be back with the other children. He
responded by quickly shrugging his shoulders and pouting his lower
lip. He answered that he did not care. "So what?"/"¿Y que?" He seemed
to prefer to stay by himself rather than admit wrongdoing or being
guilty.*

*After several futile attempts I walked away as I watched him long-
ingly eye the rest of the children happily playing about the room. I
could tell that he was fighting back humiliation and tears but would
not permit himself to show weakness in front of the other children. The
other children, especially the boys, often glanced his way while pretending not to really notice him. The boys kept their distance, but I
noticed that the girls rather "teasingly" kept running and playing right
in front of him as though they were vying for his attention. After a
while the teacher allowed him to rejoin the group, and he quickly
walked over to the boys' group. His look and walk were proud and
victorious.*

If this incident could be re-enacted with a different scenario, we
would find that increased flexibility in male and female roles could

benefit both genders. As girls grow up in our society their "tomboyish" behavior is often acceptable. Girls accept being called "tomboys" far more readily than boys being called "sissies." The statuses and roles for boys in our society are more clearly defined and held. Not fulfilling these expected roles can lead to more frequent and severe censure for boys than for girls.

In the same classroom it is not unusual for boys to receive more punishment and reprimands for similar infractions than girls do. The severity of the punishment can even be greater for boys than for girls. As a result of this differential socialization, boys become more defensive of their boyhood or masculinity at an earlier age than girls do of their femininity. Boys find it more difficult to display feelings of fear, doubt, or remorse. Boys are expected to repress their emotions and show control. Perhaps this also helps explain why girls so early in their school experiences identify with teachers, most of whom are females, and prefer the teachers' company and leadership, while boys tend to reject and distance themselves from teachers and other females at a younger age. Boys more often turn to their peers for direction and comfort. As a result of this differential socialization, early childhood education classrooms need the presence of more male figures (American Association of University Professors, 1990; Tavris, 1985; Shakeshaft, 1987; Gilligan, 1982; Lott, 1987).

FORMS OF BIAS IN CLASSROOMS, CURRICULUM MATERIALS, AND SCHOOLS

Biases and stereotypes are perpetuated by the following conditions:

1. Denying that they exist
2. Ignoring them or accepting them when they occur
3. Denying that they affect our lives
4. Denying that they affect other people's lives
5. Supporting them through our own behaviors

Bias is subtle and implicit but affects the attitudes and values of early childhood teachers and their intentions for classroom teaching. The materials on the following pages have been adapted from the writings and the work of Myra and David Sadker (1982, 1986) and their associates over the past decade, as well as the publications of the Anti-Defamation League's project "A World of Difference." The concepts listed below are all labels for forms of bias.

exclusion/tokenism
stereotyping

biased language
imbalance/inequality
unreality/ethnocentrism
isolation/segregation

Exclusion and Tokenism

This literally means to be out of sight or to be presented as a show of accommodation. Some groups in our society, such as women and people of color, have been excluded or made invisible in curricular materials and content and the schools' environments. At times, their presence is so minimal (token) that it becomes insignificant and meaningless, imperceptible or indistinguishable. The discoveries, the inventions, the acts of courage, and the contributions of women and people of color are often deleted from accounts of world history and from our nation's history. As we have discussed, this important information is also missing in the media's content, especially in children's programming.

Some examples of exclusion and tokenism:

Persons with disabilities are rarely portrayed in curricular materials for young children.

By the mid-1980s only 1 percent of the children's literature published was about African Americans; there was less about Asian Americans, Hispanics, and Native Americans (Reimer, 1992).

"Hypersensitivity" in children's books led to "watering down" or removing any cultural traits in children's literature, which, in the end, seemed to result in devaluing cultural diversity rather than valuing and celebrating it (Reimer, 1992).

Stereotyping

This form of bias occurs when individuals or groups are portrayed as having no individuality. Only one or a few "token" individual members of a group are presented as representative of all members of that group.

Some examples of stereotyping:

Persons with disabilities are portrayed as helpless and rarely in situations of leadership or where they demonstrate strength and self-reliance.

When a female is cast in a role against many male characters, the female is portrayed as the representative spokesperson for the rest of womankind.

African Americans and Hispanics are often cast as criminals or as indigent recipients of public assistance.

Native Americans are represented as unmotivated, lazy, and drunken.

Biased Language

This form of bias is often imperceptible and tends to pass unnoticed. We must keep in mind that verbal and written messages, although subliminal, still carry strong impressions and consequences that unconsciously affect us. Language shapes our thoughts and behaviors. Since the majority of linguistic symbols in use in our culture originally were developed by members of the dominant society, it is not surprising that our language is punctuated with biased images.

Some examples of biased language:

Referring to the pioneers as "settlers" who won a "victory" while referring to the Native Americans as "savages" who carried out a "massacre" creates a distortion.

Describing children whose parents are members of the blue-collar workforce as being "from the other side of the tracks" is a derogatory reference to their socioeconomic station in life.

Calling an African-American male "boy" is a negative and explosive carryover from the time of slavery and Jim Crow segregation.

Referring to people of Asian descent as "Orientals" hearkens back to the days of British colonization.

The generic use of "he" to represent both males and females tends to exclude the existence and contributions of women. Such words as forefathers, spokesman, chairman, and policeman can be construed as setting occupational parameters that preclude the participation of women.

The use of the word "handicapped" has its roots in the days when disabled beggars sat on street corners with "cap in hand" asking for alms (Derman-Sparks, 1989). The use of terms such as "lunatic" or "deformed" is demeaning and inappropriate when identifying children who are exceptional.

Imbalance and Inequality

This means to present or give value to only one side of an issue or event. This form of bias promotes limited perspectives and interpretations of the contributions and/or issues affecting certain groups in our society.

Some examples of imbalance and inequality that teachers encounter:

> When children study Martin Luther King, Jr., and his contributions to the Civil Rights Movement, they often do not hear about the women such as Rosa Parks whose action was the catalyst for the movement.

> When children study American colonization and the Westward Movement, they may learn little about the people who were already settled in this country before the arrival of the Mayflower. Did Columbus really discover America? We do not study the "Northward Movement," "Eastward Movement," or "Southward Movement" of Native Americans or Spanish settlers, people who were already here before "Americans" decided to move West into their lands.

> Children are seldom taught about how women helped our nation in times of war or about women's concerns and requests during the writing of the American Constitution.

Unreality

Textbooks and curriculum materials used in our schools may portray issues and events in inaccurate and generalized ways. Controversial issues tend to be glossed over or homogenized to the point where they are rendered insignificant.

Some examples of unreality that teachers and adults encounter in their training:

> Children do not learn about the sovereignty of the Native American Indian Nations or the rights and treaties violated nor that our form of representative government was modeled after the established government of the Native American Iroquois Nation.

> Children do not learn that the writers of the American Constitution did not mean to include or protect women and their interests or rights. Yet we study that it is the document that established our democratic, representative government guaranteeing equal rights and protection under the laws for all citizens. They may not see accurate coverage of women's or minorities' subsequent struggles for these same rights and protection.

Children may not be told about the internment of Japanese American citizens during World War II and the terrible social, economic and political consequences for our entire nation.

Isolation and Segregation

To isolate means to set aside from others, to stand alone and detached from others with negative impact. This is also the meaning of segregation. These concepts also are found in curriculum materials and school environments. Special groups' histories, contributions, concerns, and struggles are relegated to separate chapters or end of units of study as if they were not important to the subject. This places those issues, histories, and groups in a position of lesser significance. Since these groups are presented at the end of a lesson or as "extra credit," many teachers do not get around to them. Their content is usually not included in standardized tests (which so often drive schools' curricula) and often is overlooked, glossed over, or rushed through.

Children in early childhood education programs are affected by all the forms of bias in classrooms, schools, and the wider society through the adults who promulgate and reinforce these biases and stereotypes. Prejudice and discrimination start early in the thinking of young children and are implanted in their minds and in their actions by adults who carry these social messages to the youngsters as they model prejudiced behavior. The negative impact is the same whether the modeling is done consciously or unconsciously.

When examining storybooks, primers, and other curriculum materials designed for young children to ascertain any glaring biases or stereotype in their content, the following guidelines are recommended:

1. Look at the copyright date. Publishers are beginning to reduce bias in curricular materials. Although date is no guarantee of bias-free materials, the more current the publication, the more likely it is to be inclusive and fair.
2. Consider the author's or illustrator's background.
3. Consider the author's, story's, or material's perspective.
4. Examine the story's or materials' setting.
5. Examine the language, particularly the use of he and she and "loaded" words.
6. Check the illustrations for tokenism, stereotyping and role models. Are individuals and diverse groups represented accurately, in nontraditional roles, working together cooperatively and in leadership roles?

7. Check the story line for role models, standards of success, resolution of problems, and life-styles.
8. Examine the interpersonal relationships between the characters or persons presented.
9. Note the main characters and the contributions and achievements of persons presented.

(Adapted from the Council on Interracial Books for Children, 1984)

AN INCIDENT ON THE PLAYGROUND

Young children are more aware of prejudice, injustice, and inequality than adults realize. Young children are continually heard asking: "It is fair?" "Does she have more than I do?" and "Why?" Young children notice and are as concerned as adults about issues of difference. Children ask: "Why are people different?" They want to know why other people look, speak, or behave differently. They often ask questions about gender differences. When children leave home they are suddenly confronted with a world full of complex issues and questions. They are expected to share and empathize with others. Seeing the world through the eyes of others and treating others fairly are not actions children learn automatically. Empathy and compassion require adult guidance.

As adults we have been conditioned to consider some issues "taboo" and not proper topics for discussion between adults and young children. How often do we brush sensitive and controversial questions aside by either ignoring them when young children ask, refusing to answer, or even giving incorrect answers. "Because," "That's just the way it is," "Children do not ask those questions," "Children are to be seen, not heard," and so forth are some of the responses adults give to young children's questions about inequalities and injustice. We have all heard these statements as we were growing up.

Unfortunately, without accurate and reasonable answers, young children sometimes become derisive of unexplained diversity and mock, taunt, or even physically abuse other children they consider "strange." This account of an incident on the playground involving a group of linguistically and ethnically diverse young children clarifies this point.

A group of first graders played in the school's playground while the teacher and a parent sat on a bench conversing. The teacher's aide and a student-teacher were supervising some of the children, helping them climb up the slide steps and slide down. Other children played in the sandbox or on the climbing equipment. The students appeared to be mainly white except for one Asian boy and a light-skinned African-American girl.

Two girls sat on another bench watching the various groups of children at play. They were Ana and Luisa, both "Limited English Proficient" (LEP) students. Ana had arrived from Puerto Rico a few weeks earlier and spoke no English at all. She stayed close to Luisa, her friend, seeming to rely on her for support and security. Luisa came from Nicaragua and had been in the school for approximately four months. She spoke Spanish, but knew at least a few words of English.

The two girls were absorbed in watching a group of other girls. This group of five girls persistently attempted to turn a long rope in order to jump. The rope turned slowly, almost lifelessly, and without rhythm. They kept stepping on the slowly turning rope and starting all over again.

Ana and Luisa were obviously interested in jumping rope as they observed the group of girls even more intently. Luisa got up first and walked over to the girls. She stood in front of them and observed them silently, while Ana watched her adventurous friend from the safety of the bench. Two girls turned the rope while three others waited in line for their turn to jump. Luisa quietly stood in the line at the back of the group of girls waiting their turn to jump. As her turn in the line came up, Luisa attempted, in broken English, to explain that she knew how to make the rope turn more easily so everyone would be better able to jump over it. She tried to take the rope from one of the girls to show her how to do this. The girls who were waiting in line did not understand what Luisa was trying to say to them and what she wanted to show them. The girls began to push her away and called her names. They called her "dirty spic." Now, Ana left her position of safety on the bench and walked over to join her friend. As she reached the group she asked Luisa, in Spanish, what was the matter. ("What are they doing to you?"/"¿Qué te hacen?") The girls stopped turning the rope and began to push and shove Ana as well, calling her names, too. Luisa, not to be denied, began to argue with two of the girls. She attempted to communicate in English but kept switching back to her native tongue, Spanish. ("Go!/¡Vete! ¡Largate!")

One girl approached Ana and stuck out her tongue. Then another girl approached Ana and began making strange noises, attempting to mimic the Spanish sounds that they heard Ana and Luisa use when they spoke Spanish to each other. The girl said, "You talk funny. You talk like this," and continued to mock her. One girl stood very close to Ana, smiled and said in a sarcastic voice, "You are dumb, right?" She kept smiling as she grabbed Ana by her head and started to moved it up and down to simulate the motion of affirmation. "Say you are dumb, you stupid spic," her detractor keep repeating, as she forced Ana to indicate that she was saying "yes" to these taunting statements. The rest of the girls laughed and encouraged the mocking behavior of the group. It was obvious that Ana did not understand the conversation but knew that she was being taunted and laughed at. One of the girls continued her actions: "Go ahead, tell them that you are dumb," she yelled and again shook Ana's head up and down indicating affirmative agreement. All of the girls in the group then burst out laughing.

Suddenly realizing what was going on, Luisa grabbed Ana's arm and pulled her away. They returned to the bench and watched as the girls continued laughing and saying, "They are so stupid. They even say so!" The girls resumed their game of jump rope. Ana and Luisa sat on the bench silently and stared at them. Luisa was visibly angry, while tears trickled down Ana's cheeks. After a few minutes Luisa stood up and, taking Ana by the hand, guided her over to the swings where they began to play by themselves in an effort to put aside the slurs and insults they had just experienced.

What does this account tell us about the nature of prejudice? What does it reveal about the origins of discrimination and stereotyping? Ana, new to this environment, was obviously still trying to understand what had happened to her and why. Luisa, who had probably learned a few hard lessons already, refused to be hurt anymore by the rejection and bigotry she had encountered.

For the most part we are unaware of our expectations and behaviors and their consequences for children. Although they often lack the facility of language and the ability to state their feelings accurately, we can not assume that young children are not hurt by prejudicial treatment or biased words. We can not be lulled into thinking that young children understand only simple ideas and uncomplicated issues. Young children are forced to deal with an increasingly complex world where people look, act, sound, and feel different. Children are faced daily with contradictions, competing value judgments, and difficult choices to make, often on their own and without adult guidance. Young children need the modeling and support of adults.

Not only are children hurt by ethnic and racial slurs and by prejudicial treatment but their teachers can experience intolerance and racism expressed by the children they teach as an extension of the attitudes learned at home and in the community. The following two anecdotes illustrate such situations. A Black-Hispanic elementary school principal experienced the following incident:

A first-grade Hispanic boy had been misbehaving in his class and was sent to my office by his teacher. Although this was the last month of the school year and this boy had never been so naughty that he needed to be sent to the principal's office, the teacher felt that this time his misdemeanor required a reprimand from the principal. When he approached the office door the child broke out in tears and refused to enter the room. Finally, with extreme reluctance he came into my office and sat on a bench crying all the while. A teacher approached the boy and asked him why he was so concerned, trying to reassure him that his principal was only going to talk with him and try to get to know him better. As the child continued to cry the teacher became concerned that something was certainly awry. Finally, the boy revealed to her that he could not speak to this principal because she was "black" and his mother had told him NEVER *to talk to black people. When the child's remark was reported to me by the teacher, I was very sad and wondered if we have really changed at all in this society.*

Another teacher reported an incident that occurred in her suburban classroom shortly after the school year began.

Four kindergarteners were playing at the clay table. As I walked by, I overheard one of the children casually say to the others, "Did you know that we're not going to learn anything in class this year?" I bent down and asked the child why he had made that particular comment. The little boy continued molding the clay figure in his hand and, without a moment's hesitation, candidly replied, "That's what my daddy said at dinner last night. He told my mom that I probably wouldn't learn anything at all this year because I have a black teacher."

Though stunned, hurt, and angry, this veteran educator realized that the greater harm had been done to the child, because his parents were planting the seeds of bias and prejudice early in his life.

SUMMARY

This chapter focused on the subtle nature of socialization, discrimination, and stereotyping as it affects young children and their teachers.

Anecdotes demonstrated how the forces of socialization shape our attitudes, expectations, and behavior very early in our lives. We then pass this on to the young. The primary agents of socialization are the home, community, school, peers, and the media. These were examined for their crucial roles in shaping society. This led to a discussion of the perpetuation of biases, stereotypes, and prejudice, in classrooms and curriculum materials. The chapter closed by recounting incidents that exposed the deep vulnerability of young children and their teachers to inequality, injustice, and discrimination in society today.

KEY CONCEPTS

Socialization This is the dynamic process that brings human beings into a human group and causes an individual to internalize, accept, and affirm the values, traditions, folkways, mores, and attitudes of a culture (also see chapter 1).

Gender socialization Initially based on biological distinctions between males and females, gender socialization includes those processes that structure gender-appropriate behavior and activities in a society and become further developed and interpreted through culturally defined norms, attitudes, and values.

Bias A mental learning, inclination, or preference that often inhibits impartial judgment.

Prejudice A judgment or opinion formed before facts are known and examined. A prejudice is a preconceived notion, usually unfavorable and unreasonable.

Stereotype A form of bias that occurs when individuals or groups are portrayed as all the same and as having no individuality or uniqueness.

Imbalance and inequality To present or give value to only one side of an issue or event.

Unreality To portray issues and events in curriculum materials and textbooks in inaccurate and generalized ways.

Language bias A form of biased language, often imperceptible or unnoticed that negatively portrays or excludes groups of people as another form of discrimination.

Isolation A form of bias in curriculum materials and textbooks that segregates the histories, contributions, concerns, and struggles of certain groups to separate chapters or to the end of units of study as if they are not fully appropriate for general study and consideration.

This form of curriculum isolation was prevalent particularly in regard to women and people of color.

ISSUES AND ACTIONS

It has been stressed in this chapter that socialization begins early in life and is an imperceptible and unexamined process. Scenarios involving teachers of young children are presented below. These incidents provoke discussion about the appropriate actions of teachers, student teachers, paraprofessionals, parents, or care givers. Read each scenario. Write down your reactions, comments, and the implications the incidents have for early childhood education. Discuss your opinions and reactions.

Scenario 1

In the teachers' lounge at the noon break, Ms. P, the first grade teacher discussed the morning's hectic classroom experiences with her student teacher.

"Charlene is a very sweet little girl. She always gets her work done, and it is always correct. She never causes any problems, and she seems so mature and responsible, too."

The student teacher replies that she noticed Ms. P does favor Charlene, often asking her to help other students with their work. Ms. P points out to her student teacher that having students help each other is also a strategy for learning. Ms. P goes on to say that she really appreciates having children like Charlene in her class because "she is a great help, especially with the slower learners, most of whom are boys."

The first grade teacher sighs as she reiterates how unruly the boys in this class are, "always shouting out the answers even when I don't call on them. They just can't control themselves and they won't give others an opportunity to participate. It doesn't matter to these boys whether I send them to the office or keep them after school. They cannot seem to work alone without getting into fights. The girls are all so much more quiet and cooperative! Why can't the boys in this class be like that?"

How could the student teacher help Ms. P to become aware of the traditional attitudes and values she holds about gender-related behaviors of young children? What actions would encourage Ms. P to take a different viewpoint about the "nice" girls' versus those "naughty" boys' behavior in this first grade class?

Scenario 2

John G. has just completed all the requirements and received his teacher certification for the new school year. He has accepted a position as the kindergarten teacher in a suburban elementary school. John is excited about the beginning of the new school year. Over the summer he spent many hours thinking and planning for his first real teaching job—the kindergarten teacher at the well-known Washington Primary School! John wants to ensure that from the moment the children arrive they become excited and motivated about being in his room. He searches out various sources of educational materials for decorating the kindergarten classroom for the children's arrival. He selects the very popular Mutant Ninja Turtles posters and large cut-outs of dragons for the boys, because he had learned that boys like adventure and challenges. For the girls he purchases pictures of Muppets and Care Bears, because he thought they would prefer looking at cute animals. John had learned in his teaching methods courses that to encourage and stimulate children the teacher needs to provide a rich classroom environment replete in contemporary materials with which the children are familiar.

Discuss how this teacher's selection of curriculum materials reflects his own preconceived notions. How could John use his position as a man and a kindergarten teacher to break old stereotypes about what are appropriate gender occupations and gender behavior? What difficulties and problems might John run into in his new career as a male kindergarten teacher? If you were the parent of a child in John's kindergarten class, what would you do to help him in this initial year of teaching? if you were his principal? if you were a teacher in his school building?

Scenario 3

Dorelle, a paraprofessional in Mrs. W's third grade classroom, noticed a disturbing pattern in her interaction with the children. During directed lessons, Mrs. W. unconsciously gave less attention to the three ethnic boys in her small group. When asking questions, she allowed shorter "wait time" for them to respond and provided fewer verbal prompts if they seemed hesitant in answering. Dorelle became aware that Mrs. W. often ignored these students even when they waved their hands in front of her for recognition. Further, she asked them questions that required merely a "yes" or "no" answer rather than ones that were open ended and required critical thinking.

To her amazement, Dorelle observed the same phenomenon occurring when she visited Mr. A's second-grade classroom down the hall. In general, he created an atmosphere that was less academically favorable to his students of color.

What are the ramifications for the students in these two settings? Discuss ways in which each of the teachers could become aware of their teaching styles and the differential treatment found in their classrooms.

REFERENCES AND SUGGESTED READINGS

Allport, Gordon. *The Nature of Prejudice.* Garden City, NJ: Doubleday, 1954.
American Association of University Professors. *Shortchanging Girls, Shortchanging America,* Washington, DC: Author, 1991.

Anti-Defamation League of B'nai B'rith. *A World of Difference.* New York: Author, 1985.

Best, Raphela. *We've All Got Scars.* Bloomington, IN: University of Indiana Press, 1985.

Chera, Susan. *Report Says Too Many Aren't Ready for School. New York Times,* December 16, 1991, p. 18.

Council on Interracial Books for Children. "Quick Ways to Analyze Children's Books for Racism and Sexism." New York: Author, 1984.

Elkin, F., and Handel, G. *The Child and Society* (5th ed.) New York: Random House, 1989.

Elkind, David. *The Hurried Child.* Reading, MA: Addison Wesley, 1981.

Gilligan, Carol. *In a Different Voice.* Cambridge, MA: Cambridge University Press, 1982.

Grayson, Dolores and Miller, Pamela. *Gender/Ethnicity in Student Achievement.* Earlham, IA: Graymill, 1990.

Hochschild, Arlie. *The Second Shift: Working Parents and the Revolution at Home.* New York: Viking Press, 1989.

Kilbourne, J. Beauty and the Beast in Advertising. *Media and Values.* Winter, 1989 (No. 49), pp. 8–10.

Lott, Bernice. *Women's Lives.* Mountainview, CA: Mayfield, 1987.

Michigan State Board of Education. Office for Sex Equity in Education. "The Influence of Gender and Role Socialization on Student Perceptions," mimeographed report, 1990.

Milner, David. *Children and Race: Ten Years On.* London: Ward Lock, 1983.

Noddings, Nel. *Caring: A Feminine Approach to Ethnic and Moral Education.* Berkeley, CA: University of California Press, 1984.

Osborn, B. How Television Changes Childhood and Challenges Parents. *Media and Values,* 1990 (No. 52–53), pp. 2–3.

Reimer, K. M. Multiethnic Literature: Holding Fast to the Dream. *Language Arts.* (February 1992, Vol. 69), pp. 14–21.

Roman, L., et al. (Eds.). *Becoming Feminine: The Politics of Popular Culture.* Philadelphia: Falmer Press. 1989.

Sadker, M., and Sadker, D. *Sex Equity Handbook for School* (2nd ed.). New York: Longman, 1982.

Sadker, M., and Sadker, D. Sexism in the Classroom: From Grade School to Graduate School. *Phi Delta Kappan,* March 1986, pp. 512–515.

Sapiro, V. *Women in American Society.* Mountainview, CA: Mayfield, 1986.

Shakeshaft, Charol. *Women in Educational Administration.* Newbury Park, CA: Sage, 1987.

Spender, Dale. *Man Made Language,* 2nd ed. London: Routledge, 1985.

Tavris, Carol. *The Longest War—Sex Differences in Perspective.* New York: Harcourt, 1985.

8

A SOCIOLOGICAL VIEW OF
THE YOUNG CHILD

In chapter 1 we stated that we mainly are concerned in this book with developing sensitivity to ethnicity, gender, and social class affiliation as these forces affect young children. However, the diversity perspective also includes concern for "special needs" children. In this chapter we present a way of looking at human behavior that provides additional insights into understanding the life space of children and those who teach them. Using a perspective developed by social psychologists to examine how "most people" carry out and experience life in schools leads us to examine how children with special disabilities—also a form of diversity—are impacted.

The analogy of life as a stage and individuals as actors dates back to Shakespeare's immortal rhetoric that all the world's a stage and all the people merely players upon it, and perhaps even earlier. Occasionally in the literature, teachers have been referred to as actors, playing out their dramas in the classroom. Life in classrooms has been the topic and the theme of many films, novels, and plays. Some high school and college teachers have developed a reputation for dramatic histrionics in the classroom, as though they were truly "on stage" giving a performance. Some of these teachers are considered outstanding and dedicated by their students and their colleagues. A highly dramatic and theatrical technique in the appropriate context in teaching can be a vehicle to optimum learning rather than a distracting condition. Sometimes teachers of young children employ a theatrical stance when telling or reading stories to children. The whole tradition and art of the storyteller has been an integral part of early childhood learning for centuries.

Rare in the literature on teaching methodology and practice, however, is an examination of the day-to-day experience of teachers and students in the metaphor of theatrical performance. To develop such an analysis it is useful to have a framework of concepts or forms to categorize and analyze just what is going on between individuals. It is at this point, then, that we turn to the writings of sociologist Erving Goffman as a pertinent prototype for examining life in classrooms. Goffman's theories originally were developed to view men and women in everyday social interactions. He employed this metaphor of the theater and the dramatic to examine people as they present themselves and their activities to others and try to guide and control the impressions they create. This sociologist saw the individual as employing certain techniques to sustain the performance, just as the actor presents a character to an audience. This method of "people watching" has been built on painstaking research and observation of social customs in many regions of the United States and in Europe. The result has been an adroit and insightful examination of the conventional cultural hierarchies of everyday life.

APPLYING FORMS OF DRAMA TO EARLY CHILDHOOD CLASSROOMS

To apply this unique theory to the everyday life of teachers and students in early childhood classrooms, it is useful to describe the labels or terms that the sociologist has developed to examine groups of people and their social customs. The following definitions of terms and "concepts" as used by Goffman have been taken from *The Presentation of Self in Everyday Life* (1959), one of his most stimulating writings. These labels for everyday behavior and their definitions will help readers to grasp the power and insightful analysis of human behavior offered in this theatrical model.

We begin with the most obvious term, the *performance*. In this application of the theatrical model a performance refers to all the activity of an individual that occurs during a period marked by continuous presence before a particular set of observers and that has some influence on the observers. Next follows the idea of a *front,* that part of the individual's performance that defines the situation for those who observe the performance. It is the expressive equipment of a standard kind, either intentionally or unwittingly employed by the individual during the performance. The performance takes place in a *setting*—a standard part of the front involving furniture, decor, physical layout, and other background items that supply the scenery and stage props for the human action played out before, within, or upon it. Human beings put forth a *personal front,* which refers to the other items of expressive equipment, the items that we most intimately identify with the performer: gender, age, racial characteristics, size and looks, posture, speech patterns, facial expressions, bodily gestures, and insignia of office or rank and clothing.

Additional terms in this framework of the theater include "dramatic realization" and most importantly, "audience." *Dramatic realization* is used to describe how the individual typically infuses the performance with signs that dramatically highlight and confirm what might otherwise remain unapparent or obscure. The *audience* is the observers who view the performance. If the individual's activity is to become significant to others—the audience, then the individual must mobilize activity so that it will express *during the interaction* what the individual wishes to convey.

How can we apply this theatrical model to teachers and students and, more specifically, to education in the early childhood setting? We begin with the performance. The teacher is providing a performance in the class room when he or she is engaged in the activity of teaching during a period of time—the school session. Further, the teacher is in the continued presence of a set of observers—the students—and influences their behavior.

To continue the analogy—the teacher—(the performer) constructs a *front* that incorporates a personal front and is enacted within a setting. The setting in which the teacher plays out the performance is a classroom whose decor or physical layout includes walls, bulletin and chalk boards, furniture—the teacher's desk; the smaller, child-sized tables and chairs; the bookshelves, cupboards, and closets stocked with materials; the housekeeping center or playhouse; the games area, science corner, and so on. These elements have been arranged carefully by the teacher. The teacher's personal front consists of far more maturity in age, greater size and strength, and greater wisdom and experience than the young students before whom the performance takes place. The teacher's personal front might also include the dress, mannerisms, style of speech, and expressions that have been cultivated for this performance, the instruction of young children.

When we think of teachers of young children we invariably picture a *woman*—with a sweet smile and a gentle demeanor. Often a given social front becomes stereotyped and institutionalized. This expectation of front, social or personal, of the teacher of young children is certainly characteristic of American society. When men choose to become teachers for groups of children under eight years of age, they must establish a personal front that is part of a new performance in the society, while also counteracting a long-standing stereotypical role, the female kindergarten teacher.

We have used Erving Goffman's concepts of the performance, front, setting, and personal front in application to teachers of young children. Now let us see how his term *dramatic realization,* fits into life in classrooms. *Dramatic realization* has been described as a technique that the performer uses to infuse the performance with dramatic highlights, emphasizing what might otherwise remain obscure. One has to underscore the activity to impress on observers or the audience aspects of the performance. Goffman describes how students try to impress teachers by being extremely attentive. Students rivet their eyes on the teacher, exhaust themselves playing the attentive role and end up not actually learning anything.

To illustrate dramatic realization with the teacher giving the performance, we describe an early childhood teacher who keeps a mirror in a stand on her piano. The mirror is arranged at an appropriate angle so the teacher can see her four-year-olds even though her back is turned to them while she plays the piano. As the children sing and request numbers, the teacher merely glances in the mirror to see whom to call on next. This teacher has developed the technique of actually being able to survey her pupils reactions even when her back is turned to them. As Goffman describes dramatic realization, if the activity is to become significant to others, the performer must mobilize the actions *during the performance* to heighten what is intended to be portrayed. To the observer, this clever teacher provides dramatic realization of the role of the young child's teacher by being ever watchful, even when her back is turned to them.

Others Join in the Performance

The performer can function alone or be a member of a troupe or cast of players. An example comes from proper etiquette in business settings. One addresses coworkers in the office or one's administrative assistant by "Mr." or "Ms." when outsiders are present, although everyone in the office may be on a first name basis during the daily routine of activities. The school is also a type of business setting. Teachers greet each other by their first names in the classroom, the hall, the office, or the teachers' lounge when no children are within hearing. Yet, if a child appears on the scene, it constitutes a breach of etiquette to refer to Ms. Green, the art teacher, as "Blanche." One way to refer to a member of your clique or particular group on a large school faculty is to refer to the individual always by his or her first name when that individual is not present but is mentioned in the conversation. These small, but really significant actions reveal the subtleties of the "performance team" who are considered the members and those who are labeled outsiders, or the audience for the team.

Performance teams are flexible and the cast of characters in the troupe can shift and change. At times the teacher and the students become a team and the outsiders or the audience can consist of parents, other teachers, supervisors, the principal, or other administrators. We are not referring to the traditional school performance situation, where parents are invited to see the rhythm band play several numbers just before Christmas. Rather, let us look at a more subtle but commonplace situation in the public school setting. A teacher new to the system must be evaluated by superiors. It is known that the coordinator, supervisor, or principal will be coming around to observe the classroom. The teacher allies the students to perform in the manner that will be expected by the evaluator, even to the extent, in some cases, that the threat of the teacher's classroom evaluation is used as a means of discipline for the pupils in the classroom. This is especially effective with young children. The teacher may say, "Oh, you know Mr. Brown, our principal, is coming in one of these days and he doesn't like to see messy tables and noisy children." And, when the principal does arrive for a brief inspection, the cast of characters, children and teacher alike, are alerted to provide him with the performance he seems to be expecting.

What is being said here of the new teacher on the job can also be used to characterize the student teacher, perhaps even more so. For example, in the setting of the open pod-style school, with 150 to 200 children in a large, carpeted space sectioned off by many styles of dividers, the supervisor can observe the candidate to be evaluated in a very casual and unobtrusive manner. Yet five- and six-year-olds in this setting will look up from their reading or their projects and remark, "Here comes the lady from the university to see if Miss Blue is teaching us all right." The children were alerted to the performance that was expected when the "outsider" arrived by a member of their team, their student teacher.

Regions: The Setting for the Performance and Its Staging

In the traditional elementary school, regions are usually designated, such as "Room 102" or "The First Grade." Goffman's writings adroitly denote a "front" and a "back region," where the team performs. In this theatrical model both the traditional school and the more innovative open-space school can become settings with front and back regions. The front region is referred to as the place where the performance is given, while the back region is a place, relative to a given performance, where the impression, fostered by the performance, is knowingly contradicted as a matter of course. The teachers' lounge would eminently qualify for the example of a back region. It is here that, at times, emotions are fully expressed, from sobbing declamations of failure to the exhilaration successful teaching can bring. Teachers of young children often feel the fatigue of being "on stage" for hours on end. In some situations, the elementary school teacher's "day" can equal six to seven hours of unrelieved duty with children. Yet, the teachers' lounge provides the backstage area where the adult can relax from the performance.

Do the children in the school have such a "back" region? The playground or outdoors sometimes functions in this way, but often this area is but another sector of the front region for teachers and students alike. Then we wonder why young children in the school setting become so restless by the end of the day. There is really no back region for them. There is no place to let go and relax from pressures of the performance in school!

Remember that this way of examining and explaining human interactions does not need to be applied in a negative, sarcastic, or deprecating mode. Do not focus on human fallibilities but, rather, on trying to find explanations for the behavior of children and adults. This was the purpose and goals of this school of sociologists, led by Erving Goffman, in the development of this approach to understanding human behavior and the motivations behind it.

THE YOUNG CHILD WITH SPECIAL NEEDS

Another area discussed by the sociologist Erving Goffman, related to students with special needs. When some children demonstrate their inability to perform in the group, special categories are set up by educators to channel these children into educational programs that can accommodate what have been labeled their "learning disabilities." There is growing concern in both the private and public sectors of American education about categories of special education. Students may be labeled as learning disabled, mentally retarded, emotionally disturbed, speech impaired, physically disabled; or as having Attention Deficit Disorder (ADD), fetal alcohol syndrome, among other labels. Gifted and talented children are also included in programs for students with special needs.

Specialists in the field, Jane Mercer (1973) and Christine Sleeter (1985) have provided research and written widely about the biases in categorizing children as "special education" candidates. These educators have taken the standpoint that labeling children's behavior as nonstandard or deviant just because it does not fit the prevailing norms and rules of the kindergarten or early years of the elementary school is rather a problem of the broader society's attitudes and values, and not inherent in the nature of the child. Mercer and Sleeter have asserted that categories such as "learning disabled" or the labeling of children as mentally retarded can be used as an excuse to place children in a different track or educational provision altogether, which isolates and ostracizes them. In contrast, children of color are *under* represented in classes for the gifted and talented.

This phenomenon of over-representation presents a nationwide crisis, especially for African-Americans and Hispanics. Students may be labeled with "the three D's—dumb, deviant, and distrubed" before they reach second grade and become trapped in special education classes for years. Not all are able to break out of the labels given them. These at-risk students often become school dropouts due to frustration and the continual repression of their intellectual abilities. This is reflected in the low numbers of black and Hispanic males found in college (Chipman, 1990).

Much of the problem can be attributed to biased perceptions on the part of adults in the early childhood setting. Consider the following scenario:

Mrs. Stewart smiled to herself as she walked around her first grade classroom, noting the hum of activity coming from her students. She noticed Suzette and Alecia with their blond heads bent over the art table, working happily together. A few moments later she heard a cry and turned to see Suzette's round eyes fill with tears. "Alecia took the crayon I wanted to use," she said. Mrs. Stewart encouraged the two little girls to "share and play nicely together," and in a short while the incident was forgotten by both. Soon Alecia moved on to another activity, and Dominic came to the table. A few moments later, once again Suzette's cry brought the teacher to her side. "Dominic took the crayon I wanted to use," she said. Mrs. Stewart turned to Dominic and, with stern reprimands, sent him to the "time-out" chair. Later that morning she documented the incident in writing, noting that Dominic was "prone to steal from the other children." She added this to the list of infractions she was keeping regarding this boy. At the special education staffing meeting, she would present all of this information to substantiate her belief that Dominic needed to be removed from the regular classroom due to his persistent "disruptive behavior," indicative of emotional disturbance.

Suzette's explanation of the actions of both Alecia and Dominic were precisely the same. Yet the *teacher's* response was drastically different in each case. Sometimes a teacher may be offended by such unconscious cultural mannerisms as speaking in louder voices, frequent jesting or bantering, or walking with a certain gait. When the child is unable to modify his or her behavior to suit the teacher's preference, this may be perceived as rebellion. Referrals for special education under the heading of emotional problems often follow.

Here again we can bring the sociological perspective to examine what the categorization of "special education" can mean in the life of a young child.

Given the current theory and practice of teaching in many American public schools, teachers have found themselves unprepared to educate increasing numbers of ethnically diverse children. In mandating special education programs, the rationale is created that the new placement will help the child. In theory, the "special" children are given a seemingly better placement. Some school officials find it easier for all those involved to place such children in special education rather than to accept a failure in the regular education system—and to alter it to include strategies and curriculum to meet the needs of widely differing school populations.

Though initially conceived to benefit youngsters, the special education track maintains and perpetuates the "spoiled identity" of many young children who overwhelmingly happen to be ethnic, poor, and living in the inner city. The result may be the segregation and under-education of disenfranchised children in our society.

THE TEACHER AND A CURRICULUM
OF "INCLUSION"

There is a nationwide move towards "inclusion," that is, the placement of children with exceptionalities in the regular classroom. Part of the impetus for this move has been brought about by budget constraints affecting the hiring of special education teachers and class size. However, another primary factor has been the plea of many parents for their youngsters to be accepted into the learning activities found in the broader school environment.

As with all school reform, there are issues surrounding "inclusion." Among them is the fact that most teachers have not been trained specifically to work with children with special needs. Another is that, traditionally, special education programs include small class size to provide maximum individual attention. Some fear that the needs of youngsters who are mainstreamed into regular settings will not be addressed. Still another issue is that of acceptance by the other children.

For teachers in early childhood classrooms where exceptional children are served, the *diversity perspective* is critical. We have seen that attitudes toward difference are formed during the young years. Little children will notice and be affected by the *teacher's* responses to children with disabilities. Though some reactions may be unintentional on the part of the adults, the effect will be just as detrimental.

For instance, teachers may treat exceptional students as *infantile,* "talking down" to them by changing their tone of voice or even their vocabulary. They may treat these students as *invisible,* unconsciously overlooking them when calling on students for answers to questions or to perform tasks. They may treat them as *totally disabled.* This may take the form of speaking to a child who is blind in a loud voice as if she is deaf also, or assuming that a child in a wheelchair also needs help in holding a pencil.

Just as teachers model acceptance of ethnic and gender diversity, they can take responsibility for students with special needs as well. This can be done first of all by recognizing that very young children may have genuine concerns surrounding this area of difference. They may experience feelings of *curiosity* ("Why does Johnny wear that heavy brace on his leg every day?"). They may deal with feelings of *confusion* ("I don't understand why Shelly can't answer me when I try to talk to her."). They may be beset by *anxiety* ("I bet Mark can't hold his head up because he was bad one day. Sometimes I'm bad, too. Will this happen to me?"), or *fear* ("Can I catch that like catching chicken pox from someone?"). Such emotions may lead to *rejection,* a refusal to play or work with the child who is differently-abled.

By being aware, teachers can help all of their students to interact in ways that are more positive.

Things to avoid:

- Do not deny that the physical, linguistic, or emotional differences exist
- Do not criticize a child for noticing these differences
- Do not lightly dismiss their sincere questions by telling them, "Don't worry about it"
- Do not make up words or stories to explain the disability

Things to practice:

- Introduce disabilities through storybooks, dolls, and posters
- Include adaptive equipment among items in the playhouse or role-playing center
- Invite exceptional adults to speak to the class
- Encourage the parents of the mainstreamed children to talk to the class if they feel comfortable in doing so
- Highlight the contributions of people with disabilities who are musicians, civic leaders, artists, and so forth

Societal prejudices and acts of discrimination may be more harmful than actual physical or emotional differences. By developing the diversity perspective, early childhood educators can actively counter stereotypes and misconceptions regarding children with special needs. It is a certainty that our schools and nation will benefit when exceptionality is viewed as another form of cultural diversity to be valued by all.

THE REALIZATION OF SOCIAL CLASS INEQUITY IN THE YOUNG CHILD

Another area examined by Goffman in his writings refers to the realization of difference, based on social class, early in an individual's life. For instance, he writes that the orphan learns that other children have parents and a home. By the same token, children from single parent families may be stigmatized. When a child begins public school, this may be the occasion of first learning about this difference from the taunting, teasing, and ostracism that might result when joining a new group. From a remarkable and moving account of a kindergarten founded in 1889 comes this touching story of Patsy. Written by Kate

Douglas Wiggins (1894), this story of a crippled, orphan boy, Patsy, was written and sold for the benefit of the Silver Street Free Kindergartens in San Francisco during the 1890s. Kate Wiggins' description of the first meeting with Patsy illustrates so well the child's early recognition of difference.

A boy, seeming—how many years old shall I say? for in some ways he might have been a century old when he was born—looking, in fact as if he had never been young, and would never grow older. He had a shrunken, somewhat deformed body, a curious, melancholy face, and such a head of dust-colored hair that he might have been shorn for a doormat. The sole redeemers of the countenance were two big, pathetic, soft dark eyes, so appealing that one could hardly meet their glance without feeling instinctively in one's pocket for a biscuit or a ten-cent piece. But such a face! He had apparently made an attempt at a toilet without the aid of a mirror, for there was a clear circle like a racetrack round his nose, which member reared its crest untouched and grimy from the center, like a sort of judge's stand, while the dusky rim outside represented the space for audience seats.

I gazed at this astonishing diagram of a countenance for a minute, spellbound, thinking it resembled nothing so much as a geological map, marked with coal deposits. And as for his clothes, his jacket was ragged and arbitrarily docked at the waist, while one of his trousers-legs was slit up the side, and flapped hither and thither when he moved, like a lug-sail in a calm. "Well, sir," said I at length, waking up to my duties as hostess, "did you come to see me?"

"Yes, I did."

"Let me think; I don't seem to remember; I am so sleepy. Are you one of my little friends?"

"No, I hain't yit, but I'm goin' to be."

"That's good, and we'll begin right now, shall we?"

"I knowed yer fur Miss Kate the minute I seen yer."

"How was that, eh?"

"The boys said as how you was a kind o' pretty lady, with towzly hair in front." (Shades of my cherished curls!)

"I'm very obligated to the boys."

"Kin yer take me in?"

"What? Here? Into the Kindergarten?"

"Yes, I bin waitin' this yer long whiles fur to git in."

"Why, dear little boy," gazing dubiously at his contradictory countenance, "you're too-big, aren't you? We have only tiny little people here, you know; not six years old. You are more, aren't you?"

"Well I'm nine by the book; but I ain't more'n scerce six along o' my losing them three years."

*"What do you mean, child? How could you lose three years?"
cried I, more and more puzzled by my curious visitor.*

*"I lost 'em on the back stairs, don't yer know. My father he got
fightin' mad when he was drunk and pitched me down two flights of
'em and my back was most clearn broke in two, so I couldn't git out
o' bed forever, till just now."*

"Why, poor child, who took care of you?"

"Mother, she minded me when she warn't out washin'."

"And did she send you here to-day?"

*"Well! however could she, bein' as how she's dead? I s'posed you
knowed that. She died after I got well; she only waited for me to git
up, anyhow."*

*O God! these poor mothers! they bite back the cry of their pain
and fight death with love so long as they have a shred of strength for
the battle!*

"What's your name, dear boy?"

"Patsy."

"Patsy, what?"

*"Patsy nothin'! just only Patsy; that's all of it. The boys call me
'Humpty Dumpty' and 'Rags' but that's sassy."*

(Wiggins, 1894, pp. 12–16)

As the story develops, Patsy joins the Silver Street Kindergarten and
proves to be an invaluable as well as endearing aid to Miss Kate, the
teacher. Toward the end of the school year, Patsy develops a fatal illness
and the book closes with the scene of Patsy on his death bed, as poignant and touching as any in the literature. Miss Kate sings a hymn and
recites a little prayer as the dying child, with gasps of his last breath,
sighs, "I've got enough o' this, I tell yer, with backaches, 'nd no gravy
on my pertater;—but I hate to go 'way from the Kindergartent—only
p'raps Heaven is just like, only bigger, 'nd more children—Sing about
the pleasant mornin' light, will yer, please—Miss Kate?" (p. 66)

From this nineteenth century portrayal of social class inequity, we
now turn for a twentieth century example of social class stereotyping in
the public school setting. Consider the following conversation between
teachers during lunch.

*"I've had it up to here," sighed Steve as he sat grading spelling and
math papers from his third-graders. Tony came and sat next to him.
Steve continued, "Look at this. Laneisha just can't do the work. She
missed over a fourth of these words, the lowest score in the entire class.
There's more, though. Look at Jareem's paper. He can't get even these
simple problems right."*

Tony looked at Steve and shook his head affirmatively. "I know exactly what you mean. Jim and Sally are in the same boat in my class. They just can't seem to learn anything. I've tried lots of strategies, but nothing seems to help. The other children in my class need me, and I can't justify taking time away from them for these kids.

Steve said, "The problem isn't with your strategies, Tony. It's at home. These kids are bussed in from the housing project in that poor section of town, and their parents really don't care anything about them. I bet they don't have a single book or game in the house."

Beth, the first-grade teacher, came in at that moment. She joined the conversation. "I never expect those parents to show up for Back-to-School Night anymore. They don't care about parent-teacher conferences either. I sent a long letter home to all my parents and asked them to send three different kinds of fresh fruit or vegetables for a unit we were doing on health. Can you imagine! Only two of those parents sent anything. If they won't even do that, you know they're not going to help their children with homework. When I asked the children why their mothers didn't send anything, they just looked at me and didn't say a word!"

Steve said, "I read an article about possible brain damage to the kids when these teenage mothers are on drugs. If I thought they could learn, I'd give them extra attention, but what's the use?"

In this case, the biased perceptions of the teachers involved were based on stereotypes regarding not just the ethnicity, but also the social class of the young children and their parents. It must be noted that one of the most basic tenets of early childhood education is that the relationship between the school and the home should be fostered positively (Bredekamp, 1987). Teachers often assume that lower income parents do not love their children. Such assumptions usually are based on the parents' lack of participation in school events. Yet a closer look at the circumstances surrounding such non-participation can serve to undo the stereotypes.

The first-grade teacher, Beth, was insensitive to the fact that if the children were bussed from another part of town, their parents might not have transportation to travel the distance to attend the conferences. Parents in the proximity of the school could walk there. Some of the economically deprived parents may have felt they lacked proper clothing for the occasion, while others may have been embarrassed to come because of their inability to communicate adequately with the teachers.

The request for three different kinds of fresh fruit or vegetables might have been beyond the realm of possibility for a parent struggling to pay her rent, while for other parents it meant simply taking these items from the refrigerator. Additionally, some parents may have been unable to read Beth's "long letter," especially if they were not English literate. Perhaps some would have complied with her request if they had understood. Steve's comment concerning the article seemed to imply that all of the children in the neighborhood were the result of teenage pregnancies, or their mothers had been on drugs.

Early childhood educators are not justified in making comments or in asking the children questions that seem to condemn or negate the "value" of their parents. In most instances, the mother is the child's first teacher and the first real role model that they see. As their world expands from the home to the community and to the classroom, little children especially want to please the adults who are most prominent in their lives—parents and teachers. If these are perceived to be at odds with each other, it can create confusion and distress for youngsters. Parents and teachers are "partners" in the education of the young child.

SUMMARY

Whether we dip back into the descriptions of child's life a century ago or focus on labeling the special needs child, the power and potential of the sociological perspective bring new insights and new sensitivities to the educational scene. In this chapter we have used a form of sociology that describes life in terms of the theater to study the interaction between students and teacher. We have drawn on analogies and incidents in classrooms of young children and with teachers of young children to illustrate sociologist Erving Goffman's conception of sociology as drama. We then turned to a sociological view of young children with exceptionalities. Our discussion was two-pronged. We focused upon the harmful trend reflected in the overrepresentation of children of color in special education classes. We also highlighted the role of the teacher as modeling acceptance of children with special needs in the inclusive classroom. The chapter concluded with an examination of social class differences and of how both young children and their parents are discriminated against based on this factor.

KEY CONCEPTS

The Theatrical Model The use of the metaphor of the theater in sociological analysis. This approach in sociology examines people as they present themselves and their activities to others, attempting to guide and control the impressions they create.

Some terms used by Goffman's model include:

performance   The activities of an individual in the presence of others.
front/personal front   The aspects of the performance and additional expressive equipment that identify the performer, such as specific clothing, speech patterns, facial expressions, bodily gestures, size, and looks.
setting   The part of the front involving furniture, decor, physical layout, the background scenery, stage props.
audience   The observers who view the individual's performance.
performance team   Others who join the performance and the performer functions as a member of a troupe or cast of players.
region   The larger setting of stage for the performance, usually involving the performance team.

Social Class   The combination of a person's education, occupation, and income in order to derive that person's ranking in the social structure.
Inclusion   The placement of children with disabilities in the regular classroom setting. This mainstreaming increases the degree of interaction with children who fall within the "range of normality," and provides an environment with enhanced educational experiences for all.

ISSUES AND ACTIONS

1. Examine an event in your school in the light of the theatrical model. First, think about who are the "actors" in the scenario. Describe their personal fronts and the performances they give. Decide who is the audience for the performance. Is the performance provided by a single actor or a team? What is the setting? Does the setting have only a front or is there also a back stage region where the performers can relax, and "let off steam"?

2. Contact a public school district in your area and review its statistical data regarding the demographic make-up of students identified as having special needs. Compare the percentages of ethnic composition of those in "emotionally disturbed" and "learning disabled" classes with their percentage in the general student population. Discuss your findings with your classmates.

3. Interview parents from the inner-city. Discuss their aspirations for their children, and their perception of the relations between home and school.

REFERENCES AND SUGGESTED READINGS

Backler, Alan and Sybil Eakin, editors. *Every Child Can Succeed: Readings for School Improvement.* Bloomington, Indiana: Agency for Instructional Technology, 1993.

Banks, James, and Banks, Cherry McGee (Eds.). *Multicultural Education: Issues and Perspectives*. Needham Heights, MA: Allyn and Bacon, 1989.

Bredekamp, Sue (Ed.). *Developmentally Appropriate Practice in Early Childhood Programs Serving Children from Birth to Age 8*. Washington, DC: National Association for the Education of Young Children, 1987.

Chipman, Marilyn. *An Identification of Factors Perceived as Affecting the Recruitment and Retention of African American Students Attending a Predominantly-Anglo University*. Unpublished doctoral dissertation. Denver: University of Denver, 1990.

Cuzzort, R. W., and King, E. W. *20th Century Social Thought* (4th ed.) Ft. Worth, TX: Holt, Rinehart and Winston, 1989.

Fallen, Nancy and Umansky, Warren, *Young Children with Special Needs*, 2nd edition. Columbus, Ohio: Merrill Publishing, 1985.

Goffman. Erving. *The Presentation of Self in Everyday Life*. Garden City, NY: Doubleday, 1959.

Goffman, Erving. *Stigma: Notes on the Management of Spoiled Identity*. Englewood Cliffs, NJ: Prentice-Hall, 1963.

Grant, Carl, and Sleeter, Christine. *After the School Bell Rings*. London: Falmer Press, 1986.

Hilliard, Asa G. and Sizemore, Barbara. *Saving the African-American Child: A Report on the Task Force on Black Academic and Cultural Excellence*. Washington, DC: The National Alliance of Black School Educators, November 1984.

Lerner, Janet, Mardell-Czudnowski, and Golderberg, Dorothea. *Special Education for the Early Childhood Years*, 2nd edition. Englewood Cliffs, NJ: Prentice-Hall, 1987.

King, Edith. *Educating Young Children . . . Sociological Interpretations*. Dubuque, IA: W. C. Brown, 1973.

Mercer, Jane. *Labeling the Mentally Retarded*. Berkeley, CA: University of California Press, 1973.

Milner, David. *Children and Race: Ten Years On*. London: Ward Locke, 1983.

Sleeter, Christine (Ed.). *Empowerment through Multicultural Education*. Albany, NY: State University of New York, 1991.

Sleeter, Christine. Learning Disabilities: The Social Construction of a Special Education Category. *Exceptional Children*, 1986; 53(1): pp. 46–54.

Wiggins, Kate Douglas. *The Story of Patsy*. Boston: Houghton, Mifflin, 1894.

9

THE IMPORTANCE OF
RESEARCH FOR TEACHERS
OF YOUNG CHILDREN

Early childhood teachers may feel that they are so immersed in their daily classroom activities and responsibilities that they could not possibly have time for such esoteric commitments as research in their classrooms. This type of thinking is misplaced. In actuality, research in the classroom and school setting can go on as part of daily and weekly teaching and in the context of the continual interactions with parents, other teachers, and support staff. Investigating the classroom climate for the results of learning; for the interactions of student groups; or for the impact of a particular topic, project, specific curriculum material, or intensive program can be exhilarating and deeply informative for a teacher of young children. Teachers can build a component of research into any activity, unit, or project—many times we call it "evaluation" and carry out a form of research without even realizing it.

Educational researchers note that the teachers involved in their research can truly interpret the relevance of the study being carried out, since it is the classroom teacher who really knows what goes on in the classroom. This chapter is devoted to encouraging early childhood teachers to consider opportunities to design and carry out projects, taking on the role of teacher as researcher.

THE CONCEPT OF NATURALISTIC RESEARCH

Teachers of young children have much knowledge about what is happening in their classrooms. They understand the dynamics of the interactions among children and between children and adults. Employing this expertise in the implementation of educational research is logical and natural for early childhood practitioners. Therefore, it follows that the concept of *naturalistic* research is one that we emphasize. Just what is it that constitutes the type of research labeled naturalistic, qualitative, or ethnographic? Sometimes referred to as *field research* or *ethnographic methods,* these research techniques aim to represent everyday life in classrooms studied in all its various layers of social meaning. Ethnographers and naturalistic researchers try to rid themselves of any presuppositions they might have about the situation under study. They go into the field to observe people and their actions in the natural setting and frequently become participant-observers in the ongoing actions as a member of the group. Some characteristics of naturalistic or qualitative research in education are:

1. The researcher works in a natural setting such as a school or a classroom.

2. Research studies are designed and redesigned, as the investigator formulates and then reformulates the research questions, the data-gathering techniques, and even the data being gathered.
3. Data collection and data analysis occur simultaneously. The theory is therefore not superimposed on the data but emerges from the data that are collected.
4. The research is concerned with social process and with meaning, so that qualitative studies focus on how definitions or meanings are established by those whom the researcher is investigating.

The techniques stressed for naturalistic, qualitative studies function to bring educational research and theory more in line with educational practice. The investigators ask questions about how teachers, administrators, and students in the school setting interpret the meanings of their experience and how the educational process affects their lives. The subjects participate directly and have an impact on the questions as well as the results or findings. In his seminal book on qualitative methods *Inside Schools: Ethnography in Educational Research* (1986), Peter Woods writes that teachers as researchers are in the optimum position to look at what lies beneath the surface detail of what is going on in a classroom. The teacher can observe alternative views and can perceive patterns in accounts or in observed behaviors that may suggest varying interpretations of what is happening.

This approach to educational research is drawn from the social science disciplines of anthropology and sociology, which focus on the crucial nature of the culture of the group, the social structure and shared traditions, and the customs and values of a society—large or small. As an educational sociologist and ethnographic researcher, Peter Woods emphasizes that teachers can bring ethnographic (naturalistic) techniques to bear on the evaluation of their work, on student motivation and learning, and on their own careers and development. He posits that naturalistic, qualitative methods offer teachers a large measure of control over their efforts. The researcher is the chief investigator for the study, who designs the questions to be studied, gains access to subjects (the students), organizes the data gathering (the curriculum and daily classroom activities), and verifies the results with those involved in the study. "Ethnography [naturalistic] research thus offers teachers an engagement with research and a direction over it" (1986, p. 9). How is successful research in early childhood classrooms carried out? What are some of the designs and methods used by teachers of children ages three to eight years to investigate aspects of the curriculum; the links between the school, the family, and the community; or the values, attitudes, and goals of the early childhood educational program? Who becomes involved in the investigations? What is the duration of such studies? How are these projects actually initiated, developed, and then implemented?

One such research project in Britain (Huxley, 1990) examined the links among practice, research, and educational policy. The project involved collaborative research that developed from a yearlong inquiry into anti-bias strategies with preschool children. The aim of the project was to establish teaching approaches to challenge racism and sexism and to develop effective intervention strategies in early childhood classrooms.

Naturalistic Research Strategies as Practiced in England

Naturalistic or qualitative research has been highly regarded in educational circles in Britain over the past several decades. Here it is frequently termed *collaborative* research and is favored in school and classroom investigations for its small sample, in-depth, closely watched, active participation characteristics, rather than the broadly generalized, large population and sample, and little researcher involvement that characterizes the traditional quantitative, experimental-control group designs of educational research. In Britain the impetus for a teacher researching his or her own teaching practice was developed from the work and writings of Lawrence Stenhouse in the 1970s. Stenhouse (1975) and other prominent British educators promoted the teacher-researcher role because it encouraged reflective analysis of teaching, and enhanced professional growth as well as evaluation of learning outcomes. Through collaboration and negotiation Huxley used the process of identifying issues to stimulate reflective teaching and professional growth for those involved in the study. Additionally, naturalistic, qualitative, or as termed here, collaborative, research often enlists the input of key informants and the "critical" friend or critical community to validate the information collected by the researcher through observations and interviews. This is a form of collaboration from the participants, as well. Hence, naturalistic research emphasizes using every possible technique to obtain the viewpoints, the interpretations, and the meanings of the participants in the research study.

Huxley's research stimulated the development of a similar project in the United States. Following is an account of one such project carried out by a teacher who took up the challenge to become an educational researcher. This teacher had the desire to design and implement naturalistic, qualitative research for the insights her efforts would bring to better practice and new knowledge in early childhood education.

NATURALISTIC RESEARCH IN A BILINGUAL EARLY CHILDHOOD CLASSROOM

Naturalistic, qualitative research studies do not have to be conceived as major, year or longer, projects. One of the authors, intrigued by the possibilities and the applications of naturalistic research in early childhood education, designed and carried out a small-scale action research in a classroom of bilingual four-year-olds. She took on the role of an adult helper in an early childhood class while fulfilling her objectives as the teacher-researcher. These are excerpts from her field notes, her general findings, and her research paper.

Background and Plan of the Small-Scale Study

A series of five visits to an early childhood education classroom were made in April and May. I did not prepare specific research questions or issues to tackle for this study. I wanted to observe the naturally occurring sequences of events and happenings in this bilingual early childhood classroom and see what "popped out" at me. However, I did have three general areas of investigation in mind. These were:

1. What are the teacher's intentions?
2. What conditions do the teacher and other adults in the classroom provide for students to undergo educational experiences?
3. Do students actually participate in these educational experiences designed by the teacher and the other staff members?

The classroom was composed of twenty predominantly Spanish-speaking children of Hispanic ethnicity. It was housed in an elementary school that included kindergarten to grade 5 with a total enrollment of just over 500 children. Five of the children were dominant English speakers, nine were dominant Spanish speakers, and six children were bilingual speakers. The school neighborhood was Hispanic. The teacher, Ms. A spoke both English and Spanish fluently. The paraprofessional aide, Ms. G, was also bilingual. Both women exhibited a deep understanding of the students' home culture and communicated well with the parents. Ms. A was an energetic and enthusiastic person who expressed an interest in multicultural education. With the researcher, she shared a concern about the status of the Hispanic community in this large city in the American West. It was this interest that prompted me to visit her classroom.

Procedures for Data Collection

After several days of observations, my focus narrowed as I observed that Ms. A regularly voiced her expectations to the children and modeled appropriate behaviors. I watched as the children repeated her statements and acted in ways that would gain her approval. I began to pay closer attention to the teacher's statements and responses to the children. Ms. A's language was filled with positive assertions that both encouraged and supported collaboration among all students and particularly between boys and girls. Her language was nurturing. It built up rather than limited the children's self-esteem and expectations.

Here are some excerpts from my field notes as examples:

I observed the following interactions. Three students were playing. The conversation was recorded as:

First Child: Adios, me voy a trabajar. (Bye, I am going to work.)

Second Child: Adios, hasta la vista. (Bye, see you later.)

Third Child: Adios. (Bye.)

The first child walked out and immediately came back into the Playhouse and said, Se me olvidaron las llaves. (I forgot my keys.)

Second Child: No te olvides cerrar la puerta, papá. (Don't forget to close the door, dad.)

The child reached into the closet again, grabbed the keys, and walked out the door.

Another time, I observed the following interaction with the same three children.

Girl (holding a doll): Vamos a salir. (We are going out.)

All three children walked out of the playhouse and pretended to get into a car. They had placed four chairs together, two in front and two behind. One child sat behind the imaginary driver's wheel while another sat in the passenger's seat with the doll. The third child sat on one of the back seats. They told Ms. G that he was taking the baby for a drive.

Boy: Voy a sacar el bebé para que se duerma. (I am taking the baby out so it will fall asleep.)

Ms. G: Muy bueno. Muy bueno idea. Le gustará al bebe. (Very good. A very good idea. The baby will like that.)

Following my series of observations in this early childhood classroom, I interviewed the teacher, Ms. A, and the classroom aide, Ms. G. They had worked together for over three years. They spoke of their similar ideas and goals for the education of young children. These included:

Early childhood education must prepare children for the real world. The world is changing and children need to learn to respect other people, regardless of gender, language, or other backgrounds.

Young children's learning must support the acquisition and development of positive self-esteem.

Teaching and learning must be fun and motivate children to want to come to school.

During my interviews Ms. A indicated that she wanted to make her intentions clear. She affirmed:

"I want to make everyone as equal as possible. I expect my English speakers to learn Spanish and vice versa. I help the children and I give them time. Whenever I ask a question in English or in Spanish I expect an answer in that language. By the end of the school year all the children feel very comfortable with their second language—English or Spanish—and I expect the same from all students, whether they are a boy or a girl. I expect the same behavior and apply the same discipline. So you tell me what you see."

Her aide, Ms. G, supported these aims. "She explains things to me. I never have to second-guess her. At first, I did not dare ask, but now I do, and I have learned to ask 'why' just like the kids."

Results and Outcomes

Although Ms. A, the early childhood teacher, must be guided by the school district's curriculum, she still believes in exploration and self-selection as crucial to the wholesome development of young children. She balances children's independence with both physical and instructional structure in her classroom. Ms. A often brought all the children together in a common meeting area for chanting, story time, social activities such as dancing, or for guidance and general orientation. The classroom learning centers were clearly defined by dividers such as bookcases, tables, and cabinets. The researcher observed that activities were carefully presented and explained to the children before implementation. The children were not separated by language spoken because the teacher moved from one language to another swiftly, making it easy for all the children to understand. Further, children were not separated by gender except to use the lavatories. Clear classroom rules and expectations were voiced regularly.

The researcher's field notes revealed subtle patterns of behaviors. The girls continually vied for Ms. A's and Ms. G's attention more often than the boys did. The girls tended to "cuddle up" next to these adult women. Being sensitive to children's needs for affection, it is often difficult for young children's teachers to deny them this attention. They need to be cautious not to favor the girls to the exclusion of the boys. Adults need to be aware of these patterns of behavior demonstrated by girls and encourage boys, as well, to express their needs for closer physical proximity and affection. This concern has been voiced before by early childhood educators. "It is important for adults who interact with young children to become aware of how they contribute to the socialization of children. It is the responsibility of educators of young children to find ways to prevent and counter the damage done before it becomes too deep" (Derman-Sparks et al., 1989, p. 5)

Finally, this small-scale research project reinforced the researcher's conclusions that the teacher does exert a strong and lasting influence on young children. Therefore, early childhood teachers need to recognize the crucial roles they play in young children's lives and the resultant impact they have on the future educational success of such children.

Implications for Naturalistic Research in Early Childhood Classrooms

This small-scale naturalistic or ethnographic research provides an example of how a teacher-researcher can design and carry out a project in just one classroom that is of importance in bringing insights and new understandings to teaching young children. Through well-planned observations and interviews, and through the review of the actual words and actions of the teachers and children as recorded, the researcher revealed how daily practice impinges on the life of children and adults and shapes their attitudes, values, beliefs, and abilities to learn and grow.

The power of naturalistic research in capturing this immediacy is expressed by Elliot Eisner in his book, *The Enlightened Eye: Qualitative Inquiry and the Enhancement of Educational Practice* (1991). Eisner writes that Erving Goffman was one social scientist who made social life vivid in important social institutions; Bruno Bettelheim was another, whose work on autistic children enlightened the field of naturalistic research:

> *These scholars not only study intact settings in their "natural state" but they try to make sense of those settings through language that is not tied to formalism or to theories that abstract the vivid particulars into oblivion. Each tries to tell a story that has the ring of truth without compromising figurative or interpretive language. (1991, p. 3)*

The author of the naturalistic study reported in this chapter is an example of this qualitative research tradition. Teacher-researchers are literally turning enlightened eyes on the young child's classroom and educational experiences.

SUMMARY

This chapter has been devoted to encouraging teachers of young children to undertake projects in their classrooms and with their groups of young students. Through the methods and strategies of naturalistic research, teachers can realistically function as teacher-researchers. A small-scale study of the pivotal nature of the teacher in an early childhood bilingual classroom was examined in detail as an example of effective research projects. The implications for naturalistic research in early childhood classrooms were discussed and underscored.

KEY CONCEPTS

Naturalistic (Qualitative) Research sometimes referred to as field research or ethnographic methods. Research techniques that aim to represent people and the real world in all the various layers of social meaning. Drawn from the social sciences, naturalistic research emphasizes the role of the researcher as an observer and interviewer who goes into the natural setting to gather data in the investigation of the issues and research questions posed in the research study.

Teacher-Researcher Classroom teachers who undertake research projects in their own classrooms and their own schools, or former teachers who return to the classroom in the role of adults participating in the ongoing daily activities of the classroom as they carry out their research through observing and interviewing.

Collaborative Research Classroom investigations that feature research design characteristics of a small sample that is closely watched. The subjects participate and collaborate with the investigator in re-

searching the issues or questions of the study and in the analysis of
the data, as well as evaluating the findings and the outcomes of the
research.

Critical Friend or Critical Community Individuals involved in the study
who provide the researcher with critiques that validate the data
collected or provide differing views and insights for the researcher
on the information being collected for the research.

Participant Observer A teacher-researcher who functions in the classroom as a participating adult while gathering information and data
for the research study.

Nonparticipant Observer A teacher-researcher who observes classrooms
and school settings but does not participate in the ongoing activities.

Field Notes A research strategy for capturing the immediacy of the
situation by writing down the researcher's observations, document-
ing ongoing activities and experiences, impressions, remarks of subjects being observed, general and specific details of the setting, and
location of the study.

Data Collection The techniques used in a research study to gather information about the problem or issues under study. These include
activities such as analyzing field notes where observations, interviews, and comments on the setting, location, and other details have
been noted; compiling information gathered from documents, records, photographs, and other archival materials about the students
or people under investigation; and retrieving information from key
informants and critical friends involved in the study.

ISSUES AND ACTIONS

1. We have presented a qualitative, naturalistic research study that focused on
   young children and the early years of schooling. Find other such qualitative
   research reports. What were the research questions, student populations
   and samples, geographical locations, and settings for these studies? Consider undertaking a similar project in your own classroom or school.

   Hundreds of research reports and newsletters are stored in the ERIC
   Clearinghouse in Early Childhood Education, housed at the University of
   Illinois-Urbana campus. Their address is:

   ERIC Clearinghouse on Elementary and Early Childhood Education
   University of Illinois at Urbana-Champaign
   805 W. Pennsylvania Avenue
   Urbana, IL 61801-4897
   Phone: (217) 333-1386 Fax: (217) 333-5847

2. Any type of social science research involves people and therefore ethical
   issues and concerns about human subjects. Discuss with your fellow teach-

ers or students what some of these issues and concerns might be. In your discussions list some of the problems that might occur if you decide to become a teacher-researcher. How would you plan to overcome these objections or barriers? Who would be of support and assistance to you and your research efforts? Who might want to thwart such projects and efforts?

3. Discuss with your colleagues or fellow students the advantages and rewards of planning and carrying out a research project with young children or on topics in early childhood education. Why do you think more research is not taking place in early childhood education?

REFERENCES AND SUGGESTED READINGS

Berg, Bruce. *Qualitative Research Methods for the Social Sciences*. Needham Heights, MA: Allyn and Bacon, 1989.

Best, Raphaela. *We've All Got Scars: What Boys and Girls Learn in Elementary School*. Bloomington, IN: Indiana University Press, 1983.

Bogdan, R., and Biklen, S. *Qualitative Research in Education* (2nd ed.) Needham Heights, MA: Allyn and Bacon, 1992.

Carr, W., and Kemmis, S. *Becoming Critical: Knowing through Action Research*. London: Deaking Press, 1986.

Derman-Sparks, Louise, et al. *Anti-Bias Curriculum: Tools for Empowering Young Children*. Washington, DC: National Association for the Education of Young Children, 1989.

Eisenhart, Margaret, and Borko, Hilda. *Designing Classroom Research*. Needham Heights, MA: Allyn and Bacon, 1993.

Eisner, Elliot. *The Enlightened Eye: Qualitative Inquiry and the Enhancement of Educational Practice*. New York: Macmillan, 1990.

Huxley, Margaret. *A Report on Anti-Sexist Strategies*. Manchester, England: City of Manchester Educational Committee, 1989.

Huxley, Margaret. Practical Steps toward Gender Equality with the Under-Fives. *Early Years* 1990; 10(3).

Kidder, Tracy. *Among Schoolchildren*. Boston: Houghton Mifflin, 1989.

Lareau, Annette. *Home Advantage: Social Class and Parental Intervention in Elementary Schools*. Philadelphia: Falmer, 1989.

Lubeck, Sally. *Sandbox Society: Early Education in Black and White America. A Comparative Ethnography*. Philadelphia: Falmer Press, 1983.

Stenhouse, Lawrence. *An Introduction to Curriculum Research and Development*. London: Heinemann Publishers, 1975.

Whyte, H. *Beyond the Wendy House: Sex Role Stereotyping in Primary Schools*. London: Schools Council and Longman Publishing, 1983.

Wolcott, Harry. *Writing up Qualitative Research*. Newbury, CA: Sage, 1990.

Woods, Peter. *Inside Schools: Ethnography in Educational Research*. New York: Routledge, 1986.

Woods, Peter. *Teacher Skills and Strategies*. Philadelphia: Falmer Press, 1990.

Woods, Peter. *The Happiest Days?* Philadelphia: Falmer Press, 1990.

10

YOUNG CHILDREN AND
EDUCATION FOR AN
INTERDEPENDENT WORLD

EARLY CHILDHOOD EDUCATION AND THE
NEED FOR WORLD AWARENESS

Everywhere in our modern world, social forces are propelling the individual into a worldwide culture. Never before in history has the world seen such upheaval and mobility in its population. Technology has made it much easier for whole populations to be transplanted and relocated to lands or regions far from their native soils. Today it is the task of the schools and colleges, as much as any of the other institutions of society, to develop a world perspective for our students so they will be able to function in this worldwide culture.

What is a world perspective? It is a way of looking at events, issues, happenings, and experiences to see their inter-relationship to the world as a whole. A world perspective leads us to examine perceptions, ideas, concepts, and information in new ways that our growing interdependence now dictates. All around us is evidence that we cannot escape this worldwide culture. Very few items in daily use and few activities we engage in do not have international and global dimensions. Those of us who are involved in education must be constantly aware of this world milieu, not only for the practical implications of learning, but also for broader humanitarian purposes. Therefore, we must infuse our teaching from now on with world awareness, or *worldmindedness.*

We have presented much data to document how theory and research clearly indicate the importance of early socialization, the strength of values and attitudes internalized in those first eight years of life. A highly regarded study by the Population Reference Bureau of Washington, DC (1992) has documented that a half century of change in the American family has seen the demise of the "Ozzie and Harriet" model. This classic family of 1950s television fame featured a bread-winning husband and a wife who stayed at home with the children, once the dominant pattern in American family structure. Social forces that have combined to reshape the typical American family of the 1990's include the following data:

The average age at first marriage is highest in a century—26 years of age for men and 24 years of age for women.

The marriage rate fell nearly 30 percent between 1970 and 1990, while the divorce rate increased nearly 40 percent.

More than half of all mothers with preschool children worked outside the home in 1991, compared with one in five in 1960.

One in four babies was born to an unmarried mother in 1991, compared with one in twenty in 1960. (Population Reference Center, 1992)

As a result of these statistics, the most common family unit in America at the close of the twentieth century is the married couple with *no* children living at home. This group constituted 42 percent of "families"—families that were made up of younger couples planning to have children, older couples whose children had left home, couples childless by choice, or "others." Additionally, about a quarter of all children (more than sixteen million) lived with only one parent in 1991. That is double the percentage of 1970 and nearly three times that of 1960. The United States is not the only highly prosperous nation to manifest this change in the family phenomenon. Similar increases in births to unmarried mothers were charted in Canada, in France, and in the United Kingdom over the past thirty years. As the baby boomers—those individuals born in the United States from 1946 to 1964—enter their graying years the number of childless households and the number of people living alone will increase. Also by the turn of the century, one in three school-age children will be from a family of color—African American, Hispanic, Native American, Asian American—compared with one in four in the 1990s. If child poverty rates continue to be two to three times higher for these families than for majority society families, a much larger group of children will be growing up in households with limited resources precluding access to the largess of a worldwide culture. Therefore, it is imperative that teachers of young children begin in the early years of schooling to incorporate a world perspective in all aspects of their teaching.

Some Sources of a World Awareness Curriculum

World events are pushing us toward developing the world awareness curriculum for students at all grade levels. It is useful, therefore, to investigate the authoritative sources whose initiatives have contributed to recognizing the need for those working with young children to include education for global responsibility. Those leaders committed to multicultural and global perspectives in education have been emphasizing the need for world awareness and a worldminded curriculum for decades.

In recent years life in American society has provided the milieu for the joining of multicultural education with awareness. In this decade heightened feelings of self-identification are an undeniable fact. We have only to look at recent research projects and publications in all fields, as well as the titles of international, national, regional and local meetings and colloquia, to reveal a general shift from themes labeled unidimensional to "multicultural," "multiethnic," "pluralistic," "transnational," "cross-cultural," and so on. This trend focuses on examining the complexities of learning and teaching in contemporary settings in which the forces of sexism, racism, and classism are played out in multicultural social and educational systems.

The dimension of diversity is highly evident in research projects sponsored at all levels of the educational establishment—local school districts, state and regional education offices, and universities. It is a prominent theme in doctoral and postdoctoral dissertation research. Current research designs are being developed to consider how racism, sexism, and classism delineate institutional arrangements and cultural patterns that create inequalities in individual nations and in worldwide society as well (see Benavot, 1992) Some commentators on the educational scene have become so critical that they declare no education policy, curriculum, or program is ideologically or politically innocent; rather, they are inextricably related to issues of social class, ethnicity, gender, and power (McLaren, 1989).

More specifically, two outstanding social scientists have contributed writings and research to the development and philosophy of world awareness and a global perspective in the education of young children. They are the anthropologist Margaret Mead, and the sociologist Elise Boulding.

Margaret Mead's Contributions to World Awareness

Margaret Mead, the American anthropologist, was an outstanding social thinker who made major contributions to envisioning a global culture and a worldwide view of humanity. She wrote: "We have the means of hearing all of earth's diverse peoples and we have the concepts that make it possible for us to understand them, and they now share in a worldwide, technologically propagated culture, within which they are able to listen as well as to talk to us" (1970, p. xvi). Mead pointed out that today we have available to us for the first time on the "Spaceship Earth" examples of the ways people have lived at every period over the last 50,000 years. In her field work she observed that at the same time the New Guinea native looks at a pile of yams and pronounces "a lot" because he cannot count them, teams at Cape Kennedy calculate the precise second when an Apollo mission must change its course if it is to orbit around the moon.

When focusing on the education of young children and the important role of the teacher of young children, Margaret Mead was eloquent in her espousal of the seminal role teachers of young children played in the formation of the population for the world of the future. In the

School in American Culture, her lecture at Harvard University for the Inglis Lecture Series in 1950, Margaret Mead wrote that the teacher who is to help a generation go beyond their parents has a unique task. This teacher must relive her childhood and exchange the specificity of the demands that her parents and teachers made on her for a new set of demands, which she will make, in the same tone of voice, on her pupils.

Mead goes on to point out that from the most all-embracing world image to the smallest detail of daily life, the world has changed at such a rapid rate that it makes the five-year-old child further apart from his parents than ever generations were in our recent knowledge. She calls for teachers of young children to use their tried methods on new material, "a totally new kind of teaching—a teaching of a readiness to use unknown ways to solve unknown problems" (p. 40). These words, written almost half a century ago, point the way for teachers of young children to make a major contribution to shaping the generation of children that will live in the worldwide society of the twenty-first century.

Education for an Interdependent World: Elise Boulding

International educator, sociologist, scholar, and futurist, Professor Elise Boulding has lived and worked by the precepts that Margaret Mead described. In a book for teaching world awareness, *Building a Global Civic Culture: Education for an Interdependent World* (1988), she provides materials and strategies for learning and teaching about the worldwide society that *is* reality today. She labels this reality the "sociosphere," and urges teachers to imbue education with local, national, and worldwide content.

> *How do we know about the world? How do we find out what it is like? In the urban and suburban settings of the countries of the North, and for some elites of the South, children grow into adulthood without ever discovering anything about the physical and social environment beyond their own personal daily path, except through programmed secondary sources such as television, radio, the telephone, the computer, and, of course, books. They live in technologically shielded settings that cut them off from feedback about the larger environment in which they live. In fact, it is considered progress not to have to bother with getting or dealing with that feedback. (1988, p. 77)*

In writing on educating for our interdependent world, Boulding calls attention to the wide-ranging diversity and cultural pluralism in the modern nation-states. She presents strategies and methods for developing skills that are needed to deal with diversity and the conflicts that it brings. She believes that no one society can create or impose *the* universal social order; therefore, it is incumbent on societies to find creative ways of working together that acknowledge our human diversity. We must find ways to maintain an overall level of peacefulness, avoiding destructive strategies that deny our differences (1988).

Boulding has written that children have a right to have book learning relate to the world they must deal with, and they have a right to realistic presentations in their textbooks of the range of possible roles open to them in our new worldwide society. She notes that the drive to "clean up" textbooks with regard to all kinds of ethnic and gender stereotyping has been gaining momentum in the last decade. "Cutting across the increasing sterility of some classroom learning are the new developments in community based learning, community apprenticeships, and a variety of common sense efforts to bring children back into the real world they must share with adults" (1979, p. 82).

Elise Boulding's writings bring to education new resources and new thinking on the importance of dealing with differences in every aspect of the school curriculum. As Margaret Mead has urged us, we can work toward attaining a world order in which social conflicts can be handled by less than ultimate forms of threat and counterthreat. All societies can work together to solve these social conflicts.

WORLD AWARENESS AND EARLY CHILDHOOD EDUCATION IN OTHER NATIONS

Articles, studies, books, and monographs on early childhood education in other nation-states and cultures usually describe the student population of three- to eight-year-olds as a monocultural group. Often the authors of the reports and accounts assume that the programs for young children from the working classes of developing nations in African or Asian societies are living and functioning in grinding poverty. This traditional coverage of early childhood programs and the ECE curriculum in other nations is portrayed in simplistic style, eschewing the importance of ethnic diversity. Lumping all young children and their families together, without attention to diversity within groups, is dangerous and erroneous stereotyping. It is useful to examine early childhood education in various nation-states with a diversity perspective to understand the strengths and weaknesses of these programs. Further, such an examination in a cross-cultural context offers us new perspectives on our own American early childhood education system, as well.

Young Children in the Multicultural Nation of Singapore

The island nation of Singapore at the tip of the Malay Peninsula boasts a multicultural population of about two and a half million people. The four major ethnic heritages and four major languages in this multicultural nation-state are: English, Chinese, Malay, and Tamil. These four major languages are heard daily on television and radio, in the streets and markets, and in the schools of Singapore, as well. Although 70 percent of Singaporeans come from families speaking one of the several dialects of Chinese, there is still a strong Malay and Tamil (East Indian) segment in the population reflecting the preponderance of these heritages in the countries surrounding the tiny nation. However, in this multilingual nation, English is the primary language, the official language of the government and of the schools. The basic subjects of the curriculum are taught in English beginning in early childhood education, but parallel bilingual education in the three other mother tongues is offered. At a typical primary school, usually located in the center of a high-rise public housing block, children attend classes following a bilingual stream where they are taught reading, writing, math, social studies, health education, music, and physical education—all in the English language, while they also study these subjects in their mother tongue, either a Chinese dialect, Tamil, or Malay.

Not many children come from English-speaking homes; hence, for the academic work in the second language, their mother tongue, groups of twenty pupils or more are formed for each home language. Early in their school experience Singaporean children are socialized with the importance of educational attainment. Immersed as they are in school programs where basic subjects are taught in two languages simultaneously, children recognize the demands for strenuous work and serious commitment. Strict discipline and proper classroom deportment are expected at all times by Singaporean teachers beginning in preschool. Misbehavior in the classroom is seldom exhibited by even the youngest children. Doing well in school and obtaining valued educational skills, including the mastery of English, is a national duty and brings pride and recognition to one's family.

In Singapore, preschools are operated by a number of organizations. Nursery classes and kindergartens are sponsored and staffed by political and business organizations. Private organizations and church-affiliated groups operate kindergartens and preprimary classes attached to some of the Singaporean primary schools. In 1984, although preschools were not included in the state-run educational system, the Ministry of Education monitored the teaching and the facilities in all kindergartens and preprimary classes (Seng, 1992).

A nine-year longitudinal study was begun in 1983 aimed at investigating cognitive and social developmental processes of preschool children, ages three to six years. It was carried out by Singapore's National Institute of Education and funded by the Bernard van Leer Foundation of The Netherlands. This research also involved intervention strategies that attempted to enhance the children's competencies over the nine years of the study. In the first three-year phase of the study, reported in the book *Growing Up in Singapore: The Pre-school Years* (Sim and Kam, 1992), efforts were focused on collection of baseline data. Phase 2 was devoted to intervention programs in early childhood education centers. Phase 3 involved intervention in the home setting. The specific aims of the project were:

1. measuring Singaporean preschool children's cognitive growth in terms of their ability to master basic language skills, to understand simple mathematical concepts, and to perform tasks that required them to distinguish, compare, reason, and perceive relations as interpreted through performance of Piagetian tasks;
2. studying, through observation, children's social behavior in the structured environment of their classrooms; and
3. investigating and monitoring selected aspects of the children's home and school environment as they affected their cognitive and social development.

Over the period of nine years, this longitudinal study revealed that Singaporean preschoolers definitely were aware of the importance of the English language. They expressed emerging bilingual behaviors in their readiness to learn and exhibit knowledge of the English alphabet, knowledge of words in English to add to a growing vocabulary, and the ability to hold a book in the appropriate position for reading in English, rather than in the position for their mother tongue of Chinese, Malay, or Tamil. The six-year-olds in the study indicated that they knew two languages. Some of them were found to be fluent speakers of English and of the second language, which researchers attributed to the conditions in the home environment (Seng, 1992). Additionally, in the area of social development, children showed gains over the preschool years in sharing and cooperative behaviors. The children's performance on social tasks showed that young children learn through imitation and direct instruction, indicating that early childhood teachers have been successful in socializing their pupils. Unfortunately the research study did not include information on gender and social class differences in the cognitive and social aspects of the preschool child's education. In the final decade of the twentieth century new directions for research with Singaporean preschoolers have arisen that will target ethnicity, gender, and social class aspects of this widely diverse preschool population (Seng, 1992)

Early Childhood Education in Kuwait before the Gulf War of 1990

Another rapidly developing nation-state that has displayed increasing concerns and attention to the education of young children is the Arabic Gulf nation of Kuwait. One of the authors of this book had the opportunity to visit kindergartens (the Kuwaiti school facilities for children ages four to six years) and other early childhood programs in Kuwait just before the extensive destruction that was wrought on the people and the land during the Gulf War. The first kindergartens in Kuwait were established in 1954 for children from three and a half years to six years of age. By the late 1980s the majority of young children in this age range were enrolled in early childhood education throughout Kuwait, with formal schooling required as compulsory by age seven. In these kindergartens boys and girls attend classes together, but with entrance into the primary schools, boys and girls are completely separated and attend only single-sex schools throughout the rest of their educational experiences. The early childhood programs are taught by women, and women administer the schools for the girls.

The curriculum for young children emphasizes moral and religious education characteristics of the teaching of Islam in all educational programs. The early learning levels of Arabic language and arithmetic are also included. In a statement of the philosophy and aims of preschool education, officials stress that the aims of the kindergarten stem from the social values of Kuwaiti society. The children are guided in developing an understanding of certain religious beliefs and practices while instilling a sense of patriotism for their nation, Kuwait, and a deep commitment to their family. The kindergarten's curriculum also includes the aims of developing a positive self-image, enhancing cognitive growth and perceptual knowledge through exploration, experimentation, and direct manipulation of objects in the environment. *"Finally, the kindergarten stands for equal educational opportunities, taking into consideration the individual differences among the children as well as the potential inequality in the economic, social and cultural environment."* [Emphasis ours—note the familiar wording, similar to American early childhood program aims and goals statements.] (Ministry of Education, State of Kuwait, 1988)

During the 1988 visit previously mentioned, an early childhood facility serving 600 four- to six-year-olds in the port town of Ahmadi was available for observation and study. It was staffed by twenty-five teachers, a head mistress, and other support staff such as kitchen and food servers, janitor, and health workers. The ratio was one teacher to twenty-four children, comparable to American kindergarten and elementary school classrooms. Parents were evident as teacher assistants in a number of classrooms. At this school even the youngest children wore school uniforms. The children were especially proud of their prize-winning "rhythm band," which was equipped with the finest Orff instruments and beautiful costumes and sets made by parents for interschool competitions and other public programs. At this kindergarten school new curriculum materials were being introduced that gave greater attention to the local culture and traditions of Kuwait, rather than merely reflecting and copying early childhood materials from Britain or the United States. For example, the director of early childhood education and her staff, carefully adhering to developmentally appropriate practices, prepared a series of well-designed and colorful children's books that taught cognitive and language activities using settings, adults, and children drawn from the Kuwaiti daily scene in family and neighborhood. Throughout the early childhood educational system and the primary schools, attention to Islamic and specifically Kuwaiti heritage and tradition was evidenced in teaching practice, in texts, and in other curriculum materials. Before the War, the early childhood programs of Kuwait were forging ahead toward exemplary educational practice benefiting young children. Now that the rebuilding of Kuwait is in progress, it is hoped that support for early childhood education will continue into the twenty-first century.

In a stunning and unique book, titled *Traditions: The Folklore of Women and Children in Kuwait* (Wells and Al Batini, 1988), written before the Gulf War of 1990, the authors state:

> *Looking along Arabian Gulf Street (Kuwait City) with its futuristic skyline, impressive State buildings and speeding, air-conditioned limousines, it is hard to believe that along this same seafront not so long ago women came to wash their clothes, rinse their hair or anxiously await the return of their husbands on the pearling and trading dhows. Perhaps never before has a country undergone such rapid change in so short a time as Kuwait since the discovery of oil. The changes have not merely been in the physical infrastructure and technological advancement, but in the lives of the people themselves. (Preface, p. 4)*

IMPLICATIONS OF A WORLD VIEW FOR EARLY CHILDHOOD EDUCATION

We now return to the writings and theories of anthropologist and futurist Margaret Mead and evaluate their relevance to early childhood education. Beginning with her book *Continuities in Cultural Evolution* (1964) and culminating in the series of lectures cited previously in this chapter, published in the volume titled *Culture and Commitment* (1970), Margaret Mead set forth her theory about cultural learning. She states that it was her goal to explore living people, all existing at the present time but exhibiting essential differences and discontinuities. She identified these three major types of cultures:

- cultures of the Historical Past
- cultures of the Present
- cultures of the Future.

With Mead's theory of cultural continuities in hand, we will use our discussion of Singaporean and Kuwaiti early childhood education as examples of how a society can move through the stages of cultural development or continuities in less than half a century. By both detailing each stage of culture in Margaret Mead's theoretical framework and then drawing on details from the materials presented above, we will show how the importance of early childhood education amplifies the passage of societies around the globe, from postfigurative through cofigurative to prefigurative cultures.

Three Stages of Cultural Continuities

Cultures of the Historical Past

Margaret Mead believed that all three types of cultures are a reflection of the period in which we currently live. A culture rooted in the past is characterized as one in which change is so slow and imperceptible that grandparents cannot conceive of any other future for their grandchildren than that of one like their own lives. Cultures of the past are ones in which elders cannot conceive of change and so can convey to their descendants only a sense of unchanging continuities. This culture depends on the actual presence of three generations. Its continuity comes from the expectations of the old and its imprint of those expectations on the young. She gives examples from folk societies around the globe—the Samoans, the Indians of Venezuela, the Arapesh of New Guinea. She asserts that after a millennium of cultures, rooted in the past we have arrived at a new stage in the evolution of human cultures.

For example, in describing the old city of Kuwait, Wells and Al Batini note that Kuwait was originally a walled city with seven gates on the landward side, while facing a magnificent natural harbor. There was a population of about 20,000 to 25,000 people in the nineteenth century, housed in densely packed, single-story houses built of mud brick. These homes were where the women and children of Kuwait spent most of their lives behind walls with windows placed at the top to ensure privacy. Kuwait was then a society of the past where formal education, especially in the early childhood years, was unheard of.

Cultures of the Present

Mead characterizes cultures of the present as ones in which the prevailing model for members of the society is the behavior of their contemporaries. What causes society to change from a culture of the past to one of the present? Mead explains the change thusly: a culture oriented in the present has its beginning in a break in the old system. Such a break may come about in many ways, for example, through a catastrophe in which a whole population, but particularly the old who were essential to leadership, is decimated, or as the result of the development of new forms of technology in which the old are not experts. We could attribute the evolution of Kuwaiti society from the "folk" or past-oriented stage to the present-oriented stage as the result of the discovery of oil and the wealth and tremendous strides in modernization and technological advancement that this brought to the society in just a few decades. In the case of Singapore, the evolving changes to the old era are not as dramatically evident, but still the rapid adoption of extensive technology and business management in a strategically located city-state has led to the same results as the discovery of oil in Kuwait.

Mead points out that change occurs when the experience of the younger generation is radically different from that of their parents, grandparents, and other older members of their immediate community. The transition to a new way of life in which new skills and modes of behavior must be acquired occurs faster when there are not grandparents present who remember the past, shape the experience of the growing child, and reinforce all the unverbalized values of the old culture. She contends that the mere condition of rapid change can produce a culture of the present in nations such as India, Pakistan, and the new states of Africa, as well as Arabian Gulf states such as Kuwait. Mead reminds us that children become the authorities on the new ways in these situations, and parents lose their power to judge and control. She writes:

> . . . suddenly, because all the peoples of the world are part of one electronically based, intercommunicating network, young people eve-

rywhere share a kind of experience that none of the elders ever have had or will have. Conversely, the older generation will never see repeated in the lives of young people their own unprecedented experience of sequentially emerging change. This break between generations is wholly new; it is planetary and universal. Today's children have grown up in a world their elders never knew, but few adults knew that this would be so. (1970, p. 64)

Cultures of the Future

Thus, Mead sets forth the third stage of her theory of cultural continuities, the future-oriented culture, a totally new concept of living in which adults learn from their children. Since change has occurred so rapidly, within one person's lifetime, a condition arises where the older generations can no longer teach the young. Specifically, she points to the entrance of all humanity into the nuclear era; we have left behind our familiar worlds to live in a new age under conditions that are different from any we have ever known, but our thinking still binds us to the past. As we enter the twenty-first century we are living in this future-oriented era still not knowing just what astonishing changes it will bring to humanity. We are beginning to realize that the roles of men and women in all societies of the world are undergoing new and unexpected conditions and these dynamics are irreversible.

SUMMARY

As Patricia Ramsey reminds us, "young children cannot decenter from their own point of view in order to see their way of doing things as simply one of many possibilities, yet teachers can use their greater receptiveness to introduce them to a variety of cultural conventions. Later, when they can understand cultural relativity, they will have more content and experience to support those insights" (1987, p. 31). In 1959 the United Nations drew up the Declaration of the Rights of the Child. This document applies to the rights of children worldwide.

United Nations Declaration of the Rights of the Child

The right to affection, love and understanding.
The right to adequate nutrition and medical care.
The right to free education.
The right to full opportunity for play and recreation.
The right to a name and nationality.
The right to special care, if disabled.

The right to be among the first to receive relief in times of disaster. The right to be a useful member of society and to develop individual abilities.

The right to be brought up in a spirit of peace and universal understanding.

The right to enjoy these rights, regardless of race, color, sex, religion, national or social origin.

The time has come for teachers, parents, and all those who work with young children to bring world awareness and worldmindedness into the young child's classroom. Those of us in early childhood education must champion with renewed emphasis the need to prepare children to live on an interdependent planet and in a worldwide society composed of diverse traditions and cultures.

This chapter opened with a call for awareness of the contemporary situation of life in a worldwide society. The need for teachers of young children to incorporate a world perspective and the teaching of world awareness in the early childhood classroom was presented. Sources of the world awareness curriculum were discussed. This included the writings of anthropologist Margaret Mead and sociologist Elise Boulding. World awareness and early childhood education in the developing nation-states of Singapore and Kuwait were described with attention to impact of modern life in an interdependent world.

We then returned to the theories of Margaret Mead that detailed her conception of the evolution of cultural continuities. This theory was related to the implications for early childhood education on our planet and for the world's population, this widely diverse humanity.

KEY CONCEPTS

World Awareness/Worldmindedness The way of looking at events, issues, happenings, and experiences to see their relationship to the world as a whole.

World Awareness Curriculum The application to teaching and to the subjects of the curriculum of world awareness (i.e., looking at events, issues, and experiences in relation to the entire world).

Sociosphere Term coined by Elise Boulding for learning and teaching about the worldwide society that is a reality of today.

Stages in Cultural Continuities A concept developed by anthropologist Margaret Mead referring to cultures of the historical past, cultures of the present time, and cultures of the future.

ISSUES AND ACTIONS

1. It is well known that the rate of change in our world has become exponential. Yet it is difficult for people to realize just what this means in their lives in a personal perspective. To get a sense of what Margaret Mead and others have said about social change from generation to generation and from decade to decade, spend a short time with this activity.

   Write down on a piece of paper several major events of worldwide importance that have occurred in your lifetime. Then try to think about where you were at the time of this major event. How old were you at the time? How did you learn about this event? the radio? the television? the newspaper? from a friend or relative? What were you doing at the time of the event and did this interrupt or change your activities? Did the happening have a longer range effect on your life? Discuss your list and your reactions with others to see if they concur with your comments. What has been the impact of these events on world awareness and global sensitivity?

2. Read and discuss the U.N. Declaration of Human Rights (presented in this chapter) with a group of children. Point out that these rights apply to them personally as well as to all children.

   Devote time to each right and illustrate it with appropriate examples. Have the children voice their own interpretations of the rights and why they think each one is important. Discuss situations in which certain rights are denied to children. Why are they denied? What effect does it have on the children? on their families? Are there children in the world who are not given these rights? Can you give examples? Why do you think some children don't have these rights? What might happen to them?

   Have the children in your group or class look for pictures that may relate to any of the rights, or have them draw their own pictures. The pictures may illustrate rights given to children or the rights denied to children. You or other adults can also try to obtain posters and drawings that illustrate the rights of the child.

3. Other materials relating to international programs for children may be obtained from: U.S. Committee for UNICEF, Field Services Department, 331 East 38th Street, New York, NY 10016. Write for information and select projects of personal interest to you as an educator of young children.

REFERENCES AND SUGGESTED READINGS

Benavot, A. Education, Gender, and Economic Development: A Cross National Analysis. In *Education and Gender Equality,* edited by J. Wrigley. Bristol, PA, and London: Falmer Press, 1992.

Boulding, Elise. *Building a Global Civic Culture: Education for an Interdependent World.* New York: Teachers College Press, 1988.

Boulding, Elise. *Children's Rights and the Wheel of Life*. New Brunswick, NJ: Transaction Books, 1979.

King, Edith. *Teaching Ethnic and Gender Awareness*. Dubuque, IA: Kendall/Hunt, 1990.

McLaren, Peter. *Life in Schools*. New York: Longman, 1989.

Mead, Margaret. *Culture and Commitment*. Garden City, NY: Doubleday, 1970.

Mead, Margaret. *The School in American Culture*. Cambridge, MA: Harvard University Press, 1950.

Ministry of Education, State of Kuwait. *Kindergartens in Kuwait*. Kuwait City, Kuwait: Author, 1989.

Population Reference Center. *Report, 1992*. Washington, DC: 1992.

Ramsey, Patricia. *Teaching and Learning in a Diverse World*. New York: Teachers College Press, 1987.

Seng, S. H. The Cognitive and Social Development of Preschool Children in Singapore. Paper presented at the American Educational Research Association Meetings, San Francisco (unpublished), 1992.

Sim, Ko Peng, and Kam, Ho Wah (Eds.). *Growing Up in Singapore: The Pre-School Years*. Singapore: Longman, 1992.

Wells, S., and Al Batini, B. *Traditions: The Folklore of Women and Children in Kuwait*. Kuwait: Kuwait Bookshops Limited, 1989.

Index